PRIMACY IN THE CHURCH FROM VATICAN I TO VATICAN II

Primacy in the Church
from Vatican I to Vatican II

AN ORTHODOX PERSPECTIVE

Maximos Vgenopoulos

Foreword by
His All-Holiness Ecumenical Patriarch Bartholomew

NIU PRESS
DeKalb, IL

Library of Congress Cataloging-in-Publication Data
Vgenopoulos, Maximos.
Primacy in the church from Vatican I to Vatican II : an orthodox perspective / Maximos Vgenopoulos ; foreword by His All-Holiness Ecumenical Patriarch Bartholomew.
pages cm
Includes bibliographical references and index.
ISBN 978-0-87580-473-6 (cloth : alk. paper) — ISBN 978-1-60909-098-2 (e-book)
1. Popes—Primacy. 2. Episcopacy. 3. Orthodox Eastern Church—Relations—Catholic Church. 4. Catholic Church—Relations—Orthodox Eastern Church. 5. Catholic Church—Doctrines. 6. Orthodox Eastern Church—Doctrines. I. Title.
BX1805.V44 2013
262'.13—dc23
2013012132

Contents

Foreword

His All-Holiness Ecumenical Patriarch Bartholomew

It is with great delight that we welcome the publication of *Primacy in the Church From Vatican I to Vatican II: An Orthodox Perspective* by the Grand Archdeacon of the Ecumenical Patriarchate, Very Reverend Doctor Maximos Vgenopoulos.

Indeed, we greet the volume at hand not only as being the result of the devoted scholarly research by one of the promising younger theologians of our Church, but also as the focus of imperative debate on one of the most divisive theological issues in relations between the Roman Catholic and Orthodox Churches. Moreover, we rejoice in this publication inasmuch as it presents to a wider readership the important and insightful contributions of recent and contemporary Orthodox thinkers, who are compared and paralleled to their instrumental and influential Roman Catholic peers and colleagues of the last decades.

In relating the subject of primacy to the experience and thought of the Church, especially as this developed in the two latest Vatican Councils, Fr. Maximos has provided us with a deeper and clearer understanding of primacy as the most controversial and critical theological topic, which has inevitably also determined the course of the official theological dialogue between our two Churches.

It is our fervent conviction that the eradication of this impediment regarding our understanding of the concept of primacy will greatly facilitate our journey toward unity. Consequently, the study of Church history during the first millennium of united Christendom and reflection on the key milestones of the development of papal primacy in the West, especially during Vatican I and Vatican II, will provide the touchstone for a re-examination of what truly unites us.

What we must learn is that primacy is not so much a concept that affects specific individuals or offices, but rather a principle that guides ministries of service. It is only when *the primacy of a kenotic ethos* prevails convincingly in the Church that we shall not only be able to re-establish our deeply desired unity in faith, but also render ourselves worthy of experiencing all that God's revelation has promised to those who love the Lord, namely "a new heaven and a new earth."

In this context, it is well known that the Orthodox Church attaches fundamental ecclesiological importance to the synodal system. Together with primacy, synodality constitutes the backbone of the Church's government and organization. Furthermore, as the Joint International Commission on the Theological Dialogue between our Churches expressed in the Ravenna document of 2007, this interdependence between synodality and primacy permeates all levels of the Church's life: local, regional and universal.

It is our sincere hope and prayer that this book will provide occasion for further scholarly research and serious reflection on the part of all those interested in the history and essence of ecclesiology and involved in the life of the Church as the living body of Christ, who alone is "the Alpha and Omega, the first and the last" (Rev. 22.13).

Acknowledgments

Several people have helped me in one way or another to complete this study. First, I would like to thank His All Holiness, the Ecumenical Patriarch Bartholomew, to whom I am profoundly grateful for his having given me the opportunity to complete my doctoral dissertation at Heythrop College in the University of London. Throughout the work, His All Holiness has provided me with His fatherly support in countless ways.

To His Eminence Metropolitan John Zizioulas of Pergamon, I am profoundly thankful for inspiring me, for honoring me with the opportunity to have the lengthy discussions noted in the text, and for his contribution to my theological formation. Metropolitan John read earlier drafts of some sections of my thesis and offered some substantial suggestions. Many thanks go to my professor Constantine Delikonstantis and also to my former professors of the High Theological School in Athens and the Theological University in Belgrade, to whom I owe my theological education.

I am also deeply grateful to my supervisor, Reverend Professor Paul McPartlan, now of the Catholic University of America, Washington, D.C., not only for reading and rereading the whole of this book as it was written, offering constructive and substantial criticism and giving me valuable advice regarding the shape of my research project, but also for his inspiring lectures on ecclesiology given at Heythrop College, which tremendously enriched my ecclesiological thinking. I thank him especially for his love and constant support throughout. Particular thanks are due to His Eminence Archbishop of Australia Stylianos Harkianakis and to His Eminence Metropolitan of Tyroloe and Serention Panteleimon Rodopoulos for their fatherly support and for giving me valuable advice in regard to my research.

I would like to thank Reverend Professor Hermann Pottmeyer, emeritus professor of Fundamental Theology at the Ruhr Universität Bochum, who kindly helped me to understand certain points of Vatican II's teaching on papal primacy and collegiality and who read drafts of certain sections and offered constructive criticism. Many thanks also go to His Eminence Metropolitan of

Kydoniai Athenagoras, who is in charge of the patriarchal library, for kindly providing me with many books and a great quantity of material related to my research. I wish also to thank all the fathers of the patriarchal court of the Ecumenical Patriarchate, whose love, support, and encouragement during the years of my research go far beyond anything I could possibly express.

I also wish to express my thanks to His Eminence Archbishop Gregorios of Thyateira and Great Britain, to the former Dean of the Greek Cathedral of the Holy Wisdom (St. Sophia), Bishop of Nazianzos Dr. Theodoritos, and to the parish council of the Cathedral, as well as to Very Reverend Archimandrite Theonas Bakalis, for their love and support during my studies in London. It goes without saying that none of those mentioned should be held in any way responsible for any shortcomings that may remain. Finally, for their constant love and prayers, I owe a great debt to my family, and especially to my mother, Helen.

PRIMACY IN THE CHURCH FROM VATICAN I TO VATICAN II

Introduction

The primacy of the bishop of Rome as it was finally shaped in the Middle Ages and later defined dogmatically by Vatican I and II has been one of the thorniest issues in the history of the Western and Eastern Churches and has always been a topic in ecumenical dialogue. It appears to be an insurmountable obstacle to the realization of full unity between the Roman Catholic and the Orthodox Churches. As His All-Holiness, the Ecumenical Patriarch Bartholomew, stated clearly, "The ministry of the pope has become the biggest and most scandalous stumbling block" to dialogue between Orthodox and Roman Catholics.[1] In so saying, the Ecumenical Patriarch was expressing the unanimous Orthodox position on the matter. A primacy of jurisdiction over the whole Church contradicts the ecclesiological principles of the undivided Church and as such is rejected by the Orthodox Church. Needless to say, the issue was a primary cause of the division between the two churches and the tragic events that followed the schism of 1054—the sack of Constantinople by the crusaders in 1204, the appointment by Pope Innocent III of a Latin patriarch of Constantinople, the establishment of Uniatism as a method and model of union—as well as certain events in recent times. All these events fostered fear, mistrust, and anti-Roman feelings among the Eastern Orthodox churches and a polemical attitude toward the Roman Catholic Church.[2]

That attitude notwithstanding, in 1980 an official theological dialogue began between the two churches. This theological dialogue is the most important historical event in the relations between Roman Catholics and Orthodox since the tragic Council at Florence (1439), which was rejected by the Orthodox. This irenic rapprochement is a result of the ecumenical spirit and commitment to unity with other Christians that was adopted by the Roman Catholic Church at Vatican II, of a spirit of reconciliation between Rome and Constantinople, and of the unanimous readiness of the Orthodox churches to initiate a dialogue of truth and love with the Roman Catholic

Church. Despite the difficulties the dialogue has faced over time, it has produced very important texts on the nature and structure of the Church, upon which both sides have agreed.[3] At the last meeting of the international commission for the theological dialogue in Ravenna (October 2007), a text on ecclesial communion, conciliarity, and authority was approved, and it was decided that the theme for the next plenary session would be "the role of the Bishop of Rome in the communion of the Church in the first millennium."[4]

In addition, the late Pope John Paul II, in a surprisingly open encyclical letter, *Ut unum Sint* (1995), asked other Christians for an ecumenical study of the petrine ministry. After the promulgation of the encyclical, there were official replies from non–Roman Catholic churches and numerous responses to that invitation.[5] In line with the request made in the papal encyclical, the Pontifical Council for Promoting Christian Unity convoked an important symposium on the petrine ministry in 2003, the aim of which was to contribute to the work of the theological dialogue.[6]

Roman Catholic Reflections on Primacy since Vatican II

Vatican II established an ecclesiology of communion of local churches alongside a universalistic ecclesiology that supports a juridical view of the Roman primacy. Like Vatican I, Vatican II did not complete its work or the reform of the Roman Catholic Church. As we hope to demonstrate, eminent Roman Catholic theologians have contributed to the rediscovery of an ecclesiology of communion. Since Vatican II the ecclesiology of communion has become part and parcel of Roman Catholic theology and ecclesiology. Distinguished Roman Catholic theologians have constructed a theology of primacy on the basis of this ecclesiology of communion, which is also a key theological concept in the ecclesiological work of the contemporary Greek Orthodox theologian Metropolitan John Zizioulas of Pergamon. A brief and general survey of the notion of primacy in the light of communion ecclesiology as articulated by certain Roman Catholic theologians after Vatican II will be helpful in order to set the scene for the research presented in my book.

In this regard, one should highlight the work of Joseph Ratzinger, the former Pope Benedict XVI, Jean Marie Tillard (1927–2000), Cardinal Walter Kasper, and Hermann J. Pottmeyer.

Because of his unique former position as Pope, Ratzinger is an influential figure who has worked in great depth on ecclesiological issues. In recent years, Kasper and Pottmeyer have made a particular contribution to an understanding of Vatican I and II in terms of communion ecclesiology, while

Tillard was a pioneer in the Roman Catholic and Orthodox dialogue who wrote a book on the ministry of the bishop of Rome.

All of these influential theologians have worked within the setting of an ecclesiology of communion that constitutes the matrix within which papal primacy and the notion of collegiality are today being discussed. Moreover, the creative and critical dialogue that is occurring in recent decades, both in the Roman Catholic Church and in the Orthodox Church, has been represented in the aforementioned symposium, especially by Kasper and Pottmeyer on the Catholic side, and Zizioulas on the Orthodox side. Permit me to refer briefly to the points of convergence between the aforementioned Roman Catholic theologians and Metropolitan John Zizioulas.

Joseph Ratzinger has formulated his own understanding of collegiality, which in fact is very similar to Zizioulas's perception of episcopal synodality—that is, a notion of collegiality within the context of communion ecclesiology among the local churches. Ratzinger's notion of episcopal collegiality echoes that of the early Church as well as that of the church fathers. This is how Pottmeyer interprets Ratzinger's thought on the matter:

> This approach takes as its starting point the particular or local church; it understands the universal church to be a community or communion of churches (*communio ecclesiarum*), and this communion to be the source of collegiality. The individual church is not simply a part of the universal church, but is itself truly church because it becomes a church through the hearing of God's word and the celebration of the Eucharist. As such, it is a member of the communion of churches that manifests itself in the communion of the bishops with each other and with the pope, that is, in the college of the bishops. . . . The pope does not simply happen to be also the bishop of Rome? On the contrary, it is precisely because he is bishop of the church of Rome, which preserves the heritage of Peter and whose bishop is the successor of Peter, that he is a member and head of the college of bishops and visible head of the church. This communion of pope and bishops is an image of the communion of the churches, and the latter, in turn, is an image of the communion of the faithful (*communio fidelium*). The primacy of the pope is a primacy within a communion because he represents and is the concrete embodiment of the universal communion of local churches.[7]

After Council Vatican II, Ratzinger further explains how he understood the papal primacy in a Church as communion:

> The Church consists of many churches in communion among themselves; the network of communion that the Church thus forms finds its fixed points in

the Bishops: as the post-apostolic continuation of the *Collegium Apostolorum* [College of Apostles], they are responsible for the purity of the word and communion. With this as departure point, we can also realize the earliest meaning of the Primacy of the Roman Bishop. . . . It merely signified that the Roman Bishop of the *sedes Sancti Petri* [seat of St. Peter] was the central point of orientation in the unity of communion. . . . The Primacy of the Pope was not understood, therefore, in the administrative sense, but was wholly derived from a eucharistic ecclesiology. This means . . . that Rome incarnates the true *communio* and, therefore, is the determining point of the horizontal relationship, without which a community cannot remain truly *ecclesia*.[8]

Metropolitan Zizioulas considers the communion ecclesiology of the catholic churches as the essential context within which both synodality and primacy should be viewed.[9] Likewise, Cardinal Kasper shows that Vatican II revived the ancient communion ecclesiology of local churches as the fundamental background for the doctrine concerning the collegiality of the episcopate. Accordingly, he states:

Basically, what the council says is that the Catholic church exists in local churches and consists of local churches (*Lumen Gentium* 23). This formula, more than any other, shows how much the revival of the ancient church's concept of *communio* represents a turning point of the first order in the history of theology and the church. . . . This renewed communion ecclesiology is the background for one of the doctrines which was most discussed and most disputed at the council and afterwards: the doctrine about the collegiality of the episcopate.[10]

In his introductory paper on the academic symposium, he comments that Vatican II integrated the primacy into the whole doctrine of the Church as well as into the whole collegiality of episcopal ministry.[11] Although Kasper admits the existence of two different ecclesiologies in the texts of Vatican II, from his comments above on Vatican II we come to the conclusion that he considers a notion of primacy and collegiality within the context of communion ecclesiology of local churches as theologically legitimate. As we will indicate, Pottmeyer also supports and works with an ecclesiology of communion and urges the Roman Catholic Church "to renew and develop, more consistently than hitherto, its own form as a communion of churches." "Only if the church," Pottmeyer continues, "takes the form of a communion will the petrine office take a communal form."[12]

Jean Tillard also develops a theology of papal primacy grounded on an ecclesiology of communion among the local churches, understood as

Churches of God. In this regard Tillard develops the position of the bishop of Rome as *centrum unitatis* and his petrine primacy in a way almost identical to Zizioulas's understanding of primacy, namely in terms of the biblical notion of corporate personality. Ecclesiologically, this notion is the result of the work of the Holy Spirit in the Church—a pneumatologically conditioned Christ: "Because the risen Christ, by the work of the Spirit, became truly the communion of many in his one Body, so within the church which is his Body the One must always coexist with the many, the universal with the local, 'the primate' and the college."[13] This principle is realized in the relationship between the bishop of Rome and the college or council:

> The primate does not replace the council nor the council the primate. . . . The council gives true expression to the communion of bishops and the power which the Spirit has given it as the group of those who carry within themselves the multitude of the churches (the many). The bishop of Rome gives true expression to the unity toward which this communion and the power given by the Spirit to safeguard it is tending (the one).[14]

From what Tillard states here, it follows that the primate is an ecclesiologically indispensable person expressing unity understood as communion not only of the bishops but also of their churches.

Here it should be emphasized that while, according to Orthodox ecclesiology, each bishop is successor to Peter, as Zizioulas all too strongly affirms, this in turn does not deny the existence of a primate—of a Peter (for example, the pope) among the many Peters (namely, the bishops), whose ministry would be an expression of unity in communion.

Another point that should be taken into consideration here is the meaning given to the phrase "universal church"—the church of God or the catholic Church. If these terms are understood as equal to the worldwide or universal Church led by the pope, this is equivalent to a negation of the catholicity of each local church, since it simultaneously promotes the idea that the pope is head of the whole Church with jurisdiction over her. Such a position, however, is incompatible with the axiom of Orthodox eucharistic ecclesiology, according to which a local church is the fullness of the Church. Such a principle is based on the perception that each local church is an icon of the eschatological kingdom, as Zizioulas has amply demonstrated in his works.

Reference should be made here to the 1992 Vatican letter on the idea of the Church as communion (*Communionis Notio*), where the term "universal Church" refers more than simply to the Church in its universal perspective, which is the universal Church under the immediate jurisdiction of the bishop of Rome. In this context, I fully agree with Paul McPartlan's insightful comments on this letter, namely:

> We see that the Letter moves readily and almost imperceptibly between the transcendent and worldwide understandings of the Church, that is, between Church-mystery and the "universal Church." Belonging to the transcendent mystery of the Church, which is the very core of our Christian identity, effectively translates into membership of the worldwide fellowship of the Church under the jurisdiction of the Pope. A little further on, the Letter explicitly recalls the definition of Vatican I that papal primacy essentially involves "a truly episcopal power, which is not only supreme, full and universal, but also *immediate*, over all, whether pastors or other faithful."[15]

The letter continues with the following statement:

> The ministry of the successor of Peter as something *interior* to each particular church is a necessary expression of that fundamental *mutual interiority* between the universal church and the particular Church.[16]

By adopting the definition of Vatican I on the immediate papal jurisdiction over all other churches, the letter presumes that the interiority between the local and the universal Church is based on the assumption that each local church is a microcosm of the Church universal, that is, the Church worldwide under the leadership of the pope, and this mutual interiority and unity that the pope expresses is a universalistic one. Therefore, we may deduce that such universalistic unity under the pope in fact negates the catholicity of each local episcopal church. Thus, this universalistic understanding of the petrine ministry is something innate to each local church, that is, an ecclesiological element within each local church. While, as already seen, Ratzinger supports an understanding of the papal primacy as the expression of communion among full local churches, he also reflects an ecclesiology in which the universal church precedes the local church.[17] This has particular analogous implications for the realm of ecclesiology. The oneness is represented by the one visible head of the Church, namely the pope as head of the universal church. Zizioulas is critical of Ratzinger's approach, claiming that it is based on a trinitarian model in which otherness is secondary to unity and understood as subservient to unity. For Zizioulas this priority of the one over the many is confirmed by Vatican I and modified by Vatican II, while the last council failed to achieve a proper balance between the one and the many, namely between the local churches and the universal Church.

The letter on communion links the papacy intimately to the eucharistic character of the Church. Indeed, McPartlan notes that "Zizioulas could, perhaps, make a rather similar statement, for he too, from a rigorously eucharistic standpoint, regards a universal primacy as something required 'in an ecclesiology of communion.'"[18] As will become evident in the pages that follow, Zizioulas similarly believes that a eucharistic ecclesiology of communion leads to a ministry of primacy on the universal level, as an expression of unity between fully *catholic* local churches throughout the world.

In this context we should refer to the Ravenna Document, which comprises an important and indispensable document for future discussion in the Roman Catholic–Orthodox dialogue on the controversial and sensitive issue of papal primacy. This document places the ministry of primacy within the context of conciliarity, which is itself a manifestation of ecclesial communion: "The authority of a synod is based on the nature of the episcopal ministry itself, and manifests the collegial nature of the episcopate at the service of the communion of Churches" (Ravenna 25).[19] Thus, the document implies that primacy, understood within the context of collegiality, is an expression and representation of the communion of the local churches.

As we shall see, for Zizioulas the function and the purpose of the ministry of primacy is a *diaconia* that serves and expresses the communion of local churches though the synodical event and can never be understood as direct jurisdiction over the local churches. The primate cannot intervene in the internal affairs of a local church. If a local church faces a difficult situation or cases of disturbance or anomaly, the primate can intervene only when asked to do so.[20]

The teaching of Vatican I on the papal primacy of jurisdiction has been rejected by the Orthodox Church as well as by other non-Catholic confessions. This persistent and pervasive rejection has created an obstacle to the reunion among Christians. Within the ecumenical spirit created by Vatican II, certain Roman Catholic theologians endeavored to interpret the papal claims of Vatican I in the new context provided by Vatican II, while others have sought a solution in a clearer and more authentic understanding of Vatican I. However, these efforts have not proved very successful.[21] Luis Bermejo notes in this regard:

> The present Catholic attitude as regards the ecumenical obstacle to Vatican I is clear enough: a praiseworthy attempt on the part of single theologians to reinterpret the doctrinal claims of that Council, on the one hand, and the uncompromising adherence to them on the part of our present Roman authorities, on the other.[22]

Nevertheless, the Orthodox participants at the aforementioned symposium on the petrine ministry observed, regarding Vatican I, that the interpretation of this council in the light of Vatican II, namely in the context of communion ecclesiology, opens up real possibilities for further discussion and understanding.[23] In this regard, mention should be made of the recent publication by Greek Catholic professor Adam A. J. De Ville on the subject of Orthodoxy and the Roman primacy, which is addressed to both Roman Catholic and Orthodox readers.[24] After presenting a general survey of the pertinent Orthodox literature on papal primacy, particularly that of the postwar period, as well as of Orthodox reactions to the papal encyclical letter *Ut unum Sint*, De Ville offers certain practical suggestions regarding the position of the bishop of Rome as universal primate in a future unified Church.[25]

Despite the regrettable removal of the title "Patriarch of the West" to describe the jurisdiction of the pope from the 2006 Pontifical Yearbook, De Ville's attempt to understand the papal function in a patriarchal manner opens up realistic and positive perspectives for Roman Catholic and Orthodox agreement on such thorny issues as that of Roman primacy. Referring to Roman Catholic proposals—especially in the period after Vatican II—calling for a differentiation between the patriarchal and papal offices, he notes that none of these proposals has ever examined the idea of how such a patriarchate would function. He then proposes the creation of regional patriarchates within the Latin Church.[26] These Latin continental patriarchates would have a full and permanent synod and assume sometimes patriarchal, sometimes papal, and at other times purely local responsibilities, all of which have hitherto been undertaken by the papacy.

Furthermore, De Ville differentiates the patriarchal from the papal functions, reflecting on the specific responsibilities that would belong to the pope as pope—that is as a universal primate. After quoting the list of six papal responsibilities cited in *Ut unum Sint* and the crucial section 95 of the same papal encyclical, which states that all this must always be done in a spirit of communion, De Ville comes to the real issue of how a papal primacy should be exercised within a unified church. First, he notes that an emphasis on the centrality of a relationship between the bishop of Rome and the other bishops of the world is consistent with Orthodox arguments and approaches. Second, by taking into consideration Orthodox sensitivities, he discusses the possibility of a papal primacy that would function in the spirit of Apostolic Canon 34 as originally proposed by Ukrainian Catholic theologian Andriy Chirovsky and Orthodox theologian Thomas Hopko.[27] He then refers to the particular responsibilities of the pope in his unique capacity as universal primate, as these are listed in the encyclical *Ut unum Sint*; these responsibilities would be exercised by the pope in what he calls a permanent "ecumenical synod." The patriarchs of the West and the East would participate in this so-called ecumenical council under the presidency of the pope. This synod would deal with issues regarding the universal church and transcending patriarchal particularities. Accordingly, it would assume responsibility for the unity of the whole church.[28] Since such a proposal situates the papal primacy within the concept of synodality, I cannot see—at least from an Orthodox theological perspective—any objections to it. Therefore, I fully agree with De Ville that this synod would not exist as a body above the patriarchs and their synods, which in turn, I hope, implies that this synod would express the agreement and unanimity of the episcopate throughout the world. Finally, De Ville refers to unique papal responsibilities that the pope would perform without having to consult with or wait for the consent of the ecumenical council. For example, the pope has the responsibility of summoning full, permanent, and ecumenical synods, of presiding over their sessions, and of promulgating their decisions at a time and manner of his choosing.[29]

Thus, from an Orthodox canonical viewpoint, in a unified Church, the pope would *ipso jure* possess the right to preside over the sessions of an ecumenical council, as well as the right to convoke such a council with the consent and consensus of the other bishops. As Zizioulas puts it, the primate who convokes the council is the mouthpiece of all the bishops.[30] In a unified church the pope would have to announce and promulgate the decisions taken unanimously by this so-called ecumenical council, albeit not at any time or manner of his choosing, as De Ville proposes. For a primate cannot veto the decisions of the council, as De Ville suggests, unless the synod acts and decides without the presence of the primate.

Regarding the pope as head of the Vatican city-state,[31] it should be pointed out that such a role has been questioned on the Orthodox side. In the eyes of many Orthodox theologians, the existence of the Vatican as a state identifies the Roman church with secular organizations, something that is contrary to the spirit of the Gospel. However, this discussion also clearly lies beyond the scope of the present work.

Orthodox Eucharistic Eccesiology in the Twentieth Century

Before the neopatristic revival, Orthodox ecclesiology had been influenced by Western scholastic theology, while dogmatic manuals treated the Church in terms of a pyramidal or juridical Catholic view.[32] Thus instead of the pope, a council was considered as being the highest authority in the

Church.[33] However, in the twentieth century certain prominent theological figures, such as Nicholas Afanassieff (1892–1966), professor of canon law and church history at St. Serge Orthodox Theological Institute in Paris; Georges Florovsky (1893–1979), dean of St. Vladimir's Theological Seminary in New York and professor of patristics; Alexander Schmemann (1921–1983), dean of St. Vladimir's Theological Seminary and professor of church history and liturgical theology; John Zizioulas; and John Meyendorff (1926–1992), dean of St. Vladimir's Theological Seminary in New York and professor of church history and patristics, contributed to a biblical and patristic understanding of Orthodox ecclesiology. This new phenomenon—of Orthodox theologians working in the West and seeking a renewal of their own theological tradition in engagement with the West—developed a eucharistic ecclesiology.

It lies beyond the scope of the present work to offer an overview of the Orthodox ecclesiological developments and trends of the twentieth century up to this day.[34] However, since the present book relates the issue of primacy to a eucharistic ecclesiology of communion, as presented mainly by Zizioulas, it is helpful to offer some brief introductory remarks on why eucharistic ecclesiology is the Orthodox preference.

The identification of the Church with the eucharist is in principle a common position in the contemporary orthodoxy. As Aristotle Papanikolaou has observed: "In contemporary Orthodox theology, the claim that the Church is constituted in the eucharistic assembly has the status of a first principle in ecclesiology."[35] Nevertheless, such an identification, as Zizioulas admits, has not sufficiently permeated contemporary Greek Orthodox academic theology,[36] which was formerly influenced by Western scholasticism. This can been seen in the fact that Zizioulas's doctoral dissertation, entitled "The Unity of the Church in the Divine Eucharist and the Bishop during the First Three Centuries," met with certain objections and was thus regarded by some theologians as an inherent weakness in the foundations of Orthodox ecclesiology.[37] While Zizioulas himself has criticized the one-sidedness of Afanassieff's ecclesiology,[38] on the other hand he praises Afanassieff's identification with the Eucharist.[39] By appealing to biblical and patristic sources, Zizioulas has sufficiently proved in his works the importance of this identification.[40] Zizioulas considers it important that, in the conscience of the Orthodox people, the essence of the Church is identified with the place where the eucharist is celebrated; this can be seen in the popular expression used by Orthodox faithful: "I am going to the Church," which signifies, "I am going for the celebration of the Eucharist."[41]

Nevertheless, this eucharistic ecclesiology does not share an unchallenged consensus among Orthodox theologians. Vladimir Lossky (1903–1958),

Russian Orthodox theologian and dean of St. Denys Theological Institute in Paris and professor of dogmatic theology; and Dumitru Stăniloae (1903–1993), Romanian Orthodox theologian and professor do not adopt a strict identification of the Church as the body of Christ with the Eucharist.[42]

Although Lossky would see the Church as a communion of persons, he would not accept Zizioulas's perception of the Church as the body of Christ in the sense that Christ is the one hypostasis that is simultaneously a communion of many hypostases.[43] This is in fact the Zizioulas principle concerning "the one and the many," which is grounded in the life of the Holy Trinity, as we shall see below. I am convinced that Zizioulas—faithful to the biblical and patristic teaching on the Holy Trinity—presents a coherent triadology.[44] There is a clear ground of unity in the Holy Trinity, and that is the Father in communion with the Son and the Holy Spirit.

As we shall see, such a triadology has implications in ecclesiology and forms the basis of a theology of primacy understood within an ecclesiology of communion of local churches. The primacy is not just an administrative matter because, according to the canonical rules of the Orthodox Church, no synod can function without the presence of the primate. If it were simply an administrative matter, primacy could disappear from the life of the Church, but the canons do not allow such a possibility. This implies that primacy is essential to the life of the Church for ecclesiological-theological reasons. There is a theological grounding that necessitates the existence of primacy.

Metropolitan Kallistos Ware notes that:

> I find the use that Zizioulas makes of the concept of "corporate personality" to be unclear and confusing. The authors that he cites for the use of this notion in the Old Testament, such as H. Wheeler Robinson and A. R. Johnson, were writing more than half a century ago. How far are their ideas still accepted by contemporary Old Testament specialists?[45]

Though it is true that Zizioulas has not yet offered a revision of the idea of corporate personality in the light of new biblical and probably critical research on the issue, the concept of "the one and the many" is a very traditional idea rooted in the life of the Church. This is evident in the fact that the Church, from its very existence, has always recognized a certain hierarchical order, i.e., the "one" or the first as a sign, servant, and expression of the unity of the many.[46]

For Stăniloae, the Church may be seen in the eucharistic assembly but also outside of it.[47] What follows from such a position is that, although for Stăniloae baptism means death to the world or preparation for the eucharist, as in Zizioulas's thought, for Stăniloae baptism assumes a greater meaning and becomes a fundamental principle for ecclesiology. The Son and the Spirit perpetually abide in the Church primarily through the sacrament of baptism.[48] If a greater or particular importance is attributed to baptism *in itself*, this contradicts the fact that in the ancient Eastern tradition baptism led to the eucharist, which means that the completion of baptism was the eucharist.[49] Nevertheless, between these two theologians, there is a meeting point inasmuch as both affirm the ecclesial fullness of every local church.[50]

In an ecclesiological comparison made recently between Stăniloae and Zizioulas, the latter's eucharistic ecclesiology has been criticized for a lack of proper integration between Christology and pneumatology. It is argued that Stăniloae's understanding of the Spirit eternally resting on the Son provides a satisfactory integration and synthesis between Christ and the Spirit, leading to the simultaneous presence of Christ in each believer and outside the eucharistic event, that is, in asceticism, prayer, and good works.[51] As we shall see, Zizioulas's eucharistic ecclesiology derives precisely from a proper synthesis between Christology and pneumatology. In this respect, A. Papanikolaou accurately observes as follows:

> In other words, I don't think Zizioulas and Stăniloae are so far apart on the simultaneity of the presence of Christ and the Spirit. The difference lies in the fact that for Zizioulas the Christ that is made present is the resurrected Christ and, thus, the corporate Christ. Because of his emphasis on Christ as the one in whom all are united, Zizioulas finds it difficult to move toward the notion of the presence of Christ and Holy Spirit in individual believer.[52]

I have a feeling that Zizioulas attributes a certain value to individual prayer and asceticism, although he insists on the centrality of the eucharist in the life of the Church. All other activities outside the eucharist are rather individual, while the eucharist offers a communal life.[53] He admits that, outside the eucharist, the Church contains many other elements that constitute its essence—such as doctrine, asceticism, preaching, holiness, and repentance—as well as other sacraments, such as marriage, holy unction, and the holy services in general. However, in quoting the famous ecclesiological axiom of St. Nicholas Kabasilas, that the Church is only revealed in the sacraments (particularly the holy eucharist), Zizioulas comments that if, according to Kabasilas, the Church draws its identity from the eucharist, then all the aforementioned elements cannot be considered in isolation from the eucharist but instead must be incorporated into the eucharist in order to "become Church." If all these elements are considered outside the eucharist, then they cease to be ecclesial acts.[54] I conclude with Kallistos Ware's general appreciation of Zizioulas's eucharistic ecclesiology, which I would fully endorse:

> Afanasiev and Zizioulas advanced their eucharistic understanding of the Church over 45 years ago; indeed, Afanasiev had already adumbrated his characteristic viewpoint as long ago as the 1930s. It may therefore be asked: in the period from, say, 1965 onwards, has there emerged within Orthodox theology a new ecclesiological "model", to replace or to rival the "eucharistic" approach upheld by Afanasiev and Zizioulas? It would appear that this has not in fact happened. The "eucharistic ecclesiology" of Zizioulas continues to prevail almost everywhere. Admittedly it has been extensively criticised, but what its opponents have done is to suggest modifications on points of detail rather than to propose a fundamentally different alternative. For myself, I continue to find Metropolitan John's vision of the Church and of the human person deeply convincing, and I believe that he has indicated the path along which Orthodox theology should continue to progress in the future.[55]

In the context of current ecumenical dialogue on the papal primacy, this book proposes to review and reflect on Greek Orthodox reactions to the definitions of the first and second Vatican councils on this issue. Two groups of theologians will be identified: members of the first group (all Greek) argued against the papal primacy of jurisdiction, and members of the second group (both Greek and Russian) disputed in various ways the arguments brought by members of the first group, either demonstrating the inconsistency or incoherence of the arguments or pointing out the inauthenticity of the arguments in the light of Orthodox tradition. The distinctive position of this book is that it presents a critique of the arguments invoked by the first group of Greek Orthodox theologians. It is, in fact, a critique of a critique within Greek Orthodox theology that is offered here. The views of a number of Greek (and Russian) Orthodox theologians regarding primacy have been brought together systematically and compared in this way, so as to demonstrate the gradual emergence of a coherent view of primacy, in accordance with the canonical principles of the Orthodox Church. Through a critique of the first group's critique, the second group has increasingly clarified a theological approach to primacy that truly accords with Orthodox theological principles. This book also highlights the distinctive contribution of Metropolitan John (Zizioulas), one of the most creative theologians of our time and the principal representative of the second group of theologians, who calls us to see the issue of primacy in the Church from a dogmatic and truly theological point of view.

In the first chapter I present the main points of Vatican I's teaching on papal primacy, which was criticized by the first group of Greek Orthodox theologians in the nineteenth and twentieth centuries; I also look briefly at the historical context in which Vatican I took place and which had an impact on the council itself, and I consider, from an exegetical and historical point of view, some weaknesses and defects of Vatican I's definition of papal primacy. Chapter 2 reviews the principal arguments of the first group of theologians against the main points of Roman Catholic teaching on papal primacy described in the previous chapter. These arguments, as we will see, were criticized by the second group of Greek Orthodox theologians, represented primarily by John Zizioulas and certain Russian Orthodox theologians such as Nicholas Afanassieff, Alexander Schmemann, and John Meyendorff. I demonstrate how the first group's critique of papal primacy is incoherent and inauthentic and how the second group identifies those weaknesses, articulating at the same time an increasingly coherent and authentic understanding of the issue of primacy in the Church, not in terms of honor alone but also of power. In chapter 3 I review the main theological movements, namely the ecclesiological and liturgical movements, that influenced the doctrinal approach of Vatican II, after which I present that council's teaching on papal primacy and collegiality.

In chapter 4, I review the first group's continuing critique of Vatican II's renewed understanding of primacy within the context of its teaching on episcopal collegiality. We will also see that the second group of theologians continues a critique of the first group's critique. This is followed by Zizioulas's general assessment of the Roman Catholic conception of episcopal collegiality and an explanation of his understanding of the issue of primacy. We will see that Zizioulas justifies the existence of primacy in the Church on dogmatic-theological principles that shape the life of the Church and lead directly to the institution of primacy, namely the principle of "the one and the many," which makes the existence of primacy ecclesiologically and dogmatically necessary. In chapter 4 I also present the views of Afanassieff, Schmemann, and Meyendorff on the issue. There are two reasons for bringing these three Russian theologians into the discussion. First, while Zizioulas appreciates the main principle of Afanassieff's eucharistic ecclesiology that "whenever the Eucharist is celebrated there is the Church,"[56] he is on the other hand critical of Afanassieff's failure to heed the requirement for unity between local eucharistic churches. Through Zizioulas's critique of Afanassieff's eucharistic ecclesiology, we will see that Zizioulas's own view of eucharistic ecclesiology makes the existence of a universal primate indispensable for expressing the unity of the Church on the universal level.

Secondly, Zizioulas seems to share the views of Schmemann and Meyendorff regarding the ecclesiological justification and necessity of primacy. Nevertheless, Zizioulas gives a strictly dogmatical justification of primacy.

It is also important to note what lies beyond the scope of this book. It does not intend to present in detail how the Greek Orthodox theologians or historians of the period between the two Vatican councils interpreted and read the whole history of the papal primacy or to deal extensively with the different perceptions and interpretations of the passages from the New Testament regarding the petrine primacy or the Church Fathers' testimonies on the Roman primacy. The study is focused on specific arguments invoked by a specific group of Greek Orthodox theologians who were later critiqued by another group. My research is thus limited to a certain number of Greek Orthodox theologians who were chosen because of the position that they took on papal primacy.

The book raises some serious ecclesiological questions and issues regarding the nature and function of primacy in the Orthodox Church, including the following:

(1) Is primacy in the Church necessary *jure divino* for the Church or is it a matter of mere canonical organization, i.e., *jure humano*?

(2) Can the nature of primacy, including the universal primacy, be understood in terms of simple honor, *primus inter pares* or first in honor? Does such a simple honorific primacy accord with the canonical principles of Orthodox ecclesiology?

(3) Is a universal primate or an Orthodox universal primacy—that of Constantinople—compatible with a eucharistic ecclesiology of communion of local churches, and if so, in what sense, or is it a universalistic idea similar to that of the Pope of Rome in the Western Church?

(4) Does the Orthodox Church have an adequate structure without a single universal primate, since each autocephalous Church is headed by its own primate? Is the theory of an absolute autocephalism that excludes the existence of a universal center of the Church justified by the canonical tradition of the Orthodox Church? These final two issues pose a question pertinent to the previous questions: do the Orthodox Churches form one body united in one institutional center or is their unity purely a spiritual and invisible unity in terms of confederation?

(5) Would conciliarism as an alternative to the monarchical view of papal primacy be acceptable to Orthodox ecclesiology?

I hope, by presenting and examining these questions, to make a humble contribution to a true and coherent understanding of primacy in the Orthodox Church, including universal primacy, free from the polemical reactions of the past. I also hope to stimulate theological discussion as well as a self-critical and constructive dialogue within the Orthodox Church regarding primacy because the fact remains that the Orthodox Church lacks an exact, definitive, and coherent definition of both primacy and universal primacy, crucial issues inasmuch as they are intimately related to the unity of the Church.

CHAPTER ONE

Vatican I

In this chapter my intention is to present the teaching of Vatican I on the jurisdictional primacy of the bishop of Rome. I will present the main points of this teaching, which led to the reaction of Greek Orthodox theologians of the nineteenth and twentieth centuries, which I will discuss in chapter 2. I will also review the historical context in which Vatican I took place and which, inevitably, had an impact on the council itself. Then I will outline the history of the redaction of Vatican I's constitution on the Church, *Pastor Aeternus*, with a focus on its teaching on papal primacy. Finally, I will consider from an exegetical and historical point of view some weaknesses and defects of Vatican I's definition of papal primacy.

The Driving Forces behind Vatican I and the Historical Situation in the Nineteenth Century

Vatican I was convoked to deal with issues of the widest importance, but its main concern was the papacy, and its outcome was a settlement of the long controversy over the position and authority of the pope in the Church.[1]

This controversy can be traced back to events in the fourteenth and fifteenth centuries, especially the Great Schism in the Western Church (1378–1417). These events led to a long-term weakness of the primacy of the pope and a debate on the constitution of the Church: which is the last and the ultimate resort in the Church—the pope or a council?[2] The Council of Trent (1545–1563) discussed these issues but was not able to settle the debate over the constitution of the Church or over the relationship between the universal Church and the particular churches and between primacy and the episcopate.[3]

Although the papacy was strengthened in the post-Tridentine period,[4] the theory of conciliarism in both its moderate and radical forms found representatives in Germany (episcopalism) and especially in France (Gallicanism).[5]

The four Gallican articles adopted and passed by the French clergy congress of 1682 were the "Magna Carta" of Gallicanism.[6] The Gallican and episcopalist currents aimed at emphasizing, over against papal centralization, collegial realities such as consensus and reception and the autonomy of the individual churches.[7] Gallicanism in its pure theological form pertinently referred back to the *Ecclesia primitiva* as its model.[8]

On the other hand, the Gallican and episcopalist movements were not politically neutral, and it is no exaggeration to say that governments and princes exercised an influence on matters related to the Church. Gallicanism was both theological and political, opposed to the papal claim of temporal and absolute, as well as religious, power over the whole world. This claim found an eloquent expression in Pope Boniface VIII (1294–1303).[9] We may aptly recall here Napoleon's success in subordinating completely the Church to the state. The four Gallican articles became law. The events following the French Revolution brought about a radical destruction of both political and ecclesiastical life as well.[10] The 1790 French constitution imposed on the Church was likewise an "extraordinary radicalising of episcopalist and state church ideas."[11]

French Gallicanism was divided into two parties. One party accepted the new constitution and agreed to an ideology of a state church. The other opposed the constitution, believing that the origins of Gallicanism sprang from the episcopal and collegial constitution of the ancient Church. It is noteworthy that those who refused to take an oath to the constitution were forced to accept the papal position.[12] Likewise, the French church/state model became a model for other European countries in the nineteenth century, and Gallicanism would be seen as tantamount to a system of state control of the church.[13]

In addition to events in France, the Roman Catholic Church suffered from a certain loss of authority after the Enlightenment. The development of the sciences and the humanities led to conflict with the Church. This was reflected in the autonomy claimed both for reason and for freedom and in the development of naturalism, empiricism, relativism, the subjection of all traditions and authorities to criticism, and finally in atheism.[14] Furthermore, the revolutionary movements of 1848 in most countries of Western Europe, and especially in Italy, were characterized by strong anticlerical, anticatholic, and antireligious attitudes.[15]

In light of the above, it comes as no surprise that Ultramontanism,[16] as a movement looking beyond the Alps and supportive of papal primacy, gained in strength, becoming a mass movement in the middle of the nineteenth century.[17] It was a dynamic popular movement against powerful institutions of bureaucratic state religion and the antireligious calamities and errors of the time (i.e., atheism, naturalism, rationalism, and materialism). With Pope Gregory XVI assuming leadership of the Ultramontane movement, as Hermann Pottmeyer explains, Ultramontanism was linked not only to the struggle against the state-controlled church but even more to the struggle against modern errors. The popes understood themselves and their teaching authority as a bulwark against the penetration of modern thought into the Church.[18] This self-understanding found eloquent expression in the Syllabus of errors in 1864.

In such a situation, with the world in turmoil, a need emerged within the Catholic Church at the time of Vatican I for the strengthening of the primacy and authority of the pope. It appears that the novel concept of "sovereignty" based on Roman law, which was applied to papal primacy in the nineteenth century, had two advantages. Thus Pottmeyer explains:

> Appealing to his external sovereignty, the Pope could claim his independence of princes and states; by reason of his internal authority he could claim a position of absolute independence in relation to councils and bishops within the Church. This concept was thus a suitable means of rejecting, on the one hand, conciliarism and Gallicanism, and, on the other, state control of the Church and other limitations on the primacy by the states. The success of this concept can be seen in the fact that the Pope was more and more named as "Sovereign Pontiff". . . . Thus it was the struggle for the freedom of the church that seemed to demand an absolute primacy and a centralised government of the church. Conciliar theory and Gallicanism seemed to be necessarily disavowed as being the gateway to the system of state control of the church.[19]

The defenders of papal authority took the concept of sovereignty, already existing in some European countries prior to the middle of the nineteenth century, and applied it to the primacy.[20] The idea of the sovereignty of the pope found its chief expression in the book by Mauro Cappellari (1764–1846), *The Triumph of the Holy See and the Church over the Attacks of Innovators, Who are Rejected and Fought with Their Own Weapons*,[21] which was written to counter Piero Tamburini's book *The Authentic Idea of the Holy See*,[22] in which Tamburini combined conciliarist and Gallican concepts with the idea of popular sovereignty and democracy.[23] In fact, Cappellari's reasoning was entirely novel. It was based on the conviction that the present provides an interpretation of the Tradition and there is no need to return to the "confusion of antiquity." What is today has always been. Accordingly, the present form of the Church is its "essential-unchangeable form."[24] His only concern was to support and secure papal sovereignty. He thus determined that the form of Church government given by Christ was that of the second millennium, putting aside the whole Tradition of the first millennium and the testimonies to this tradition.[25] In Cappellari's mind, the only way to settle all disagreements between the Ultramontanists and the Gallicans was through an understanding of papal primacy as sovereignty.[26]

Cappellari claimed that the episcopal college, along with the pope, has universal jurisdictional authority in the Church. However, it is to be understood that this authority is entirely dependent on the pope, and the collegial jurisdictional authority is shorn of its legal effectiveness.[27] Thus, the episcopal college has no real status in his ecclesiological model. Cappellari took a specific position on this important question and did not leave it open. In his view the pope was superior to the college of the bishops, and the collegial character of the episcopate was dependent on him. It thus appears that Cappellari borrowed the idea of sovereignty from the state and applied it to the Church. His novel analogy between the Church and the state made it possible to accept the concept of sovereignty, which is not to be confused with despotism.[28] According to Cappellari, God as "sovereign ruler" of the Church has given to the Church, in the person of the pope, a sovereign government.[29] Pottmeyer concludes as follows:

> True enough, even Cappellari rejected any papal despotism, since the pope is bound by Divine law. However, the bishops would have no way of resisting a despotic or heretical pope except by rebelling or by praying for a divine intervention since he provided no institutional way in which the bishops could regularly exercise their universal responsibility except with the permission of the pope. Cappellari's position went a step beyond that of the thirteenth century because it claimed the pope's infallibility was an element in his sovereignty.[30]

Once Cappellari became Pope Gregory XVI (1831–1846), he put his own ideas into practice.[31] The modern conception of sovereignty was likewise part and parcel of the Ultramontanist movement.[32] Among the main figures of this movement were the French philosopher Joseph de Maistre (1753–1821) and Felicité Lamennais (1782–1854), the founder of "liberal Catholicism" and an Ultramontanist leader from 1830 to 1832. In Lamennais's view, the sovereignty of the pope was the basis of the Church's freedom from the state.[33] De Maistre firmly located the existence of the Church in the person of the pope. As might be expected, he had no ecclesiology of the episcopate, the laity, the sacraments, or the conciliar life of the Church.[34] Congar states emphatically that "thus begins the career of a theory of authority, in fact of the monarchical authority of the Pope, without a true ecclesiology."[35] Bishop Henri Maret's book, *Du concile général et de la paix religieuse*, which criticized de Maistre's absolute conception of the primacy, led to a vehement discussion three months before Vatican I.[36] In order to refute de Maistre's conception of the primacy, Maret proposed the idea of a "complex sovereignty."[37] After an investigation into the history and structure of the Church, Maret considered that Peter and the other apostles formed a "collective unity,"[38] just as the pope and the bishops do in a council. Sovereignty belongs, therefore, neither to the pope alone nor to the bishops but is shared by both of them.[39] Maret's notion of "sharing sovereignty" was rejected by Vatican I in its categorical statement: "If anyone says that the Roman Pontiff has only the principal part but not the absolute fullness of this supreme power . . . let him be anathema."[40]

Although De Maistre and Lamennais both had primarily political goals, they nevertheless wielded a widespread influence among Catholics before Vatican I, and through them Cappellari's ecclesiological ideas became influential after 1831.[41] On a popular level the unique personality of Giovanni Maria Mastrai Ferreti, Pope Pius IX, furthered the Ultramontanist movement. It would be no exaggeration to say that he was the object of a particular devotion.[42] Further, Tillard considers that "the personality of Pius IX interacted with ultramontanism to the point of osmosis."[43] Nichols defines Ultramontanism from a theological point of view: "Ultramontanism was theologically derived from Neo-Scholasticism, especially the ecclesiologies of Aquinas[44] and Bellarmine,[45] and was poorly grounded in either church history or scripture."[46] In spite of this, one thing was clear: on the eve of Vatican I, the novel idea of papal primacy as indivisible sovereignty was, in the thought of many Catholics, a traditional teaching.[47]

We can conclude that Vatican I was strongly influenced by its historical context. In this context, the pope and many in his flock felt threatened by political and modern scientific developments, and the papacy took a defensive stand against them. In order to represent the Church as a refuge in such a situation, the papacy had to be strengthened.[48]

Thus, marked by this context, Vatican I was on the defensive.[49] The pope and the bishops at the council considered that rescue could be effected only by the pope and a centralized view of papal primacy. This defensive attitude of the Roman Catholic Church explains why Vatican I defined the papal primacy of jurisdiction in a consciously one-sided manner. The Roman Catholic Church in Europe could no longer rely on kings as defenders of faith or on feudal structures to safeguard its independence. With the end of papal states immediately after Vatican I the papacy lost its feudal basis.

But it no longer needed this, since in the meantime the council had turned papal primacy into a dogma and had thereby ensured its practical acceptance within the Roman Catholic Church.[50]

The Dogmatic Definition of Papal Primacy
THE HISTORY OF THE CONSTITUTION AND THE CONCILIAR DEBATE

Pope Pius publicly announced the forthcoming council on June 26, 1867, when the bishops were gathered in Rome to celebrate the eighteenth centenary of St. Peter's martyrdom. The council was "to bring necessary and salutary remedies to the many evils which oppress the Church."[51] The bishops replied with a congratulatory address that exalted the role of the Roman pontiff as teacher and judge of the universal Church. One of the passages of the address speaks of the pope as follows:

> For we fully accept what the Fathers of the Council of Florence defined in the decree of union: That the Roman Pontiff is the Vicar of Christ and Head of the whole Church, and Father and teacher of all Christians, and to him in blessed Peter has been given by Jesus Christ full power of feeding, ruling and governing the Church.[52]

Two years before the announcement of the council, Pius IX decided to consult a number of bishops on the feasibility of holding an ecumenical council and on the matters they felt needed treatment by such a council. Among the replies were requests for the condemnation of Gallicanism and for a definition of papal primacy.[53] On this, Dewan quite significantly notes the following:

> Regarding all the replies received, one is not struck by any unanimity of requests to define the power and nature of the papal Primacy. It goes without saying, of course, that bishops of anti-Roman or anti-centralisation tendencies would not mention this point. But we have here—considering only the Western Bishops—with very few exceptions, men of Ultramontane sympathy, eleven alone from Italy. The group could scarcely be called representative, there being, for example, only one Bishop from all the English-speaking lands—and that, Archbishop Manning, the most Ultramontane of them all.[54]

The Eastern Catholic bishops, on the other hand, hoped that the forthcoming council would be a wonderful means of promoting reunion with the Eastern Orthodox churches, but it must be pointed out that not one of them asked for a definition of primacy to assist in this regard.[55] Attitudes and opinions also were influenced by the issuing of a papal bull, *Reversurus* (1867)—which required papal confirmation before the ordination of bishops—and by the events that followed.[56]

The draft Constitution on the Church consisted of fifteen chapters in total, which treated all aspects of the Church—as the Mystical Body, as the true religion, as perfect society, as visible, as necessary for salvation, as indefectible, as infallible. Chapter 10 was on the power of the Church, chapter 11 on the papal primacy, chapter 12 on temporal power, and chapters 13–15 on Church and the state. There was no reference to papal infallibility, although chapter 9 was on the infallibility of the Church. Later, during the council, chapter 11, on the papal primacy, was taken from the rest of the draft and expanded to include reference to papal infallibility, so as to form the stand-alone text, "The First Constitution of the Church of Christ." Finally, this separate single Constitution was the sum content of Vatican I's teaching on the Church.[57]

As soon as Pope Pius IX decided to proceed with the council, the nomination of canonists and theologians to prepare the schemata for the council took place. The consultors chosen were assigned to various commissions, while to the Dogmatic Commission was confined the work of formulating a schema on the primacy. The four consultors who were entrusted with the drafting of a schema on the primacy were Phillip Cossa, Franz Hettinger, Giovanni Perrone, and Clement Schrader.[58] They were all Ultramontane, albeit to varying degrees.[59]

These consultors wrote their reports on the nature of papal primacy, but no formal schema was composed.[60] On the basis of the reports and recommendations, Hettinger composed a schema on the primacy and infallibility of the Roman pontiff. In it the word "episcopal" was not used to describe papal jurisdiction. The schema was discussed by Hettinger and by the special deputation, which was charged with looking after uniformity and evenness of style in the schemata. In the end, for reasons of prudence, the text on infallibility was deleted.[61]

Finally, a new redaction was committed to Schrader. Dewan explains that it is to Schrader that we owe the schema on the papal primacy as it substantially was enacted by Vatican I.[62] In this schema the pope's supreme power of jurisdiction over the particular churches as well as over the Universal Church is qualified as "true" and "proper," "ordinary," and "immediate."[63]

According to the Dogmatic Commission, the first qualification, "proper and true," was directed against the followers of Febronius, Tamburini, and the Pistoians, who claim the power was only of inspection and direction.[64] The third qualification (i.e., ordinary) was directed against J. V. Eybel,[65] who said that "the whole power of the ecclesiastical primacy is contained in this one prerogative, namely, of supplying for the negligence of others by exhortation, example, and the counselling of a unity that must be preserved"; and again, that "the Pontiff cannot act in other dioceses except in extraordinary cases."[66] Finally, the fourth qualification (i.e., immediate) opposed Tamburini's position that "the Primacy is not episcopal and immediate jurisdiction in each and every diocese." Tamburini maintained that "the spiritual authority of the primacy must not be confused with episcopal authority. They are distinct things. . . . If the Primacy must be one and the same thing as episcopal authority, it would logically follow that the Pope is the universal and only bishop, since the authority of the primacy would extend to the whole Church."[67]

The schema asserted that "all are bound by the duty of hierarchical subordination and true obedience to submit, so that the Church of Christ may be one flock under one supreme Pastor."[68] The words "one flock" indicate the end and the effect of the primacy in the view of the consultors. Thus, the form of rule was settled by divine institution. It must enable the pope, who was made supreme and universal pastor of both lambs and sheep, to rule the whole flock and to keep unity. Therefore, the power of primacy must be ordinary and immediate over each and every member. Nor does it suffice, as some claim, to limit this unity to dogmatic unity. No, it must extend to a unity based on obedience to the Supreme Pastor, not only in matters regarding the faith but in discipline as well.[69] Moreover, this papal power extended even to the bishops united in the General Council.[70]

In January 1870 the schema on the Church, *De Ecclesia*, including chapter 11 on the primacy, was distributed to the council's bishops for their written comments.[71] Many were dissatisfied with the absence of mention of rights of the bishops from the schema, which took no account of hierarchy, episcopate, ministry, or ecumenical councils.[72] It was felt that a statement should have been made that the episcopate is of divine origin and that the bishops are the successors of the apostles and not vicars of the pope.[73] According to Hans Küng, Vatican I left open the question as to whether episcopal jurisdiction derived from the pope or from Christ; for Küng this question is a controversial one for Roman Catholic theology.[74] However, some years after Vatican I, Leo XIII's encyclical letter *Satis Cognitum* (1896) declared that the bishops are not to be accounted vicars of the Roman Pontiff.[75]

Some of the bishops objected to the description of the pope as the principle and source of unity. For them, Christ is the "essential principle of unity" in the Church, and Peter is the subsidiary principle of unity in the college of the apostles.[76] In addition, there were demands to delete the phrase "visibile fundamentum" (visible foundation) and to add "praecipium fundamentum" (principal foundation) in the chapter on the primacy, for Peter is not the only foundation; according to St. Jerome, the foundation rests also upon all the apostles.[77]

The debate on *Pastor Aeternus*, the First Constitution on the Church, began in May 1870.[78] Here again, some of the bishops reminded the council that while the primacy affirmed and defended the rights of the bishops, these rights were nowhere listed. However, all of them affirmed the papal primacy of jurisdiction.[79]

As the spokesman for the Deputation on the Faith noted, the pope can exercise his immediate power directly over all believers without the permission and the intermediacy of the local bishop.[80] On the other hand, the spokesman made an effort to clarify the meaning of the word "immediate": "Certainly, if the supreme Pontiff, since he has the right to perform every true episcopal action in any diocese, were to multiply himself so to speak, and nullify in each day's decisions without the consideration of the bishop what the latter has wisely ordered, then he would use his power not for building but for destruction."[81]

With regard to the description of papal authority as "episcopal," the spokesman of the Deputation explained that the pope has the same pastoral authority in the entire Church as the bishop does in his diocese. This term was later inserted into the schema in order to make clear that the pope's authority is not limited to an office of inspection or direction but is a genuine authority of jurisdiction.[82] Episcopal authority derives from the sacrament of ordination, so that both the pope and the bishops share the same reality.[83] However, "the episcopal authority in the Pope is supreme and independent; in the bishops it is immediate and ordinary but dependent."[84] The *potestas episcopalis* does not mean that the pope is the bishop of every place and of every believer; instead, it implies a general pastoral authority. Nevertheless, this pastoral authority concerns all directly, not indirectly through the bishops.[85] Ordinary power in the canonical sense means the power that is not delegated but belongs to the pope by virtue of his office and is to be exercised "*in peculiaribus adiunctis*," that is, in special cases.[86] This explanation countered the bishops' fear caused by the general conviction that "ordinary" meant day-to-day authority.[87]

Since both Pius IX and the Deputation of Faith were afraid of anything that might make papal power vulnerable, nothing was said about practical limits to the pope's jurisdictional authority over the Church. The spokesman of the Deputation did set general principles of limitation, however, namely that the power of the pope exists for the building-up of the Church, not its destruction, and that the plenary and supreme authority is limited by divine and natural law.[88] Although there was no reference to limitations on the exercise of that primacy, the spokesman for the Deputation on the Faith pointed out that the Church must not be regarded as an absolute monarchy, for divine and natural law bind the pope. He also stated that the pope would not annul "all canonical decisions enacted with wisdom and piety by the Apostles and the Church."[89]

Moreover, the Constitution itself set limits by affirming that "this power of the supreme pontiff by no means detracts from that ordinary and immediate power of episcopal jurisdiction, by which bishops, who have succeeded to the place of the apostles by appointment of the holy Spirit, tend and govern individually the particular flocks which have been assigned to them."[90] That said, as Tillard notes, "one would like to know the actual areas where these limits come into play. The council did not delay over it."[91]

There was also no mention at all of the collegial character of the bishops in the Constitution. The two requests in this regard were rejected on the ground that the only issue for the time being was the full and immediate authority of the pope. An anti-Gallican emphasis is obvious here.[92] Nevertheless, the spokesman of the Deputation makes a clear assertion of episcopal collegiality, with Matt. 18:18 as the scriptural basis; supreme authority exists together in the pope and the bishops. An ecumenical council has supreme ecclesiastical power over the faithful, as an act of the bishops with their head.

On the other hand, he clearly admitted that this supreme and full governmental authority exists in the pope himself and that the same full and supreme power is also in the head joined with the members, i.e., the pontiff with the bishops. What is more, the pope as a head can exercise his supreme authority even independently of his joint actions with the other bishops.[93]

Küng stresses the fact that Vatican I did not take an express position on the relationship between the pope and an ecumenical council or on the mode of coexistence between these two supreme authorities that would prevent either of them from losing their authority.[94]

As we have seen, the bishops at Vatican I were critical of the fact that their rights and their collegial co-responsibility were passed over in silence. It was then decided that the composition of a second constitution on the Church would follow the first Constitution (i.e., *Pastor Aeternus*). The drafting of this second constitution was entrusted to the German Jesuit Joseph Kleutgen but was not further discussed or decided upon due to the premature suspension of the council.[95] As we shall see, it was Vatican II that would address this issue.

THE DEFINITION OF PAPAL PRIMACY OF JURISDICTION
IN *PASTOR AETERNUS*: WEAKNESSES AND DEFECTS

On July 18, 1870, the council accepted the definitive version of the first dogmatic Constitution on the Church of Christ, *Pastor Aeternus,* which contained four chapters. The first chapter treats of "the institution of the apostolic primacy in blessed Peter"; the second speaks in particular of "the permanence of the primacy of blessed Peter in the Roman Pontiffs"; the third deals with "the power and character of the primacy of the Roman Pontiff"; and finally, the fourth treats of "the infallible teaching authority of the Roman Pontiff."[96]

We will review the main points of the Constitution's teaching on the primacy, and then, in the next chapter, the reaction to and rejection of these points by Greek Orthodox theologians of the nineteenth and twentieth centuries. For now, let us note that some contemporary Roman Catholic theologians consider that the internal arguments from the Bible and church history adduced by Vatican I to substantiate its teaching on the papal primacy of jurisdiction are, in fact, weak and unconvincing. The main points of the teaching are presented below.

Chapter 1. Pastor Aeternus in its opening paragraphs declares that Christ set Peter over the rest of the apostles as the principle of unity of the episcopate and of the faithful in faith and communion. Thus, the description of the primacy of Peter and therefore of his successors as the principle (i.e., source) of unity is a manifestation of universalistic or pyramidal ecclesiology, namely a unity understood as obedience to papal authority.[97] The first chapter teaches that Peter was appointed by divine right as the visible head of the Church with a primacy not of honor but of jurisdiction over the whole Church. For the Constitution, such a jurisdictional primacy is grounded in the Holy Scriptures, namely it draws on Mt. 16:16–19 and Jn. 21:15–17:

> We teach and declare that, according to the gospel evidence, a primacy of jurisdiction over the whole Church of God was immediately and directly promised to the blessed apostle Peter and conferred on him by Christ the Lord. It was to Simon alone, to whom he had already said *You shall be called Cephas* (Jn. 1:42), that the Lord, after his confession, *You are the Christ, the son of the living God,* spoke these words: *Blessed are you, Simon Bar-Jona. For flesh and blood has not revealed this to you, but my Father who is in heaven. And I tell you, you are Peter, and on this rock I will build my church, and the gates of the underworld shall not prevail against it. I will give you the keys of the Kingdom*

of heaven, and whatever you bind on earth shall be bound in heaven, and whatever you loose on earth shall be loosed in heaven (Mt. 16:16–19). And it was to Peter alone that Jesus, after his resurrection, confined the jurisdiction of supreme pastor and ruler of his whole fold, saying: *Feed my lambs, feed my sheep* (Jn. 21:15–17). . . . Therefore, if anyone says that blessed Peter the apostle was not appointed by Christ the Lord as prince of all the apostles and visible head of the whole church militant; or that it was a primacy of honour only and not one of true and proper jurisdiction that he directly and immediately received from our Lord Jesus Christ himself: let him be anathema.[98]

The spokesman of the Deputation on the Faith, Bishop D'Avanzo, regarding Mt. 16:16–19 and in answer to difficulties raised by Cardinal Schwarzenberg, gave a restricted interpretation of the passage:

> Since the Church is to be built upon Peter as the foundation stone, it follows that in this text the relation between Peter and the Apostles is the same as that between the foundation and the building. The foundation supports the building, it is not supported by it; it rules but is not ruled; in short, the building depends absolutely on the foundation, not the other way round. Therefore the relation of the Apostles to Peter is in itself a relation of absolute dependence.[99]

In referring to Jn. 21:15–19, D'Avanzo came to the same conclusion, namely that the passage implies a subordination of the eleven to Peter.[100]

While our focus is on the Greek Orthodox rejection of Vatican I's restrictive interpretation of the petrine texts, the views of some contemporary Roman Catholic theologians are of interest as well. Luis Bermejo, for example, finds many defects and weaknesses in Vatican I's exegesis of the petrine texts. Criticizing this exegesis in the light of modern biblical scholarship, he notes that "the all-important question of Peter's successor too remains undecided, for whereas the power of binding/loosing may be the object of a transference—and in the light of 18:18 the entire community would be the successor rather than a single individual—the metaphor of the rock and foundation of the building seems rather to suggest an unrepeatable foundational role which by its very nature cannot be handed down."[101]

Bermejo also considers that Jn. 21:15–19 indeed implies a real authority, one that is spiritual and pastoral rather than juridical, but one that is not unlimited.[102] For Bermejo, "it is at least doubtful whether the other members of the apostolic college are also included in the imagery of the flock, so as to make them subordinate to Peter."[103] He notes:

In conclusion, John's text is not so far apart from Matthew's. The framework
and imagery used may be either quasi-juridical or pastoral, but both the texts
convey substantially the same meaning: Peter is placed by Jesus in a position
of authority, either to teach and govern (Mt.) or to guide and guard (Jn.). . . .
In spite of its faulty exegetical tools . . . the Council may not be so far wide
of the mark in attributing to Peter, on the basis of Mt. 16:18, a truly juridical
power; but the same cannot be said of John's text, for here the context is not
of law but of love.[104]

Thus, for Bermejo it is doubtful that the petrine texts imply an *omnimoda
et absoluta subordinatio* (a universal and absolute subordination) of the eleven
to Peter as they did for Bishop D'Avanzo, for "contemporary exegesis has established that 'in reference to the Twelve, Peter's position was nuanced and
special authority over the others is not clearly attested.'"[105] Bermejo goes on
to say that Vatican I even distorts the true image of Peter: "Instead of giving a comprehensive description of Peter as it emerges from the entire New
Testament, with its disconcerting lights and shadows, the Council zeroes in
exclusively on two texts, and these narrow conciliar perspectives cannot but
distort the true image of Peter."[106]

Chapter 2. The second chapter of *Pastor Aeternus* teaches that the Roman
Pontiff is *jure divino* successor to Peter in his primacy. The teaching is
summed up in the following canon: "Therefore, if anyone says that it is not
by the institution of Christ the Lord himself (that is to say, by divine law)
that blessed Peter should have perpetual successors in the primacy over the
whole Church; or that the Roman Pontiff is not the successor of blessed Peter in this primacy: let him be anathema."[107]

Vatican I's contention that Peter must have perpetual successors in his
primacy over the Church by divine right is disputed by Bermejo. In fact,
the second chapter does not quote a single scriptural text to support this
claim but relies exclusively on four quotes of Western authors: Irenaeus,
Ambrose, Pope Leo the Great, and Philip, papal legate at the Council of
Ephesus (431).[108] Bermejo considers that Irenaeus's expression that "it has
always been necessary for every church—that is to say the faithful throughout the world—to be in agreement with the Roman Church because of its
more effective leadership (*propter potentiorem principalitatem*)" is clearly
too controversial to be of any real value and that Ambrose's reference to
the Roman see as the center and origin from which "the rights of sacred
communion (*venerandae communionis iura*)" flow to all, is too vague and
inconclusive.[109] For Bermejo the quotes from Philip's address to the council

in 431, which state that Peter has been established as the foundation and pillar of the Church, has received the keys of the kingdom from Christ, and continues to live and exercises judgement through his successors, and those also from Pope Leo I, are an excellent testimony to the mentality prevalent in Rome by the middle of the fifth century, which attributed to Peter a kind of continual spiritual presence in his successors, a presence more quasi-sacramental than juridical.[110] Thus, none of these testimonies speaks of Peter's successors by divine right. Bermejo concludes: "Vatican I seems to be correct in not even attempting to show from the New Testament that Peter must have perpetual successors, for we have seen above that this question lies outside the purview of the biblical writers. So, deprived of any scriptural basis and amazingly weak in its selection of patristic testimonies, the contention of the second canon . . . that Peter must have perpetual successors by divine right remains highly questionable."[111]

Chapter 3. In order to provide historical support for the jurisdictional primacy of the Roman pontiff, the third chapter of the Constitution appeals to the decrees of previous councils and to the teaching of the Council of Florence on papal primacy:

> And so, supported by the clear witness of holy scripture, and adhering to the manifest and explicit decrees both of our predecessors the Roman pontiffs and of general councils, we promulgate anew the definition of the ecumenical council of Florence, which must be believed by all faithful Christians, namely, that the apostolic see and the Roman pontiff hold a world-wide primacy, and that the Roman pontiff is the successor of blessed Peter, the prince of the apostles, true vicar of Christ, head of the whole church and father and teacher of all Christian people. To him, in blessed Peter, full power has been given by our Lord Jesus Christ to tend, rule and govern the universal church. All this is to be found in the acts of the ecumenical councils and the sacred canons.[112]

Nevertheless, there were voices that demanded the insertion of some conciliar decrees of previous councils. The spokesman for the Deputation on the Faith rejected this amendment on the curious grounds that detailed citations are proper to a theological treatise but not to a conciliar decree.[113] Florence, like Vatican I, grounded its definition of the Roman primacy in the previous councils without any further specification. Some of these decrees were explicitly quoted by theologians during the Council of Florence.[114]

Even so, Bermejo notes that the uncritical way in which those important testimonies were handled by some theologians at the Council of Florence calls for extreme reserve in assessing their probative value.[115] Following a critical evaluation, Bermejo comes to the conclusion that the testimonies cited by Latin theologians at the Council of Florence, in which Vatican I found indirect support for a papal primacy of jurisdiction, cannot in fact be used as a convincing argument in favor of such a primacy.[116] Bermejo considers the early councils held in the East and finds no support in them for a papal primacy.[117]

Thus, for example, Montenero, one of the leading Latin theologians at the Council of Florence, referred to the Councils of Chalcedon, Constantinople III, and Nicea II. Montenero magnified the famous acclamation of the conciliar fathers at Chalcedon, "Peter has spoken through Leo"; he quoted Agatho's letter to the fathers of Constantinople III, in which the pope claimed to have universal teaching authority by divine right, but he omitted to say that the letter was accepted by the council after it had been subjected to close scrutiny, not before. The reference to Nicaea II is not to any conciliar enactment but to two letters of Pope Adrian II to Tarasius, patriarch of Constantinople.[118] The acclamation of the fathers at the Council of Chalcedon could be taken not as an implicit recognition of papal primacy of jurisdiction, but rather as an acknowledgement that Leo's Tome was in agreement with apostolic faith.[119] In a second speech, Montenero asserted also that Peter would have ordained his successor Anacletus, Chalcedon would have been convoked by order of Pope Leo, and Nicea I, in its Sixth Canon, would have acknowledged the Roman primacy.[120] As Bermejo notes, "These gross historical errors concerning Chalcedon and Nicea I can hardly be a convincing testimony in favour of the primacy."[121]

The Sixth Canon of Nicea I mentions the existing privileges (*presbeia*) of the Bishop of Rome, the Bishop of Alexandria, and the Bishop of Antioch, understood in the sense of legal power. Alexandria, Rome, and Antioch are on the same level, each one endowed with the same power consisting in the right to confirm the elections and to ordain all the bishops within a group of secular provinces. This power was not exercised universally but only locally.[122] With regard to the convocation of Chalcedon, it has been historically proven that "although Rome at that time considered its own consent to be necessary for the convocation of an ecumenical Council, it is the Emperor Marcian who convokes it, not the Pope."[123]

Finally, the Constitution summed up its teaching on the jurisdictional primacy of the Bishop of Rome in the following canon:

> So, then, if anyone says that the Roman Pontiff has merely an office of supervision and guidance, and not the full and supreme power of jurisdiction over the whole church, and this not only in matters of faith and morals, but also in

those which concern the discipline and government of the church dispersed throughout the whole world; or that he has only the principal part, but not the absolute fullness, of this supreme power; or that this power of his is not ordinary and immediate both over all and each of the churches and over all and each of the pastors and faithful: let him be anathema.[124]

Although the same Constitution affirms that the power of the supreme pontiff is far from standing in the way of the episcopal power by which the bishops, who have succeeded to the place of the apostles, govern the particular flocks assigned to them, the fact is that the Constitution defines the papal primacy of jurisdiction in a consciously one-sided manner. As Pottmeyer has explained, the main reasons for such a one-sided emphasis on the papal primacy of jurisdiction were the Ultramontane and anti-Gallican tendencies of the majority of bishops as well as the defensive attitude of the Roman Catholic Church prevalent at the time in a number of countries, in response to the challenges of modern society.[125]

THE ENCYCLICAL LETTERS OF POPE LEO XIII, PRAECLARA GRATULATIONIS AND SATIS COGNITUM, AND THEIR TEACHING ON THE PRIMACY

Pope Leo XIII (1878–1903) was deeply concerned with Christian unity. One of the aims of his pontificate was the promotion of unity with other Christians.[126] Thus, on the occasion of his episcopal jubilee (1894), Pope Leo XIII addressed an encyclical letter, *Praeclara Gratulationis,* to all the princes and rulers of the world, and in this letter he invited all the Orthodox to union with the Church of Rome.[127] The style of the encyclical letter was kind. In contrast with Pius IX, Leo placed emphasis on the points of rapprochement with the Eastern Orthodox:[128] "First of all, then, We cast an affectionate look upon the East, from whence in the beginning came forth the salvation of the world. . . . We hope it all the more, that the distance separating them from us is not so great: nay, with some few exceptions, we agree so entirely on other heads that, in defence of the Catholic faith, we often have recourse to reasons and testimony borrowed from the teaching, the rites, and customs of the East."[129]

Along with his insistence on the points of rapprochement, Leo XIII set out the precondition for achieving unity with the Orthodox, namely, recognition of the primacy and of the supreme power of the Roman pontiffs. Leo XIII urged the Orthodox to "look back to the early years of their existence

... and examine what the oldest traditions testify, and it will, indeed, become evident to them that Christ's divine utterance, *Thou art Peter, and upon this rock I will build my Church*, has undoubtedly been realised in the Roman Pontiffs."[130]

Referring back to the ancient time before the unfortunate division between the East and the West, Leo points out that "the East, like the West, agreed without hesitation in its obedience to the Pontiff of Rome, as the legitimate successor of St. Peter, and, therefore, the Vicar of Christ here on earth."[131]

Two years later (1896), in his encyclical letter on the unity of the Church, *Satis Cognitum*, Leo elaborated extensively on the papal primacy.[132] It must be noted from the outset that the encyclical letter speaks of the Church as a "perfect society."[133] From an ecclesiological perspective, to consider the theory of the Church as a "perfect society" means to consider it in juridical terms. Accordingly, the encyclical letter affirms that "indeed no true and perfect human society can be conceived which is not governed by some supreme authority. Christ therefore must have given to His Church a supreme authority to which all Christians must render obedience."[134] Obedience to the supreme authority is one of the norms that is to guide discussion on the unity of the Church.

The encyclical letter then states that this authority, which stems from Jesus Christ, is found in his vicars, namely Peter and his successors:

> Certainly, Christ is a King forever; and though invisible, He continues unto the end of time to govern and guard His Church from heaven. But since He willed that His kingdom should be visible He was obliged, when He ascended into heaven, to designate a vicegerent on earth. . . . Jesus Christ, therefore, appointed Peter to be the head of the Church; and he also determined that the authority instituted in perpetuity for the salvation of all should be inherited by His successors, in whom the same permanent authority of Peter himself should continue.[135]

Like Vatican I, the encyclical letter evokes the Council of Florence's definition of papal primacy, which calls the pope, successor of Peter, *vicarius Christi* and head of the Church.[136] Although its emphasis is on the pope as head of the Church and *vicarius Christi*, the encyclical letter also stresses that Christ is the head of the Church.[137] More precisely, we may say that the Church has not two heads but one, insofar as the invisible head, Jesus Christ, is represented by the pope as the visible head, his *vicarius*. The unity of the Church is based on the pope and on the obedience of all to him and to his authority as vicar of Christ.[138]

Also in line with Vatican I, the encyclical draws upon Mt. 16:18, "Thou art Peter, and upon this rock I will build my Church," in order to show that Peter, by the will and command of God, became the foundation of the Church, upon whom the whole Church rests. Peter's office consists, therefore, in supporting the Church and guarding it in all its strength and indestructible unity by jurisdictional power. According to *Satis Cognitum*, Jesus' words "and the gates of hell shall not prevail against it" (Mt. 16:18) proclaim this authority and power.[139] The encyclical also appeals to the passage from John's Gospel to show that this authority was given to Peter by Christ: "Feed my lambs, feed my sheep." These words imply a pastoral authority of Peter over the whole Church. It also quotes in support some Fathers, such as St. Chrysostom.[140]

Although it is not the purpose of this study to review in detail the views of the Fathers of the Church on Peter's position or their interpretation of the petrine texts, we will see in the next chapter that the Orthodox theologians of the nineteenth and twentieth centuries did not consider that the Fathers embraced the idea that Peter had been granted power over the whole Church by Christ.

To support its argument, the encyclical also quotes statements of Popes Leo I and Gregory the Great, both of whom had a strong belief in Roman leadership of the whole Church. Leo I's strong view on the papacy was not accepted by the East, as the story of the Council of Chalcedon clearly demonstrates. Nevertheless, Leo was not an autocrat, for he decided on important issues together with his synod.[141] As for Gregory the Great, he laid the foundations of the medieval papacy and can in fact be considered as a transitional figure between the ancient and medieval Church.[142]

In order to prove the claim that the bishop of Rome is the legitimate successor to Peter in his office and his jurisdictional primacy over the Church, the encyclical letter *Satis Cognitum* quotes, among others, St. Cyprian, traditionally viewed by Catholic ecclesiology as providing incontrovertible evidence in favor of a papal primacy of jurisdiction and of a juridical view of unity under the pope.[143] Accordingly, the encyclical asserts that Cyprian teaches that it is the Roman Church that is the root and mother of the Catholic Church, the chair of Peter, and the principal Church where sacerdotal unity has its source.[144] This claim can hardly be considered an historical truth, for the Fathers never described the primacy of the pope in juridical terms as does the encyclical letter. On the contrary, as the Russian Orthodox Alexander Schmemann notes, the Fathers and the ecumenical councils acknowledge Rome as the senior Church, the center of ecumenical agreement.[145] In the ancient Church, Rome, and not only her bishop, was recognized as the touchstone and center of orthodoxy. It is in fact in this sense that we may understand the well-known passage from Irenaeus, referred to earlier, which Vatican I proffered as evidence of the papal primacy of jurisdiction over the Church.[146] This passage need not be understood as implying a unity under the jurisdictional primacy of the pope, as *Satis Cognitum*, like Vatican I, inferred.[147]

In support of the pope's jurisdictional authority, the encyclical quotes the address of the papal legate Philip to the fathers of the Third Ecumenical Council, which implies that the bishop of Rome as a successor of Peter exercises a juridical authority over the East, and also mentions the acclamations of the fathers at the Third and Fourth Ecumenical Councils.[148] However, the conception of jurisdictional primacy reflected in the address of the papal legate was ignored and set aside by the Third Ecumenical Council,[149] and the acclamations at the councils are not to be taken literally, as Bermejo notes.[150]

Regarding the bishops' authority, the encyclical letter affirms that the bishops "are not to be looked upon as *vicars* of the Roman Pontiffs; because they exercise a power really their own, and are most truly called the *ordinary* pastors of the peoples over whom they rule."[151] However, it indicated that their authority must be understood within the pyramidal ecclesiology of Vatican I: "But the authority of the Roman Pontiff is supreme, universal, independent; that of the bishops limited, and dependent."[152]

It should also be noted that in *Satis Cognitum* the relation between the pope and the councils is characterized by the dominance of the pope over the councils and the episcopal college. The highest authority resides in the pope and not in the councils:

> Christ the Lord, as we have quite sufficiently shown, made Peter and his successors His *vicars*, to exercise forever in the Church the power which He exercised during His mortal life. Can the Apostolic College be said to have been above its master in authority? This power over the Episcopal College to which we refer, and which is clearly set forth in holy writ, has ever been acknowledged and attested by the Church, as is clear from the teaching of General Councils.[153]

In order to prove the superiority and the authority of the pope over the councils, the encyclical also refers to statements by Pope Hadrian II (867–872) and Pope Nicolas I (858–867), claiming that "the Roman Pontiff has pronounced judgements on the prelates of all churches; we do not read that anybody has pronounced sentence on him."[154]

This principle is summed up in the famous phrase "*prima sedes a nemine iudicatur*" (the first see is judged by no one) that appeared much earlier in the letters of Pope Gelasius (492–496) in the context of the Acacian schism.[155]

It is important to stress the fact that, at the time of Gelasius, the Eastern Church considered such a view as contrary to tradition.[156] The principle, which was incorporated into Western canon law in the ninth century through the Symmachian forgeries, would in the Middle Ages expand into the claim of Roman infallibility.[157] Nichols criticizes the method of grounding a monarchical view of papacy upon false documents:

> Many of the arguments for a command model of papal authority have depended on false historical assumptions or on forged documents. . . . The principle that *"Prima sedes a nemine iudicatur"* (the first see is judged by no one), though it appears in two letters of Pope Gelasius, actually entered canon law through the Symmachian forgeries. Yet canon law and papal documents have unblushingly continued to repeat these claims with no acknowledgment of their historically specious origins.[158]

For *Satis Cognitum*, the pope's authority over the councils is also substantiated by Pope Gelasius's statement on the decrees of the councils: "That which the first See has not approved of cannot stand; but what it has thought well to decree has been received by the whole Church."[159]

Although Pope Gelasius formulated a monarchical definition of the papal primacy and prepared the way for the papal monarchy of the high Middle Ages, on the other hand he considered that the quality of a council as good or bad was not determined by its approval, or lack thereof, by the Church of Rome; other criteria, such as the approval of the other patriarchs and the consensus of the Church, were important. He said that a good council was assented to by the Universal Church and approved by the premier See (i.e., Rome); bad councils spoke against the scriptures, against the rules of the Church, were not accepted by the Church, and especially were not approved by the apostolic sees.[160]

The idea expressed in *Satis Cognitum,* that all councils and synods receive their legal authority through a confirmation by the pope, implying that the bishop of Rome possesses authority in his own right and is the final authenticator of any council, proves to be false from a historical point of view.[161] As the Roman Catholic theologian Nichols puts it: "Historical justification for the papalist model is also very weak. All major decisions in the early Church were made in councils by the principle of unanimity."[162] The Orthodox Bishop Kallistos Ware, for his part, notes:

> In Roman Catholic ecclesiology the Pope's acceptance of a council as ecumenical is clearly an indispensable, and indeed decisive, criterion. Eastern Orthodoxy, on the other hand, has always been reluctant to isolate the Pope from his

brother bishops and from the whole body of the Church. . . . The Pope, then, cannot act in isolation as the final arbiter of conciliar ecumenicity."[163]

With regard to the position of the pope at the ecumenical councils, Schatz also underlines the fact that in the East before the ninth century, union with Rome was not a particularly important criterion for the validity and ecumenicity of a council. This was due to the imperial nature of the councils. During the iconoclastic period, although Eastern authors recognized that matters of faith could only be definitely resolved in union with Rome, this certainly did not mean "only by Rome."[164]

Satis Cognitum tries again to prove the historical veracity of the pope's authority over the councils by asserting that "it has ever been unquestionably the office of the Roman Pontiffs to ratify or to reject the decrees of Councils," and it refers to some examples of such papal rejections: "Leo the Great rescinded the acts of the Conciliabulum of Ephesus, Damasus of Rimini and Hadrian those of Constantinople. The Twenty-Eighth Canon of the Council of Chalcedon, by the very fact that it lacks the assent and the approval of the Apostolic See, is admitted to be by all worthless."[165]

The Seventh Ecumenical Council proves quite the opposite of this assertion. This council was valid because it was accepted not only by Rome, which at that time was recognized as being the center of orthodoxy and as having an apostolic authority (not having a primacy of jurisdiction over the whole Church), but it was also approved and ratified by the other patriarchs.[166] The same criteria invalidated the Council of Hiereia (754); it was not approved by the pope or by the other patriarchs of the East.[167] Finally, the Fifth Ecumenical Council did not accept the pope's demand to follow his teaching and responded that matters of faith had to be decided by communal discussions.[168]

The sweeping papal statement about the Twenty-Eighth Canon of Chalcedon is also not accurate. It is true that Pope Leo I (440–461) opposed the canon that elevated Constantinople to a place after Rome and was never incorporated into Western canon law.[169] However, the canon was not disputed in the East. The power of the patriarch of Constantinople that was given to him by the Twenty-Eighth Canon was not disputed by Alexandria and Antioch.[170] In times of tension, Rome disputed the ecclesiastical rank of Constantinople and recalled the unalterable ordering of the Church— Rome, Alexandria, Constantinople—but that did not change the existing order. In times of good relations, however, Rome kept silent about Constantinople and its rank.[171] The Eastern Church received this canon into its official canonical collection at the Council of Trullo in 692.[172]

Finally, the encyclical refers to a statement of the Fifth Lateran Council (1512–1517), which declares the subordination of the councils to the pope: "The Roman Pontiff alone, as having authority over all Councils, has full jurisdiction and power to summon, to transfer, to dissolve the councils, as is clear, not only from the testimony of holy writ, from the teaching of the Fathers, and from the decrees of the sacred canons, but from the teaching of the very Councils themselves."[173] This council adopted in its teaching a universalistic and pyramidal view that held that the juridical power of the Church was concentrated in the pope and flowed from him, that the unity of the Church and even of civil society issued from the pope, and that the councils were subordinated to him.[174]

In line with *Satis Cognitum*, various Roman Catholic priests of the time, for instance M. Malataki,[175] John Baur,[176] and Soterios Brandi,[177] who wrote against the Orthodox encyclical letter of the patriarchate of Constantinople (1895),[178] used the same line of argumentation. Quoting the classical petrine texts, the ancient councils, and some passages from the Fathers of the Church, Malataki, for instance, claimed that Christ instituted Peter as a center, the principle of unity in the Church and its visible head, and that in order to exercise this function He gave to him a jurisdictional primacy over the Church, while this function was continued in his successors, the Bishops of Rome.[179]

CHAPTER 2

The Aftermath of Vatican I

This chapter will consider the main points of the arguments contained in the official Greek Orthodox encyclical letter of the Ecumenical Patriarchate issued in 1895, as well as those of selected Greek Orthodox theologians from the same period. I will present the arguments invoked by Archimandrite Grigorius Zigavinos (1835–1910), who was professor at the Theological School of the Ecumenical Patriarchate on the island Halki; John Mesoloras (1851–1942) and Anastasios Kiriakos (1843–1923), who were both professors at the Faculty of Theology of the University of Athens; and Spiridon Papageorgiou (1850–1918), a theologian from the Greek island of Corfu, against the main points of the Roman Catholic teaching on papal primacy described in the previous chapter. The views of the twentieth-century Greek Orthodox theologian John Karmiris (1904–1992), professor of Dogmatics and Christian Ethics at the Faculty of Theology of the University of Athens, follows the same argumentation as the encyclical letter of the Ecumenical Patriarchate, and Zigavinos, Mesoloras, and Kiriakos, are also presented. As we shall see, however, these arguments were later criticized by another group of Greek Orthodox theologians, represented primarily by John Zizioulas, and some Russian Orthodox theologians such as Afanassieff, Schmemann, and Meyendorff. I will show how the first group—those of the nineteenth century and Karmiris—present an incoherent and inauthentic critique of papal primacy, whereas the second group—Zizioulas and others—identify the weaknesses in their arguments, with Zizioulas in particular articulating an increasingly coherent and authentic understanding of the issue of primacy in the Church, not simply in terms of honor but also of real power.

The Invitation to Vatican I and the Reason for the Issuance of the Patriarchal Letter of 1895

By way of preamble, it is worth recalling that Pope Pius IX in 1868 issued a letter inviting all the Orthodox bishops to Vatican I, an invitation that was declined. The Patriarch of Constantinople, Gregory VI, told the papal delegation that delivered the letter that he already knew its contents and that it contained principles that were against the Gospel, the ecumenical councils, and the Fathers of the Church, which he could not, of course, accept. For Patriarch Gregory VI, attendance of the Orthodox bishops at the council would mean a renewal of old theological disputes that would accentuate disagreement and reopen old wounds; he saw no common ground for any synodal discussion or agreement. The only basis for reunion would be the return of the Roman Catholic Church to the doctrine and norm existing before the schism, giving up all that was added after that.[1] For Patriarch Gregory VI, the main sources of disagreement between the Orthodox and Roman Catholics were the Roman Catholic claims that in the Church of Christ there is a ruler and head other than the Lord, that one of the patriarchs is infallible and superior over the ecumenical councils, that the apostles were not equal, and that the prerogatives of the patriarchs and popes are not *jure humano* but *jure divino*.[2]

The papal delegation replied categorically that Rome had no intention of changing its principles and that all these matters had been examined at the Council of Florence, which united the two Churches. The patriarch then contested the validity of that council, stating that unity was not in fact achieved there.[3]

Further, the Patriarch expressed his disagreement with the way in which Pius IX had convoked the council, without asking the patriarchs and synods for their agreement: "If his Holiness the Pope of Rome had respect for apostolic equality and brotherhood, it was fitting that, as an equal among the equals in point of dignity, but being first by canonical right and rank of his See, he should have directed a separate letter to each of the Patriarchs and Synods of the East, and not in encyclical and dictatorial form to impose it as lord and master of them all, but as a brother to brethren equal in honour and degree, to ask them how, where, and in what conditions, they would agree to the assembling of a Holy Council."[4] The other Patriarchates followed the example of Constantinople and none attended the council.[5]

Almost three decades later, for Patriarch Anthimus and the synod assembled around him, the main reason for issuing the patriarchal letter of 1895 was to show their strongly negative opinion of Uniatism as a method of proselytizing Orthodox Christians.[6] It was not their intention specifically to answer the papal encyclical *Praeclara Gratulationis*, given that, as the letter said, the Orthodox Church, through writings and through encyclical letters,

> has never ceased to intimate to the Papal Church (i.e., the Roman Catholic Church), having clearly and explicitly set forth that so long as the latter preserves in her innovations, and the orthodox Church adheres to the divine and apostolic traditions and institutions of the first nine centuries of Christianity, during which the Western Churches were of the same mind and were united with the Churches of the East, so long is it a vain and empty thing to talk of union. For which cause we have remained silent until now, and have declined to take into consideration the papal encyclical in question, esteeming it unprofitable to speak to the ears of those who do not hear.[7]

The patriarchal letter appeals to the Fathers and the ecumenical councils of the first nine centuries, the latter being an exemplary period "in which the Bishop of Rome was never considered as the supreme authority and infallible head of the Church"[8] and "the Eastern Church never recognised the excessive claims of primacy on the part of the bishops of Rome, nor consequently did she ever submit herself to them, as Church history plainly bears witness."[9] The Patriarch then stated that the Pope in his encyclical *Praeclara Gratulationis* directs the Orthodox, in vain, to the sources that "we may seek diligently for what our forefathers believed and what the first period of Christianity delivered to us."[10] Whereas the papal encyclical associates the dogma of supreme power of the pope with ancient Christianity, the patriarchal letter claims that there is a glaring contradiction between this dogma and the view of ancient Christianity on the subject. Moreover, the patriarchal letter says that the papal primacy of jurisdiction is a heretical innovation concerning the administrative system of the Church, in opposition to the ecclesiastical condition of the first nine centuries.[11]

In the following pages, I will consider the main arguments invoked by the patriarchal letter and by particular Greek Orthodox authors immediately after Vatican I in the nineteenth century, against the main points of Roman Catholic Church teaching on the papal primacy, as discussed in chapter 1. As we shall also see, these arguments are criticized by a second group of contemporary Orthodox theologians, represented primarily by Zizioulas. This second group shows up the weaknesses of the first, while at the same time moving toward a coherent understanding of the issue of primacy in the Church.

The Orthodox Position in the Late Nineteenth Century
THE PRIMACY OF PETER

In order to refute the Roman Catholic teaching that the jurisdictional primacy of Peter and of the bishops of Rome is grounded in Mt. 16:18, the patriarchal letter asserts the following: "The Papists themselves know well that the very passage of the Gospel to which the Pontiff of Rome refers, 'Thou art Peter, and upon this rock I will build my Church', is in the first centuries of the Church interpreted quite differently, in a spirit of orthodoxy, both by tradition and by all the divine and sacred Fathers without exception; the fundamental and unshaken rock upon which the Lord has built His own Church, against which the gates of hell shall not prevail, being understood metaphorically of Peter's true confession concerning the Lord, that 'He is Christ, the Son of the living God.'"[12]

In replying to the assertion of *Praeclara Gratulationis* that "Christ's divine utterance, *Thou art Peter, and upon this rock I will build my Church*, has undoubtedly been realised in the Roman pontiffs," an assertion implying in fact the jurisdictional primacy of Peter, Gregory Zigavinos says that for the Fathers, St. Chrysostom among them, the "rock" upon which Christ will build His Church is Peter's faith in the divinity of Jesus Christ.[13]

On the other hand, Roman Catholic theologians of the time, among them Malataki, who wrote against the argumentation of the patriarchal letter regarding the primacy of Peter, stated that the interpretation of Mt. 16:18 in the letter, rather than refuting the primacy of Peter, in fact proves it. The faith and the person of Peter do not exclude each other; they are in harmony and the one illustrates the other. Malataki concludes that the Fathers of the Church, when they say that Christ has built the Church upon the faith of Peter, do not consider Peter's faith as abstract and independent of his person, but as concretely signifying Peter.[14] The Russian Orthodox theologian Meyendorff would agree with such a Roman Catholic interpretation, which does not distinguish the faith of Peter from his person. For Meyendorff, to oppose the two is artificial and polemical.[15] However, as we have seen, Malataki goes a step further, claiming that Christ instituted Peter as a center, the principle of unity in the Church and its visible head, and that in order to exercise this function he gave to him a jurisdictional primacy over the Church, and this function was continued in his successors, the Bishops of Rome.[16]

The patriarchal letter minimizes the scope of Peter's title as the foundation of the Church by opposing it to other texts of the New Testament: "For other foundation can no man lay than that which is laid, which is Jesus

Christ (1 Cor. 3:11); Christ Himself is the chief cornerstone of the Church."[17] Zigavinos also asserts that the Church is not founded on Peter alone but "on the other apostles and the prophets" (Eph. 2:20); James presides at the apostolic council, and he pronounced the final judgement; Peter is not the head of the Church, but Christ is the head of the body of the Church (Col. 1:18).[18] Zigavinos says that in the passage Mt. 16:15–19 the Lord does not grant Peter a primacy of power, but rather praise, honor, and a promise of future spiritual power and authority, which were also given to the other apostles.[19] Examining Peter's place in Byzantine theology, Meyendorff considers that this particular kind of argument against the primacy of Peter, invoked already by the Byzantine polemicists of the twelfth and thirteenth centuries, and which subsequent Orthodox polemicists made their own, obviously does not give sufficient credit to the personal role of Peter that is acknowledged in the patristic tradition.[20] Moreover, Meyendorff explains that "even after the schism between East and West, Orthodox ecclesiastical writers were never ashamed of praising the 'coryphaeus' and of recognising his pre-eminent function in the very foundation of the Church. They simply did not consider this praise and recognition as relevant in any way to the papal claims, since any bishop, and not only the pope, derives his ministry from the ministry of Peter."[21]

Meyendorff asserts, therefore, that for the Fathers and the Orthodox ecclesiastical writers after the schism, the primacy of Peter involves a pre-eminent and distinct function in the foundation of the Church, and this implies that the primacy of Peter himself is not one of honor. However, each bishop is a successor of the petrine function and not exclusively the bishop of Rome.

For his part Zigavinos states categorically that in the teaching of the Church, for St. Chrysostom as well as other Fathers, Jn. 21:15–17 simply signifies a confirmation of Peter in his apostleship and not a conferral of sovereign primacy.[22] He asserts that for the Fathers (Augustine in particular) the primacy of Peter was a primacy of honor, of respect and of order (πρωτεῖον τιμῆς καί τάξεως), never a primacy of power and jurisdiction. He was the first among the other apostles, speaking in many cases in the name of the others, as noted by St. Chrysostom.[23] Many passages from the New Testament refer to Peter as being the first in honor, in respect, as the pillar of the Church together with James and John, not as prince of the apostles, vicar of Christ, or absolute governor of the whole Church, with power over the other apostles.[24]

Zigavinos refers to the period of the apostolic Fathers, up to the second century, and concludes that there is no proof therein for the jurisdictional primacy of Peter and of the bishops of Rome over the Church. One example he mentions is the first Letter of Clement, Bishop of Rome, to the Church of Corinth. Zigavinos states that this letter cannot be taken as proof for the jurisdictional primacy of the bishop of Rome, as Roman Catholic theologians interpret it. Clement did not invoke any absolute primacy or privilege, nor did he intervene by virtue of a supreme authority; rather, he replied in a fatherly way when asked by the Corinthians to instruct those who were quarrelsome.[25] For Zigavinos, the beginning of the letter—"The Church of God which sojourns at Rome to the Church of God which sojourns at Corinth"—shows that Clement is writing in a fraternal way to an equal apostolic church, with no hint of the monarchical titles of his successors.[26] Zigavinos states that the bishops of the East from apostolic times considered the bishop of Rome as equal to them, possessing like them an apostolic see and not having a supreme *jure divino* primacy and privilege, but only that one might be accorded to the bishop of the imperial capital.[27]

In support of this argument, Zigavinos refers to the Quartodeciman controversy in which the Bishop of Rome, Victor (189–199), attempted to excommunicate the churches of Asia Minor because those churches did not celebrate Easter on the same day as the Roman Church. For this he was criticized by both East and West, notably by St. Irenaeus.[28] Polycrates, the bishop of Ephesus, convoked a council of bishops, which took a decision contrary to Victor's wishes. The council claimed that their custom had been handed down to them from the apostolic tradition. For Zigavinos, this proves that Victor did not exercise any jurisdiction over Polycrates and that Polycrates was a bishop of an independent church and did not consider Victor as a supreme bishop, vicar of Christ, or visible head of the Church, but as bishop of Rome, just as he was bishop of Ephesus.[29]

For Zigavinos, the Western Fathers and authors from the end of the second century already teach that in the West the church of Rome and the Roman capital served as a religious center with which both faithful and heretics must be in agreement because of its apostolicity.[30] We recall that the encyclical letter *Satis Cognitum* quotes the famous passage from St. Irenaeus: "It has always been necessary for every church—that is to say the faithful throughout the world—to be in agreement with the Roman Church because of its more effective leadership" as evidence of the papal primacy of jurisdiction.[31] Zigavinos believes that to interpret Irenaeus as saying that the other apostolic churches in the East, like Corinth, Antioch, or Jerusalem, must be in agreement with Rome because of its more effective primacy, would be absurd. Zigavinos argues that this passage, while indicative of Roman primacy, does not demonstrate power over any other church. It refers, instead, to Rome's political importance as imperial capital as well as to its apostolicity.[32]

Satis Cognitum also refers to St. Cyprian as providing evidence in support of the papal primacy of jurisdiction.[33] For Zigavinos, this is incorrect. One of the striking indications of this among the several that Zigavinos cites is Cyprian's struggle against the Roman view on baptism.[34] We also noted earlier that *Satis Cognitum* quotes St. Chrysostom in support of the Roman Catholic teaching that Peter had a primacy of jurisdiction.[35] Zigavinos argues, instead, that Chrysostom praises Peter but never says that Peter was chief of the apostles with a jurisdiction over them or that the Roman bishop is the supreme bishop and vicar of Christ with jurisdiction over the whole church. St. Chrysostom did not anticipate the beliefs of Latin theologians after the schism. Peter had a primacy of respect, honor, and order, and not one of power and jurisdiction over the other apostles.[36]

Nor, according to Zigavinos, can the appeals made to Rome by St. Athanasius (339–340) and by St. Chrysostom (404) be taken as proof of the bishop of Rome's jurisdictional primacy. Athanasius sought protection from Pope Julius against the heretics, but this does not mean that St. Athanasius was subjected to the pope or that the pope exercised jurisdiction over him. Likewise, St. Chrysostom appealed to Pope Innocent I, claiming papal protection, but again this does not mean that the patriarch of Constantinople was under the power and jurisdiction of Rome.[37] Kallistos Ware expresses the Orthodox viewpoint of these actions as follows:

> What has been termed . . . the "all-embracing pastoral concern," exercised by the pope of Rome as elder brother may be seen visibly expressed in the practice whereby, before the schism, appeals were made to the pope from all parts of the Christian world. . . . While the fact of these and other such appeals is not in doubt, the question remains: how precisely should they be understood? More, certainly, is here involved than a bare primacy of honour. Yet it is dangerous to assume that such appeals were interpreted by the Christian East in strictly juridical terms. . . . The case was not necessarily closed when Rome had spoken, and the Byzantines felt free on occasion to reject a Roman ruling: a celebrated instance occurred in 906, when Pope Sergius III gave a decision permitting fourth marriages, which was not accepted at Constantinople. Bishops and others in the East who felt that they had been unjustly treated, turned naturally for help to Rome; but they did not turn to her as to the Church endowed with universal and supreme ordinary jurisdiction, but as to the Church which presides in love.[38]

THE REFUTATION OF THE ROMAN CATHOLIC TEACHING
THAT THE POPE IS THE HEAD OF THE CHURCH AND CEN-
TER AND PRINCIPLE OF THE UNITY OF THE CHURCH

As we have seen, Vatican I in its Constitution on the Church declared that
the pope is the head of the Church with power over her. We have seen that
the Roman Catholic priest Malataki again asserted that, according to Scripture and ancient testimonies of the Church, Christ instituted Peter as a center, the principle of unity of the Church and visible head of the Church, and
that in order to exercise this function, he gave Peter jurisdictional primacy
over the Church, which continued in his successors, the Roman bishops.[39]
Thus the unity of the Church was understood and manifested as a unity
through the power of a head, i.e., a universal center.

The patriarchal letter, on the contrary, argues that only Christ is the head
of the Church:

> But having recourse to the fathers and the Ecumenical Councils of the
> Church of the first nine centuries, we are fully persuaded that the Bishop of
> Rome was never considered as the supreme authority and infallible head of
> the Church, and that every bishop is head and president of his own particular
> Church, subject only to the synodical ordinances and decisions of the Church
> universal as being alone infallible, the Bishop of Rome being in no wise ex-
> cepted from this rule, as Church history shows. Our Lord Jesus Christ alone
> is the eternal Prince and immortal Head of the Church, for "He is the Head
> of the body, the Church" (Gal. 2:2), who said also to His divine disciples and
> apostles at His ascension into heaven, "Lo, I am with you always, even unto
> the end of the world."[40]

This argument was also in line with that of the Orthodox confessions of the
seventeenth century, which had taught that the bishops are the heads and vicars of their particular churches, while Christ is the head of the whole Church.[41]

In explaining the main difference between the Greek/Russian Orthodox position and Roman Catholic doctrine, Martin Jugie refers specifically
to this Orthodox position, clearly expressed in the patriarchal letter, that
Christ is the head of the Church, while each bishop is head and president of
his own particular church. While the Orthodox position places many visible
heads of the Church and particular vicars of Christ (i.e., the bishops) under
one invisible head, which is Christ, Roman Catholic doctrine places one supreme visible head, the Roman pontiff, under an invisible one (i.e., Christ),
as his vicar.[42]

Nicholas Afanassieff, in describing and discussing universal ecclesiology, which for him was first formulated by St. Cyprian, points to the incoherent and inconsistent logic of the above Orthodox argument:

> A single body must be crowned by a single head, showing in his own person the unity of the whole system. If we take the universal theory of the Church, we cannot refute the doctrine of universal primacy just by saying that the Church has Christ as Head; that is an indisputable truth, and supporters of primacy do not themselves oppose it. The real question is: If the Church has an invisible head (Christ), can she, or can she not, also have a visible head? If not, then why can a local church have a single head in the person of its bishop? In other words, why can one part of the Universal Church have a single head, while the entire Universal Church is deprived of one? This question should be relevant in discussing autocephalous Orthodox churches and their problems. If there is no primacy in the Universal Church, why do we allow a partial primacy within the boundaries of an autocephalous church? The head of an autocephalous Church makes manifest its unity: but how can the unity of the whole Orthodox Church be given empirical expression in the absence of a universal primacy?[43]

Afanassieff's queries serve to highlight a weakness in the above argument that the Orthodox regard only Christ as head of the Church as a whole, in that it overlooks the question of why the Orthodox acknowledge the existence of visible heads on the local level, i.e., the bishops, while on the other hand they do not accept a visible head on the universal level. We have already seen that the patriarchal letter acknowledges the bishops as heads of their churches, while on the other hand it does not accept a head on the universal level. The letter also overlooks the fact that in the Orthodox Church there has always actually been a visible head and a center on the universal level. We shall see that both Schmemann and Zizioulas affirm this fact.

Mesoloras considers that the Church has always proclaimed Christ to be both the visible and invisible head of the Church and therefore that the acceptance of any ecclesiastical person as the visible head of the Church and center of all churches is contrary to the New Testament and to the tradition of the Church.[44] Mesoloras appeals to explicit scriptural texts (for example, Eph. 5:23; 1 Cor. 3:11; 1 Pet. 5:4), in which Christ is described as the head, the foundation, and the chief pastor of the Church. Having made the claim that the Orthodox confessions are in full agreement with the Scriptures and sacred tradition on this point, Mesoloras calls upon, for example, the confession of the Patriarch of Jerusalem, Dositheos (1672), which states that the four Eastern patriarchs are equal among themselves and none of them claims to be the head of the whole Church. Only Christ is therefore the head and the ruler of the whole Church and not any mortal and sinful man.[45] Mesoloras agrees with the Protestants in saying that the Church cannot have any other head but Christ, for the Church as spiritual body must have a spiritual head. He disagrees with the Protestant position, however, that the Church is invisible and therefore does not need a visible head, namely ministers appointed by the act of ordination.[46]

Mesoloras states that in order to prove the primacy of Peter and his Roman successors, Westerners misinterpret the passages of Scripture and the evidence of the ancient Church, claming that this dogma of faith always existed and was developed later for the sake of the unity of the Church.[47] Mesoloras believes that the Church is not united by the *jure divino* power of a visible head—the pope—but rather by the same faith, the same constitution, and the same worship.[48] He explains that this was in conformity with the constitution of the ancient Church; according to the canons of the apostles and the synods, each province (*metropolis*) exercised independently its jurisdiction to ordain bishops and was united with the other churches through the same faith, rather than through one of the bishops acting as supreme ruler.[49]

By invoking the argument that only Christ is the head of the Church, Mesoloras intends to refute the Roman Catholic teaching that the unity of the Church was always understood and manifested as a unity though the power of a head or a universal center, in this case the pope.[50] In arguing against this teaching, he went to the other extreme, denying the existence of any visible universal center or head in the Church, ignoring the obvious fact, testified to by canonical tradition, that there has always existed a universal center or primacy, i.e., a head, in the Church, although this did not imply a power over the Church. We have seen that he strongly considers the existence of a specific person as center of all the churches as being contrary to Scripture and tradition. Thus Mesoloras's position that the Church never recognized a universal center is incoherent, since it contradicts canonical and ecclesiological facts of the ancient Church. This nonrecognition of a universal center in the Church on the part of the Orthodox theologians is the result of a polemical attitude, as Schmemann points out.[51] As we shall see in chapter 4, Zizioulas implicitly agrees with Schmemann, who states emphatically that, from a canonical and ecclesiological point of view, a universal primacy—center of unity and of agreement—always existed in the Church.[52] Schmemann further notes that a study of church history of the first millennium will reveal that the essence and purpose of universal primacy is to express and preserve the unity and unanimity of all the local churches.[53] We shall also see in chapter 4 that Zizioulas underlines the necessity of the existence of such a center of unity on the local and universal level, not so much from a historical point of view but from a dogmatic one.

It is interesting to note in this context that in the nineteenth century not all Greek Orthodox theologians shared the idea that the Church has no visible universal center of unity. The Greek Orthodox Metropolitan of Stavroupolis, Constantine Tipaldos (1795–1867), who was professor and dean at the Theological School on the island of Halki-Constantinople, in his treatise *The Unity of the Orthodox Eastern Church*, written before Vatican I in 1833–1834, accepts the necessity of the existence of a universal center of unity in the Orthodox Church. For Tipaldos, it is the patriarch of Constantinople who is the center of ecclesiastical unity in the Orthodox Church.[54] One of the reasons for writing this treatise was to reply to accusations that Orthodox Christians were separated from each other, and that their churches were divided.[55] In addition, Tipaldos was writing during a period when the national Greek Orthodox Church declared itself arbitrarily as an autocephalous church (1833), thus breaking its unity with the Ecumenical Patriarchate.

Tipaldos says that Roman Catholics consider "the religious unity" (i.e., the Church's unity) differently from the Orthodox. By establishing the pope as the center of unity, they come to different conclusions, introducing an absolute monarchy in the Church and considering those who do not accept this form of unity as schismatics and divided among themselves.[56] Tipaldos argues that the Orthodox Church is a unity of the same faith and of communion. No one disputes the unity of faith, but there is debate on the second issue. For Tipaldos, the hierarchical order in the Church demonstrates the unity of communion. This canonical, hierarchical order has established one of the patriarchs as first among equals, who is the center of religious unity.[57] Also, Tipaldos says that, according to the canons of the ecumenical councils, the patriarch of Constantinople is the primate among the other patriarchs, and this therefore implies that in this primate the whole Orthodox Church is united and in communion under one supreme head, Christ.[58] In other words, the patriarchs have centered in themselves the particular churches, and when the patriarchs then commune together, all of the churches therefore commune. Hence, all the Orthodox churches have ecclesiastical and religious unity.[59] The patriarch of Constantinople as a primate of the whole Orthodox Church is therefore the center of unity, which unites all the particular Orthodox churches.

Thus, for Tipaldos, as we have seen, such a unity does not necessarily imply a monarchical unity. The patriarch is not like the pope and not above the councils.[60] Tipaldos asserts, therefore, that from a canonical point of view there is a universal primate in the Orthodox Church, i.e., the patriarch of Constantinople, who unites the whole Orthodox Church, acts in a synodical context, and is not placed above the councils.

In explaining why the Orthodox cannot accept subjection to papal authority, another Greek Orthodox theologian of that time, Anastasios D. Kiriakos, argues that such subjection would distort the administrative system of the Orthodox Church. For Kiriakos, the Orthodox Church follows the administrative structure of the ancient Church, based on the canons of the ecumenical councils and of the Fathers. The whole Church is a confederation of national autocephalous churches. Each particular church is autocephalous, autonomous, independent, and self-administered. The same faith and love unites these churches. Each is governed by a synod of bishops, which is the supreme ecclesiastical authority. No bishops have the right to interfere in the affairs of other churches.[61] In arguing against Roman Catholic accusations that the Orthodox Church does not preserve unity because, administratively speaking, it consists of many different autocephalous churches, Kiriakos states that unity is spiritual and interior. It is unity in the same faith, mysteries, and administrative system; it is not a unity achieved by submission to the orders of a bishop.[62] The implication is that autocephaly, understood as a confederation of autocephalous churches, is a model opposed to the papal primacy of jurisdiction.

In recent times, however, Zizioulas has stressed that Orthodoxy does not understand the Church as a confederation. Such a view fails to see the institution and ministry of unity that expresses the unity of the church on the universal level: "Orthodox theology is wrongly understood if we simply think of the Church as a confederation of local churches. The Orthodox view of the Church, in my understanding at least, requires an institution which expresses the *oneness* of the Church and not simply its multiplicity."[63] Kiriakos's view that the administrative system of the ancient Church was a confederation of local churches is not coherent either for Zizioulas or for Schmemann, who point out that the ancient Church recognized a center of unity on the universal level from a canonical and ecclesiological point of view. Neither, therefore, was this unity simply a spiritual one, but rather a unity through the institution of a primacy.

Spiridon Papageorgiou wrote an essay, *On the Unity of the Church* (1895), which was published by the Ecumenical Patriarchate.[64] The Ecumenical Patriarchate considered Papageorgiou's thesis as a response to the papal letter *Satis Cognitum*.[65] By publishing Papageorgiou's treatise, the Ecumenical Patriarchate of Constantinople officially approved Papageorgiou's line of argumentation, which as we shall see, is inconsistent.

Opposing to an external unity under one man and a human head, by which he certainly intends the pope, a unity based on absolute obedience, Papageorgiou emphasizes a mystical unity under the one head of the Church, namely Christ. This idea of unity is witnessed in the Scripture and in the Fathers. It is a unity of all those who believe in Christ united in love, in truth, and in peace.[66]

By drawing upon the Scriptures, Papageorgiou concludes that the only principle and center of unity in the Church is Christ.[67] The Scriptures contain no evidence for an external unity in the Church. The letters of the apostles make no direct or indirect allusion to Peter being the principle of unity, even less for his jurisdiction over the Church.[68] For the Apostle Paul none of the apostles is the principle of unity; Christ is the principle and center of unity.[69] The idea that unity is the absolute, monarchical jurisdiction of the bishop of Rome over the whole Church and that the pope is the visible head of the Church is alien to the teaching of the Scriptures.[70] He also refers to the Apostolic Fathers and comes to the same conclusion, namely that, according to their teaching on the unity of the Church, Christ is the principle and center of the unity of the Church.[71] Unity is based on the same faith, love, and peace. There is no dogma about Rome being the center, foundation, and principle of ecclesiastical unity.[72] By also appealing to the period from the third up to the sixth century and to some Fathers of this period, he repeats once again that the principle of unity in this period was Christ.[73] He says emphatically that for the Fathers of this period nobody was vicar of Christ. These Fathers apply the expression "head of the Church" only to Christ. In order not to introduce an innovation in this respect, the popes invented the teaching according to which Christ is the invisible head of the Church while the pope is the visible head of the Church. But the ancient Church was not aware of this teaching.[74] He is opposed to the kind of unity promoted by the papal encyclical *Praeclara Gratulationis*, which consists not only in a unity of doctrine and faith, but also in a unity of government, which means, for Papageorgiou, an obedience without hesitation to the pope.[75]

Papageorgiou's main objection is that for Scripture and for the ancient Church the unity of the Church was not an external unity under one head (the Bishop of Rome) and under the jurisdictional primacy of the Roman bishop, who was the principle of unity, but on the contrary it was rather a mystical unity, with Christ being the center and principle of unity. Papageorgiou, like every Orthodox, cannot accept the Roman Catholic teaching that Peter and the Bishop of Rome are the principle of unity, a teaching declared at Vatican I, which, as we have seen, is a manifestation of a universalistic ecclesiology, unity being understood here as under papal authority.[76]

However, the weakness of his argument is that he does not take into account that in the ancient Church the unity of the Church was not expressed only spiritually or invisibly—a unity in Christ, i.e., a unity based on the same faith, love, and peace—but also visibly through an institution, a primate on the regional level and on the universal level as well. In fact, Papageorgiou, by asserting that in the ancient Church Christ was the center of the Church, implicitly wanted to refute Roman Catholic teaching that the pope is the center of unity with a jurisdiction over the Church. But Papageorgiou's presentation of the ancient Church's unity is not consistent with the history and the canonical life of the ancient Church, which always recognized a visible center of unity, namely primacies on the regional and the universal level, as both Zizioulas and Schmemann state.

The patriarchal letter gives its own account of the ancient constitution of the Church, in its argument against the papal claim that in the period before Patriarch Photius of Constantinople (ninth century), both East and West, with one accord and without opposition, were subject to the Roman pontiff as lawful successor of the apostle Peter and Vicar of Christ. The letter says, "Each particular self-governing Church, both in the East and West, was totally independent and self-administered in the times of the seven ecumenical councils. And just as the bishops of the self-governing Churches of the East, so also those of Africa, Spain, Gaul, Germany, and Britain managed the affairs of their own Churches, each by their local synods, the bishop of Rome having no right to interfere."[77]

Such a concept of churches as totally independent is for Zizioulas a rather Protestant one, which is not in accord with the ecclesiological principles of the Orthodox Church nor justified by the ecclesiological sources of the first three centuries. The patriarchal letter thus appears to have been influenced by Protestant provincialism, which considers local churches as totally independent. The argument is therefore anachronistic, reading a later situation back into an earlier one.[78]

The patriarchal letter also asserts that all the particular Orthodox churches are inseparably united to each other in the unity of one saving faith in Christ, and in the bond of peace and of the Spirit.[79] Institutionally speaking, since the schism the unity of the Orthodox churches has also been visibly manifested through the synods, not just invisibly as the letter implied. Nevertheless, as we shall see, the nationalism that prevailed in the Balkan countries during the nineteenth century resulted in the creation of national autocephalous churches and in their fragmentation and division.

It must be acknowledged that in the nineteenth century we encounter the autocephalism of the Orthodox national churches that transformed the legitimate ancient ecclesiastical regionalism into divisive ecclesiastical nationalism. This transformation was the result of the great revival of nationalities, which occurred in Western Europe in the second half of the eighteenth century and determined the entire history of the nineteenth century.[80] This nationalist ideology, which Meyendorff believes was promoted in Greece and in other Balkan countries by a Western-oriented secularized *intelligentsia*,[81] resulted in the creation of autocephalous national state-controlled churches in the nineteenth century.[82]

Metropolitan Maximos of Sardes notes that in the context of the nineteenth century, "*Nationality* came to prevail as a conception, bringing into being the nation-states of Europe and the Balkans. The direct consequence of this was the splitting up of the Orthodox Church in South-East Europe, its unified structure undergoing considerable external change. The most important stages of development were the creation of the national churches, which for a period were estranged from one another, and the gradual influx into the East of secularism, the intellectual movements deriving from the ideas of the Enlightenment and individualistic radicalism."[83] The nineteenth-century autocephalous churches and the ecclesiology supporting them did not provide effective structures for communion on the universal level, and this led to their division and fragmentation.[84]

THE ARGUMENT FROM CONCILIARISM

In its argument against the papal claim of a jurisdictional primacy over the whole Church, the patriarchal letter considers the Councils of Constance (1414–1418) and Basle (1431–1449) as an attempt by the people of the West to return to the ecclesiastical constitution of the ancient Church. The letter refers to the forged and spurious pseudo-Isidorian decrees, by which, contrary to the truth of history and the established constitution of the Church, it was purposely promulgated that Christian antiquity assigned to the Bishops of Rome an authority over the Universal Church, and also to Peter's denial and to heretical popes, like Pope Honorius in the seventh century, facts that prove that popes were not infallible. The letter then states:

> With these and such facts in view, the peoples of the West, becoming gradually civilised by the diffusion of letters, began to protest against innovations, and to demand (as was done in the fifteenth century at the Councils of Constance and Basle) the return to the ecclesiastical constitution of the first

centuries, to which, by the grace of God, the orthodox Churches through-out the East and North . . . , remain and will always remain faithful.[85]

Thus, the patriarchal letter implies an identification of its concept of synod-ality with the Western theory of conciliarism defined at both councils; what is more, it considers this theory as being in conformity with the ancient constitu-tion of the Church. As we shall see in the next section, however, for Zizioulas the Western theory of conciliarism renders primacy incompatible with synod-ality. The patriarchal letter seems to overlook the fact that conciliarism, taken as an argument against the papal primacy of jurisdiction, actually contradicts the canonical and ecclesiological principle of the Orthodox Church itself and makes primacy compatible with synodality. Here, then, is an instance of an incoherent argument that contradicts the ecclesiological and canonical prin-ciples of the ancient constitution of the Church, which, as we shall see, sup-ported the existence of primacy within the synodical institution.

THE PRIMACY OF HONOR

In order to reject the claim that the Bishop of Rome has jurisdiction over the other bishops, the patriarchal letter proposes an understanding of the nature of his primacy in terms of a simple primacy of honor, as *"primus inter pares,"* and refers to the Twenty-Eighth Canon of Chalcedon:

> The divine Fathers, honouring the Bishop of Rome only as the bishop of the capital city of the empire, gave him the honorary prerogative of presidency, considering him simply as the bishop first in order, that is, first among equals; which prerogatives they also assigned afterwards to the bishop of Constanti-nople, when that city became the capital of the Roman Empire, as the twenty-eighth canon at Chalcedon bears witness. . . . From this canon it is very evi-dent that the Bishop of Rome is equal in honour to the bishop of the Church of Constantinople and those of other Churches, and there is no hint given in any canon or by any of the Fathers that the Bishop of Rome alone has ever been prince of the universal Church and the infallible judge of the bishops of other independent and self governing Churches, or the successor of the Apostle Peter and vicar of Jesus Christ on earth.[86]

Thus, the letter implicitly denied the position, supported by Vatican I and by Leo XIII in his encyclical *Satis Cognitum*, that the primacy of Peter should not be conceived as being a primacy of honor but as a primacy of jurisdiction.[87]

In his critique of the use of the expressions "a simple primacy of honor" or *"primus inter pares,"* suggested also by the contemporary Greek Orthodox theologian John Karmiris, Zizioulas states that, although this expression intends to exclude the right of the primate to exercise jurisdiction over the rest of the bishops—a principle accepted by all Orthodox Churches—the description of this principle as "a simple primacy of honor" is ecclesiologically and canonically questionable.[88]

For Zizioulas, the description of primacy in terms of honor or *"primus inter pares"* suggests a lack of power and contradicts basic canonical principles, such as the Thirty-Fourth Apostolic Canon, which states that in each region there must be a primate, without whom no bishop can do anything. This canon seems to imply that the primate can even block the deliberations of the synod, leaving the other bishops unable to function.[89] The canon reads as follows: "The bishops of each nation—*ethnous*—are obliged to look up to the first among them—*the protos*—to consider him as head, and to do nothing without his consent. Each one is to do only what is pertinent to his diocese and to the villages within it. Nor, on the other hand, is the *protos* to take any action without the consent of all. For thus there will be concord, and God will be glorified, through the Lord, in the Holy Spirit, the Father, the Son, and the Holy Spirit."[90] Zizioulas also refers to a canonical provision in the Orthodox Church that, in the absence of a patriarch or during the vacancy of his throne, there cannot be episcopal elections or canonical acts. He wonders whether such primacy is then purely a primacy of honor and concludes that the phrase "primacy of honor" is very misleading if taken literally. For Zizioulas, it seems that there is, in fact, no such thing as a simple primacy of honor in the Orthodox Church.[91]

From a canonical and historical point of view, these privileges of primacy are not understood as a simple honorary distinction in the hierarchical order, as the patriarchal letter asserts, but in fact involve a power.[92] The Council of Chalcedon and its Twenty-Eighth Canon granted privileges of honor to Constantinople that are linked to the power of its bishop over the ordinations of the metropolitans in Pontus, Asia, and Thrace.[93]

Zigavinos explains that the Sixth Canon of the First Ecumenical Council establishes prerogatives, namely, a power of the primate or metropolitan of certain areas over the other bishops in that area. Thus, the Bishop of Rome exercises power over the provinces of Italy; the Bishop of Alexandria over Egypt, Libya, and Pentapolis; and the Bishop of Antioch over Syria and Kilikia. The Bishop of Rome did not have, therefore, any power or jurisdiction over the Bishop of Alexandria, or the Bishop of Alexandria over the Bishop of Rome. For Zigavinos, this canon defined the jurisdictions of these three bishops. Zigavinos says that the canon additionally determines that in the other provinces the prerogatives of the primate or the metropolitan to exercise power over the other bishops must be preserved.[94] Referring also to the Eighth Canon of the Third Ecumenical Council, Zigavinos says that this canon defined the limits of the power and jurisdiction of the Bishop of Antioch, preventing him from ordaining bishops of the Church of Cyprus.[95] What Zigavinos implies here is that the prerogatives that give the primate a power and jurisdiction over a certain area contain the right and power to ordain bishops in that area.

Curiously, Zigavinos himself states that the Sixth Canon of the First Ecumenical Council grants primacies and prerogatives of order and simple honor, without saying anything clear about these prerogatives.[96] Yet, Zigavinos's description of these privileges or primacies in terms of simple honor is in contradiction with the canonical fact that Zigavinos himself brings out and seems implicitly to accept, namely that these privileges of honor contained a real power and jurisdiction of the primate, which consisted in the right of the primate to ordain all the bishops of his area. They were not simply privileges of honor, but privileges of real power. Thus Zigavinos seems to contradict himself. By referring to the Third Canon of the Second Ecumenical Council and the Twenty-Eighth Canon of Chalcedon, which accorded prerogatives of honor to Rome and to Constantinople, he concludes that the primate in honor and in order (i.e., the Bishop of Rome) is the first among equals, presiding among equals at an ecumenical council. As we noted above, for Zizioulas, such a conception of primacy simply as first among equals contradicts the canonical principles deriving from the Thirty-Fourth Apostolic Canon. This apostolic canon implies that a real power is assigned to the primate, on the regional and by extension on the universal level, namely that the primate can block the deliberations of a synod.

THE UNDERSTANDING OF PRIMACY AS *JURE HUMANO*

Zigavinos also considers that the primacy granted by the canons (for example the Sixth Canon of the First Ecumenical Council) to a church is not a primacy *jure divino*, but a primacy due simply to ecclesiastical and political circumstances and to ancient customs. For Zigavinos, because Rome was the capital city of the Roman Empire, it received a primacy of order and honor, and then after it came Alexandria. Constantinople subsequently received a primacy of honor after Rome because that city was the new Rome (Third Canon of the Second Ecumenical Council).[97] Zigavinos intends thereby to refute the idea that the Bishop of Rome has received *jure divino* a primacy of jurisdiction. His position implies that primacy is simply a matter of human right and of canonical order, without any connection to the Church's *esse*. We shall see in the next section that Zizioulas criticizes the position, adopted by Karmiris, that considers primacy as being of human right and origin, due simply to political and historical circumstances.

Karmiris's Argument against the Papal Primacy of Jurisdiction

This section will examine Karmiris's argument against a papal primacy of jurisdiction, which overall follows the same line of argument as that of the patriarchal letter and the Greek Orthodox theologians discussed earlier. The main arguments fall into several subsections, presented below.

THE PRIMACY OF PETER

We shall see that Karmiris, in line with his Greek Orthodox predecessors of the nineteenth century, invokes the classical polemical arguments against the petrine primacy of jurisdiction that we mentioned above.

With reference to canon 1 of chapter 1 of *Pastor Aeternus*,[98] Karmiris denies the Roman Catholic classical arguments *ex scriptura* (Mt. 16:16–19; Jn. 21:15–17) for the foundation *jure divino* of a petrine primacy of jurisdiction, as proposed by Vatican I.[99] Peter did not receive directly from Christ a special power of jurisdiction over the other apostles and the Church.[100] He maintains that Peter simply had a primacy of honor among the other apostles, as *primus inter pares*,[101] always acting in agreement with the other apostles.[102] From Mt. 16:16–18 it follows that a primacy of first among equals is given to Peter and not a primacy of power.[103]

However, the arguments Karmiris invokes in rejecting the petrine primacy as taught by Vatican I are only rehearsals of those expressed by the Orthodox patriarchal letter and the Greek Orthodox theologians, like Zigavinos, in the nineteenth century. Karmiris is content to repeat those arguments that, as Meyendorff has noted, contradict the traditional recognition of Peter's personal role and function as the "rock" of the Church acknowledged in the patristic tradition.[104] Karmiris, for example, distinguishes between the person of Peter and his confession. As we observed above, Meyendorff considers such a distinction polemical and artificial.[105] Karmiris minimizes Peter's role by pointing out that the powers given to Peter by Jesus were also given to the other apostles (Jn. 20:23; Mt. 18:18).[106] He also minimizes the scope of Peter's title "foundation of the Church" by opposing it to other texts of the New Testament—the Church is not founded on Peter alone but on the apostles and prophets (Eph. 2:20);[107] or by opposing Peter to other preeminent persons of the New Testament, for example James and John.[108] This polemical style in turn leads Karmiris to minimize the titles and praises given to Peter by some Fathers, titles that are used by Roman Catholic theologians to support a papal primacy of jurisdiction or power.[109] In other words, he makes an effort to minimize the scope of these titles by opposing them with other patristic texts that praise other apostles, such as John, James, and Paul.[110] In this way Karmiris fails to see the persistence of a particularly realistic exegesis in the patristic texts dealing with Peter.[111]

Following the interpretation of St. Chrysostom and other Fathers, which was echoed by the polemicists of the nineteenth century, Karmiris concludes that Christ's words in Jn. 21:15–17 do not imply a special power conferred on Peter by Christ but rather simply Peter's restoration to his apostleship.[112] However valuable and important this exegesis is, the fact remains that because of his polemic approach Karmiris fails to acknowledge Peter's preeminent function as recognized by the patristic tradition more generally.

We have noted Meyendorff's assertion that, in line with traditional patristic exegesis, Orthodox ecclesiastical writers, even after the schism between East and West, were never ashamed of praising Peter and of recognizing his preeminent function in the very foundation of the Church. For them, however, such praise and recognition were irrelevant to papal claims, since *every* bishop derived his ministry from Peter.[113]

We notice here the tension that exists regarding the modern Orthodox critique of Vatican I's definition of the petrine primacy. Whereas the theologians of the first group deny Vatican I's definition of the petrine primacy of jurisdiction as *ius divinum*—and in this respect represent the common Orthodox position—nevertheless, for Meyendorff, who belongs to the second group of theologians, the arguments they invoke against such a primacy do not represent the traditional, patristic recognition of Peter's personal function. Moreover, the insistence of the first group on polemical arguments shows clearly that they are engaged in a sterile conflict, influenced by the controversies and disputes that caused the schism between East and West.

For Karmiris, the primacy of Peter had a personal character and was limited in time. It is precisely for this reason that the New Testament provides no proof for petrine succession.[114] Because of this, he says, Vatican I did not invoke any passage from the Scriptures to support a perpetual succession by the Bishop of Rome to the primacy of Peter.[115] We have seen that the second chapter of Vatican I's dogmatic Constitution, *Pastor Aeternus,* does not quote a single scriptural text to support its teaching that Peter must have perpetual successors in his primacy of jurisdiction.[116]

For Karmiris, it follows from the lack of evidence in the petrine texts for Peter's primacy over the other apostles and the apostolic Church that the patristic texts of the first centuries also lack any correlation between petrine primacy of power and the primacy of power of the Bishop of Rome, which developed later in the West. The apostolic Fathers and the great Fathers of the Church were unaware of such a correlation or primacy.[117] Moreover, Karmiris makes the distinction between the apostolate and the episcopal ministry: the apostles, including Peter, were not bishops of any city, and their mission was a universal mission not limited to any geographic location.[118]

THE ARGUMENT THAT CHRIST ALONE IS HEAD OF THE CHURCH: A CRITIQUE

In arguing against Vatican I's teaching on the papal primacy of jurisdiction, Karmiris refutes the idea that the pope is head of the Church in the sense of having absolute power of jurisdiction over the whole Church. Instead, Karmiris contends that only Christ is the head of the Church.[119] He emphasizes that the ancient Fathers of the Church called the Church the Body of Christ, teaching the unity between the divine and human elements in her, in which the divine takes the place of the head while the human the place of the body. The Roman bishop occupies a place in the body that is dependent on the head, even if his place is distinct.[120] By drawing upon the teaching of St. Chrysostom, Karmiris concludes that the head cannot exist without the body and likewise the body cannot exist without the head. Neither can the place of this divine head be taken by a mortal hierarch.[121] Christ is forever the only head of the Church, governing the Church through the Holy Spirit and through the pastors appointed by Him. Christ is the only teacher, archpriest, and pastor of His Church and the source of the life of the Church.[122] In support of his argument, Karmiris cites explicit New Testament texts, for example, Eph. 1:22, and Col. 1:18, in which Christ is described as the head of the Church. He also draws upon the statements of the Orthodox confessions of Critopoulos (1626) and of the Patriarch of Jerusalem,

Dositheos (1672), which state that it is only Christ, the immortal head of the Church, who governs her. No mortal man can therefore be the head of the Church.[123] In this, Karmiris is also following the Orthodox confessions of the seventeenth century, for example, that of the Metropolitan of Kiev, Peter Mogila, who taught that the bishops are the particular heads and vicars of Christ of their particular churches, while Christ is the head of the Church as a whole.

As we noted above with reference to Afanassieff's comments, the view that only Christ is the head of the Church as a whole, while the bishops are heads of their particular churches, is inconsistent since it accepts the existence of a visible head of the Church at some levels but not at the universal level and overlooks the historical fact of the existence of a visible head in the Orthodox Church at the universal level.[124]

THE ARGUMENT FROM CONCILIARISM: A CRITIQUE

In arguing against the papal primacy of jurisdiction defined by Vatican I and II, Karmiris sides explicitly with conciliarism, which considers an ecumenical council as the highest authority in the Church. For him, the Western theories of conciliarism and Gallicanism are in accord with the position of the Orthodox Church and of the ancient Church. Thus, in his view, not only did the undivided Church consider the pope to be subject to an ecumenical council, as is the view today in the Orthodox Church, but so did the Church in the West as well, through conciliarism and Gallicanism, until Vatican I was convoked to defeat them.[125] Accordingly, he asserts that an ecumenical council is above any primate, i.e., the patriarchs.[126] Zizioulas criticizes Karmiris for siding with the theory of conciliarism. He points out the incoherence of his argument as follows:

> He [i.e., Karmiris] argues more on the basis of *conciliarism*: there can be no primacy by the Church because the highest authority in it is the council or synod. The real *primus* in the Church is the Council. Karmiris explicitly sides with western *Konziliarismus* in his opposition to the primacy of the pope. He identifies the Orthodox position with that of Western conciliarism: the council, particularly in the form of the ecumenical council, is above any primate. This is certainly the view of all the Orthodox, but the question remains *whether any council or synod can exist without primacy*. There must, therefore, be a way of incorporating primacy into conciliarity, if we are to arrive at a theologically sound position on this matter.[127]

Thus, for Zizioulas, conciliarism renders primacy incompatible with syn-odality. By means of the Thirty-Fourth Apostolic Canon, Zizioulas avoids the dilemma of having to choose which is above the other, a dilemma posed by both papalism and conciliarism. As we will see in chapter 4, Zizioulas asserts that both primate and council function together and coexist, as the Thirty-Fourth Apostolic Canon clearly implies; this canon is for Zizioulas a key to understanding the role and the function of the primate. The council is not above the primate—pope or patriarch—nor is the pope or patriarch above the council.

For Zizioulas, the theory of conciliarism is not in conformity with the ancient understanding of conciliarity. The authority of an ecumenical coun-cil does not lie in some sort of institutional status. By institutional status Zizioulas means the juridical idea that a council is the highest authority in the church.[128] The ecumenical council did not exist as an institution in the history of the Church. He asserts that

> when the Ecumenical Council appeared in the history of the Church, it did not appear as an institution but rather as an *event*. The institutionalization of conciliarity—with reference to the ecumenical councils—represents a later Western phenomenon (the "Conciliarism" of the 14th and 15th centuries) and has never found its way into the consciousness of the Orthodox Churches. For the ancient Church, too, the ecumenical councils were not part of an in-stitutional machinery, but *ad hoc* events. This is evidenced by the fact that these councils lacked juridical form to such an extent that even a *local* council could be "ecumenical" (e.g., the 2nd Ecumenical Council of 381 AD) while a council institutionally qualified to be "ecumenical" could be anything but that (e.g., Ephesus 449).[129]

In contrast with Zizioulas, Karmiris regards the ecumenical council as an institution. Thus, in arguing against the teaching of Vatican I, namely that the "definitions of the Roman pontiffs are of themselves, and not by the con-sent of the church, irreformable,"[130] he claims that this teaching renders the ecumenical council useless as an institution.[131] To consider the ecumenical councils as the highest authority, as does Karmiris, is certainly to adopt a juridical conception of the synodical institution.[132]

Karmiris asserts that all autocephalous churches are equal among them-selves, united through a common faith, canonical order, worship, and mu-tual love into a larger unity, constituting thus the one Orthodox Church, which is in unbroken historical continuation with the ancient Church and completely identified with it.[133] Karmiris agrees with the view of his fellow

Greek Orthodox theologian Hamilkas Alivizatos (1887–1969), a professor of canon law at the Faculty of Theology of the University of Athens, that the Orthodox Church is organized as a confederation of local autocephalous churches united in themselves through the same faith and love, but totally independent, over which no other church has any jurisdiction; the Ecumenical Patriarch has only an honorary primacy.[134] We have seen that such a view of the Orthodox Church in terms of a confederation is for Zizioulas a mistaken understanding, for it fails to see the existence of a ministry of unity in the Church. In other words, here Karmiris in fact implies that the system of autocephalous churches—which are equal among themselves and exclude a primate as a ministry and institution of unity—is opposed to a monarchical and universalistic view of ecclesiology.

Institutionally speaking, for Karmiris, the synods, in the form of a local and ecumenical councils, express the unity of the Church and the center of that unity. He agrees with his fellow Greek Orthodox theologian Christos Androutsos (1869–1935), a professor of dogmatics at the Faculty of Theology of the University of Athens, that the synod is the unifying and binding center, rather than simply one bishop, as the Roman Catholic Church believes.[135] Karmiris rejects a monarchical and juridical unity under the pope and instead proposes a unity manifested through the councils. As we will see in chapter 4, Zizioulas likewise believes that synods express the unity of the Church, but he insists also on the necessity of the institution of primacy, which expresses the unity and the oneness of the Church on the regional and the universal levels, within the synodical context.

Karmiris believes that the mystery of unity, which unites all the particular local churches among themselves, and which is manifested in a common faith, grace, structure, worship, life, and love, originates from and is patterned upon the mystery of the unity of the three persons of the Holy Trinity among themselves. Each local church under its bishop who celebrates the Holy Eucharist possesses the fullness of the Church, making up the body of Christ in the Holy Eucharist, "the Church of God which is in Corinth, in Rome, etc." In the unity, equality, and identity of grace, faith, and structure, the Orthodox local churches form the one Orthodox Catholic Church, and its unity is expressed though the pan-Orthodox or ecumenical council.[136]

As we will see in chapter 4, Zizioulas believes that this trinitarian pattern of unity has a clear structure. For him, the trinitarian model of unity is based upon the principle of "the one and the many," a pattern of unity that has implications in the realm of ecclesiology and necessitates the existence of the primate as an expression of the unity of the Church.

THE PRIMACY OF HONOR

Karmiris, in arguing against the papal primacy of jurisdiction, suggests instead that the Bishop of Rome enjoyed a simple primacy of honor. He asserts that the Third Canon of the Second Ecumenical Council and the Twenty-Eighth Canon of Chalcedon have granted to the throne of Rome privileges of honor and to the Patriarch of Constantinople equal privileges of honor, because Rome "is the royal city" (cf. Twenty-Eighth Canon of Chalcedon) and Constantinople "is the new Rome" (cf. Third Canon of the Second Ecumenical Council).[137] For Karmiris, these canons as well as the Thirty-Sixth Canon of the Council in Trullo (692) determined the privileges of honor and the order of the five patriarchs, without recognizing in the Bishop of Rome a primacy of jurisdiction over the whole Church. These canons recognized in the Bishop of Rome an honorary primacy as first in order. The Church of Constantinople enjoyed the same privileges, followed in turn by the Patriarchs of Alexandria, of Antioch, and of Jerusalem.[138] By speaking of a primacy of honor and of order among the bishops, he clearly seeks to refute and to exclude the jurisdictional primacy of the Bishop of Rome over the entire Church. He quotes in this respect the patriarchal letter of 1895, which states, as we have seen, that "the divine Fathers, honouring the Bishop of Rome only as the bishop of the capital city of the empire, gave him the honorary prerogative of presidency, considering him simply as the bishop first in order, that is, first among equals; which prerogatives they also assigned afterwards to the Bishop of Constantinople, when that city became the capital of the Roman Empire."[139]

We have seen, however, that from a canonical point of view these privileges or primacies of honor were not simply understood as honorary distinctions in the hierarchical order. They involved a real power.[140] In referring to the ancient canonical institution of the Pentarchy, Karmiris cites another Greek Orthodox theologian, Vlasios Phidas, who points out the historical fact that only the thrones of Rome, Constantinople, Alexandria, Antioch, and Jerusalem, which were canonically endowed with privileges of honor, had jurisdiction over and the right to ordain and judge the bishops of their provinces.[141] It seems that by citing this fact from Phidas, Karmiris accepts implicitly that these privileges or primacies are linked with legal power, namely with the legal right of the primates to perform ordinations. As we noted above, in line with the patriarchal letter, Karmiris describes the primacies or privileges in terms of a simple honorary distinction in the hierarchical order but contradicts this with the canonical fact that these privileges contained also a legal power, which Karmiris seems to accept implicitly.

He also asserts that the Third Canon of the Second Ecumenical Council, the Twenty-Eighth Canon of the Council of Chalcedon, and the Thirty-Sixth Canon of the Council in Trullo (692) accorded to the bishops of Constantinople privileges of honor "because it was the new Rome" (διά τό εἶναι αὐτήν Νέαν Ρώμην), just as the Fathers had in the past accorded to the bishop of old Rome privileges of honor, conferring on him in this way a moral authority without any power of jurisdiction. For Karmiris, it is obvious that these canons and actions reject the Roman primacy of power *jure divino*.[142] However, as we have seen, primacy cannot be understood only in terms of moral authority, since it contained real power.[143]

Zizioulas does not agree with Karmiris's understanding of the privileges or primacies in terms of simple honor or of *primus inter pares*. He is particularly critical of Karmiris's description of primacy in terms of honor. He quotes a passage from Karmiris that for him sums up the position of most of the Orthodox theologians in the first half of the twentieth century:

> Because of the political importance of Rome and the apostolicity of this Church, as well as the martyrdom in it of the Apostles Peter and Paul and its distinction in works of love, service, and mission, the bishops of Rome received from the Councils and from the Fathers and the pious emperors— therefore by human and not divine order—*a simple primacy of honor and order*, as first among equal presidents of the particular Churches, since basically the popes and patriarchs and archbishops and metropolitans are simple bishops, equal with their fellow-bishops from the point of view of priesthood (*hieraticos*).[144]

He then states that Karmiris—by speaking of "simple primacy of honor"— wants to exclude the right of the primate to exercise jurisdiction over the rest of the bishops. For Zizioulas this is a principle accepted by all the Orthodox Churches, and it is indeed a stumbling block for them in relation to the claims of the bishop of Rome.[145] He emphasizes that, in spite of many examples of interventions by Orthodox Patriarchs and heads of the autocephalous churches in the affairs of the other bishops, no Orthodox would find such interventions acceptable canonically and ecclesiologically.[146]

On the other hand, Zizioulas points out the incoherence of using such a description of primacy in terms of simple honor:

> "Simple honor" seems to suggest no power and authority at all, whereas it is known from experience that the person who chairs a meeting of any kind exercises powers of great significance, including the right to convoke and dis-

cuss the meeting, to form the agenda, and so on. With regard to the Church, such a description of primacy as "simple honor" seems to contradict basic canonical principles, such as the ones contained in the 34th Apostolic Canon which states that in every region (presumably a metropolitan district, but by extension in all forms of primacy) there *must* be a primate (*protos*) without whom the bishops of the district can do nothing, while he himself can do nothing without them. This seems to imply that the *primus* can even block the deliberations of the synod, if he chooses to do so *without the rest of the bishops being able to function synodically in his absence.*[147]

In order to prove further this last implication of the Thirty-Fourth Apostolic Canon, Zizioulas refers to a canonical provision in the Orthodox Church that "in the absence of the Patriarch or during the vacancy of his throne there can be no Episcopal elections or the performance of any 'canonical acts.'"[148] Zizioulas concludes that the phrase "simple honor" appears to be useful with regard to what it intends to exclude (jurisdictional intervention), but nevertheless, it seems, in fact, that "a simple primacy of honor" does not exist, even in the Orthodox Church.[149]

On the other hand, Karmiris states explicitly that the Thirty-Fourth Apostolic Canon implies a primacy of honor. Thus, Karmiris says that in the case of an ecclesiological rapprochement with the Roman Catholic Church, the Orthodox Catholic Church would continue to recognize a primacy of honor as first among equals granted to the Patriarch of Rome by the ecumenical councils, as with the pattern of the Patriarch of Constantinople.[150] Karmiris's conception of universal primacy—that of Rome in the united Church or that of the Patriarch of Constantinople within the Orthodox Church, as based on the Thirty-Fourth Apostolic Canon—is thus an honorary one. For Zizioulas, on the other hand, the Thirty-Fourth Apostolic Canon implies a primacy, and by extension a universal one, which is not simply of honor but with real power.

After noting that the Orthodox Churches have largely accepted the idea of primacy as exercised by the Patriarch of Constantinople in the spirit of the Thirty-Fourth Apostolic Canon, Zizioulas states that "primacy of honor" is a misleading term, since such a primacy is not honorific but involves actual duties and responsibilities.[151] He refers to the responsibility of the Patriarch of Constantinople as the primate of the Orthodox Church: "The Patriarch of Constantinople could not interfere in the affairs of the other Patriarchates, but would be responsible for the canonical order within them and intervene only when asked to do so in cases of emergency or disturbance and anomaly of some kind. He would be responsible for the convocation of councils dealing with matters pertaining to the entire Orthodox Churches, always with the consent of the other patriarchs."[152]

Karmiris accepts the fact that the primacy of the popes, patriarchs, and archbishops is mainly a primacy of concern (i.e., care, solicitude), service, and witness, but not of power, which comes from the privileges of the churches of each primate.[153] Karmiris's conception of primacy in terms of solicitude therefore implies that primacy is not just one of simple honor, as he himself nevertheless asserted, but involves something more, as noted by Zizioulas. Karmiris accepts that according to the Ninth Canon of the Council of Antioch (341), which developed and completed the Fourth Canon of the First Ecumenical Council, the metropolitan in the ancient Church "was charged with concern (*phrontis*) for the whole province, because all men of business come together from every quarter to the metropolis," and he therefore had precedence in honor.[154] The concept of concern is something more than Karmiris's persistent description of primacy in terms of simple honor.

John Erickson notes in this regard that primacy on the provincial level is not just one of simple honor; something more is involved, which may be found in the concept of *phrontis, sollicitudo*.[155] For Erickson, this care, solicitude, supervision, of which the Ninth Canon of Antioch speaks, is exercised on the provincial level in a number of concrete ways but chiefly in the supervision of episcopal elections (Canon Nineteen of Antioch) and in the reception of appeals. Also, Erickson states that the metropolitan's *phrontis* is to see that the canons are observed, that due process is maintained. But for Erickson this *phrontis* is not limited to the provincial level.[156] As we saw above, Zizioulas speaks in similar terms of the exercise of such a *phrontis* of the universal primate of the Orthodox Church, the Patriarch of Constantinople, who is responsible for canonical order within the Orthodox Church and for the convocation of councils dealing with matters pertaining to the whole Orthodox Church. Also, we have seen that for Zizioulas the canonical principle deriving from the Thirty-Fourth Apostolic Canon, which gives a real power to the primate on the regional level, is also applicable by extension to the universal level, and therefore the universal primacy of the Patriarch of Constantinople is not only one of simple honor.

Karmiris quotes from the book by Maximos, Metropolitan of Sardes, on the canonical and historical position of the Ecumenical Patriarchate in the Orthodox Church and agrees with Maximos's assertion that the Patriarch of Constantinople does not have a kind of Eastern papacy; the Patriarch is not a universal bishop, and he does not claim doctrinal infallibility or a direct, absolute jurisdiction over the faithful. Instead, his position as first bishop and his jurisdiction are defined by the holy canons and by history. Karmiris then concludes with Metropolitan Maximos that the Ecumenical Patriarch exercises his duties and rights, which derive from his position as first bishop, on general ecclesiastical matters but always in cooperation with the other patriarchs.[157] Karmiris accepts therefore the fact that the primate, and in this case the Patriarch of Constantinople, exercises particular rights. This again contradicts his description of primacy in terms of simple honor. Although Karmiris accepts Metropolitan Maximos's point that rights are assigned to the primate, he continues to assert that a primacy of simple honor is accorded to a patriarch or to an archbishop who is *primus inter pares* and presides over the synod of each particular Orthodox Church—and not a primacy of jurisdiction. Their honorary primacy, he says, is balanced by the obligation not to do anything without the agreement and the consent of all the bishops and of their synods. Likewise, the Ecumenical Patriarch can act after consultation and with an agreement by all the heads of the Orthodox Churches on general ecclesiastical matters or after the decisions of pan-Orthodox conferences and councils.[158] Karmiris also implies that the primacy of honor means that all bishops, from the popes and the patriarchs down to the least of the bishops, are equal.[159]

For Zizioulas, this is a basic principle for both Roman Catholics and Orthodox but with a fundamental difference between them, namely that Roman Catholics would apply this equality only to the level of sacramental grace, which does not involve automatically the exercise of jurisdiction (*missio canonica*), while the Orthodox would make no such distinction.[160] The fact, therefore, that for the Orthodox all bishops are equal sacramentally does not in itself justify the rejection of papal primacy unless it is supplemented by the idea that episcopal sacramental grace is inconceivable without automatically involving jurisdictional power.[161] Zizioulas then asks, if that is the case, how can the Orthodox account for the existence in their Church of titular "bishops," i.e., bishops who are equal with the rest of the bishops sacramentally, but with no right of jurisdiction? Because of the existence of such bishops, Zizioulas believes that the Orthodox suffer an internal contradiction and weaken seriously their argument against the Roman primacy.[162] By borrowing from the West the institution of titular bishops, they unwittingly also borrowed the distinction between episcopal grace and jurisdiction (*missio canonica*), which distinction allows the pope to exercise jurisdictional authority beyond his own diocese without contradicting the principle of the sacramental equality of all bishops.[163]

PRIMACY AS A MATTER OF CANONICAL AND HUMAN ORDER

We have seen that Karmiris asserts that primacy in the Church is by human and not by divine order, a primacy of honor and order resulting from historical circumstances and human factors (the political importance of capital cities, distinction in service to the other churches, etc.).[164] In emphasizing that primacy is due only to human factors, and is therefore *jure humano*, Karmiris seeks to reject the Roman Catholic teaching defined by Vatican I that a *jure divino* primacy of jurisdiction is granted to Peter and to his successors.[165] On the other hand, Zizioulas is critical of understanding primacy as a matter of canonical and human order. In commenting on Karmiris's view, Zizioulas asserts that "the existence of primates in the Church is not, according to this view, a matter of divine but of human right. This means that the Church could exist without primacy, although she could not exist without bishops or synods, the latter being *jure divino* and part of the Church's esse."[166]

Zizioulas states that, for Karmiris, the actual structure of primacies, which stemmed from the Pentarchy[167] and was complemented later by the rest of the Patriarchates and autocephalous churches in the East, is due simply to historical circumstances, i.e., to entirely human and transitory factors.[168] Zizioulas notes critically that this argument "against papal primacy promoted by Karmiris and his contemporary Orthodox theologians rests upon a clear-cut distinction between *dogma* and *order*: whereas the episcopal and synodical structure of the Church is a matter of dogma (ecclesiology), primacy is not. This raises the question whether there can be such a clear-cut distinction between canonical order and ecclesiology, since the canons of the Church derive their authority from ecclesiological justification for them."[169]

Zizioulas then criticizes Karmiris for adopting in his ecclesiology a Western distinction between the human and the divine aspects of the Church. He says that "Karmiris, like Alivizatos, Trembelas, and more explicitly Mouratides (all of them drawing probably from Androutsos, who was strongly influenced by Western scholasticism), operates in ecclesiology with the idea of a distinction between the *human* and *divine* aspect of the Church. Whatever belongs to order in the Church derives from her human aspect, and whatever pertains to the dogma of the Church exists *jure divino*."[170]

Zizioulas then goes on to explain that this is "a curious ecclesiology based on an equally curious Christology":

> In ecclesiology, just as in Christology, there is an *antidosis idiomatum* between divine and human, and as there is nothing in Christ's divine nature which

does not affect decisively and permanently His humanity, so also in ecclesiology we cannot say that something is of the canonical order, and therefore inevitably *de jure humano*. Primacy, like episcopacy, synodality, and so on, belongs to the canonical order but not necessarily to the "human" aspect of the Church. The view maintained by the above-mentioned theologians that episcopacy, synodality etc. exist *jure divino*, but primacy does not, requires a great deal of explanation in order to become acceptable.[171]

Moreover, Zizioulas points out the logical incoherence of the position, adopted by Karmiris, that primacy exists *jure humano*:

> The main weakness of this position lies in that it seems to overlook the simple and obvious fact that *synodality cannot exist without primacy*. There has never been and there can never be a synod or a council without a *protos*. If, therefore, synodality exists *jure divino*, as the above theologians would (rightly) maintain, primacy also must exist by the same right.[172]

It follows then that Zizioulas accepts the position that primacy exists *jure divino* and not simply *jure humano*. He accepts the pragmatic and human-historical realities that contributed to the emergence of primacy in the Church.[173] But for Zizioulas, primacy belongs to the canonical order and is not simply *jure humano*; he goes beyond the historical-human realities, which obviously played an important role in the emergence of the primacies, and as we will see in chapter 4, he bases the issue of primacy upon the dogmatical and ecclesiological principle of "the one and the many." This principle renders the existence of primacy ecclesiologically necessary, i.e., *jure divino*, and stems from the life of the Holy Trinity. Primacy is not due simply to canonical order, which for Karmiris is related to the human aspect of the Church. Karmiris accepts the opinion of Chrysostom Papadopoulos that the privileges (i.e., primacies) of the bishops, metropolitans, and the patriarchs, etc., have to exist for the sake of canonical order and that one must precede the other in honor, but he maintains that the one who precedes in honor does not hold any power over the following ones, who are equal.[174] We shall see that for Zizioulas this hierarchical order, which implies a primate, is a matter of dogma. It originates in the life of the Holy Trinity and is reflected in the existing order between the churches.

CHAPTER 3

Vatican II

Papal Primacy and Episcopal Collegiality

In this chapter we will first look at the main theological movements, namely the ecclesiological and liturgical movements, that influenced Vatican II's doctrine on the Church and on papal primacy and episcopal collegiality, and then we will present the doctrine itself. As we will see, the ecclesiological movement developed a eucharistic ecclesiology that consolidated the biblical and patristic linkages between the Eucharist and the Church. In this perspective the Church came to be understood not in juridical categories—as a pyramidal hierarchical structure in which officeholders had jurisdiction over the members and the Vicar of Christ (the pope) was considered as ruler of the whole—but rather as a communion, based on the idea of eucharistic communion, and indeed as a communion of local churches. The liturgical movement led to the idea of episcopal collegiality and to a rediscovering of the ancient theology of the episcopate. Both these movements were reflected in the teaching of Vatican II.

Despite Vatican II's insistence on the ecclesiology of communion, however, we will see that its doctrine on primacy and collegiality contains strong reaffirmations of a juridical and universalistic ecclesiology. This universalistic ecclesiology operates in two ways: (1) the pope as head of the Church has jurisdiction over the Church and the bishops; and (2) the college of the bishops with the pope exercises a jurisdiction over the Church.

The Main Theological Movements and Trends before Vatican II and Their Ecclesiological Contributions to Vatican II

It has rightly been pointed out that in the twentieth century enormous developments took place in Roman Catholic ecclesiology. The seeds of renewal can be found in the nineteenth-century patristic revival of the German theologian, Johan Adam Möhler, but the fruit of this renewal did not appear until the turn of the twentieth century.[1] The ninety years separating the two Vatican councils, as Michael Himes notes, are part of what could be called the "century of the Church."[2] A reaction took place within Roman Catholic ecclesiology, provoked by Vatican I. As Olegario Gonzáles de Cardedal puts it, "Such a radical, complex council as the First Vatican Council tended to provoke an equally radical reaction, either prolonging the emphases adopted by the Council or directing attention toward themes which it did not treat. A mere retouching of the ecclesiological edifice was not needed; rather, a new ecclesiology was called for."[3]

It would appear that Leo XIII was aware of the partiality and ecclesiological deficiencies of the texts of Vatican I, and he thus directed the attention of Roman Catholics to the interior and constitutive elements of the Church's mystery. Hence the encyclical letters *Satis Cognitum* (1896) on the Church, the body of Christ; *Divinum illud* (1897) on the Holy Spirit as the source of the Church's sanctifying and sacramental life; and *Mirae caritatis* (1902), treating the Eucharist as the sacrament of unity and as "the soul of the Church."[4]

Although Leo XIII presents the Eucharist as the sacrament of unity, this unity is universalistic and juridical, i.e., unity with the pope. This is because the Eucharist was not considered as encompassing the whole life of the Church.[5] Nevertheless, the words of another German theologian, Romano Guardini, in 1922, reflected significant developments in Western theology: "An event with incalculable consequences has begun: The Church is awakening in people's souls."[6] Guardini implied that the Church was beginning to be seen not as something imposed on us as an external structure or organization, existing over and against us, but as something that embraces us from within.[7] Joseph Ratzinger points out that "this new awareness of the Church was articulated in the phrase 'the mystical body of Christ.'"[8] Paul McPartlan claims that Guardini's phrase indicates the move from an individualistic view of salvation, dispensed by an external organization called the "Church," to an appreciation of the corporate life of the mystical body of Christ. Instead of grace being considered as something individual and invisible, it was now seen as communitarian, as participation in the mystical body of Christ, with the Church itself now being seen "first and foremost as this mystical communion."[9]

Henri de Lubac (1896–1991), who coined the famous principle "the Eucharist makes the Church," considered that this corporate life of grace, namely the life of the Church, was not something invisible but concrete, for the Church's communitarian life was realized concretely in the celebration of the Eucharist. Seen in this light, the Church is most fully visible in the celebration of the Eucharist, which is the sacrament of Christ and the place where the Church is revealed.[10] De Lubac made clear the relationship between the Eucharist and the Church in his well-known work *Corpus Mysticum*.[11] In fact, by showing that for the Fathers the term "mystical body" meant the Eucharist and not the Church, he recovered the link between the Eucharist and the Church.[12]

Thus, for Ratzinger, *Corpus Mysticum* gave rise to a eucharistic ecclesiology or an ecclesiology of communion that "became the real core of Vatican II's teaching on the Church."[13] Vatican II took up the communional aspect of the Church in its Constitution on the Church, *Lumen Gentium*, stating that in the communities under the bishops, "the Mystery of the Lord's Supper is celebrated 'so that, by means of the flesh and blood of the Lord the whole brotherhood of the Body may be welded together'" (*LG* 26).[14] More specifically, in the opening paragraph of the Constitution on the Church, Vatican II followed de Lubac's ecclesiological thought in teaching that the Church is a sacrament and a place of grace, both communal and concrete.[15] Thus, *LG* 1 says that the Church "is in the nature of a sacrament—a sign and instrument, that is, of communion with God and of unity among all people." Vatican II uses the key concept of the Church as the mystical body of Christ in the opening chapters of the Constitution on the Church (*LG* 7).

De Lubac's principle, which, as we saw, was patristic, namely that the Eucharist makes the Church, is affirmed by Vatican II's teaching that in every celebration of the Eucharist Christ himself is present "through whose power and influence the One, Holy, Catholic, and Apostolic Church is constituted" and that local groups united with their pastors are properly called churches (*LG* 26).[16] By studying the sources, that is, the Bible and the Fathers (in this case especially Augustine), de Lubac recovered the Church's original self-understanding.[17] Ratzinger notes the influence that de Lubac had upon the council's teaching on the Church by saying that de Lubac "put the idea of the Church as the body of Christ in concrete terms as eucharistic ecclesiology and thus opened it up to the actual questions of the Church's legal order and the relationship between the local and the universal Church."[18]

The link between the Eucharist and the Church was broken in the eleventh century as a result of the eucharistic controversy started by the scholastic theologian Berengar.[19] As McPartlan shows, Catholic thought, instead of following Pauline and Augustinian trains of eucharistic thought to their ecclesial end, "got stuck half-way, following the tumultuous eucharistic controversy sparked by Berengar in the eleventh century, since when all emphasis had been placed on the fact that the elements of bread and wine are themselves changed into Christ in the Mass, by 'transubstantiation.'"[20] The consequences for ecclesiology of this broken link between the Eucharist and the Church that came about during the scholastic period were considerable. W. Kasper notes that eucharistic ecclesiology fell into general oblivion after the eleventh-century controversy, leaving the Church to be understood mainly as "a social hierarchical structure."[21] The break opened the way for social and juridical definitions of the Church, i.e., an external vision. The mystical body of Christ was thus designated the social body, which is the Church, of which the pope was the head (caput).[22] In the medieval scholastic description of the Church, as McPartlan notes, the Eucharist "is in there somewhere, but simply as one of the things done by the juridically defined Church: 'The Church makes the Eucharist.'"[23] Eamon Duffy indicates the transition that occurred in the Middle Ages, from the original and early eucharistic understanding of the Church as a communion of local churches to the pyramidal view, when he refers to "the medieval reimagining of the Church not as a communion of local Churches but as a single international organisation, with the Pope at its head."[24]

For the Russian Orthodox theologian, Nicholas Afanassieff, who likely coined the term "eucharistic ecclesiology," and his disciples, the Eucharist was seen as the constitutive element of the Church, in light of which the theology of the local Church could be developed.[25] In fact, this eucharistic ecclesiology did not originate with Afanassieff but rather was something that had continued to exist in the Orthodox Church and was revisited in the nineteenth century.[26] Afanassieff exercised a great influence on the teaching of Vatican II regarding the link between the Eucharist and the Church and on the fullness and catholicity of the local church. A footnote to the penultimate draft of *Lumen Gentium* in 1963, which explains a passage that is now part of *LG 26*—"[It is the Eucharist] from which the Church derives its life and on which it thrives"—gives an indication of Afanassieff's influence on Vatican II. It advises the bishop perusing the schema for the Constitution on the Church to read Afanassieff in order to investigate further the bond between the Eucharist and the Church.[27]

Works of Karl Rahner in 1958–1959 and of Yves Congar in 1959–1960 also postulated the need for a theology of the local church.[28] Congar showed the historical shift that had occurred in the West, from an ecclesiology of communion of local churches to a universalistic ecclesiology.[29] Gonzáles de Cardedal comments that Congar's thinking "was the thinking of a prophet, calling for the coming council to elaborate a Church which begins from below, from catholicity, which is rooted in local churches and embraces the universal Church."[30]

Another pioneer of Vatican II who shared de Lubac's view of the Church was Dom Lambert Beauduin (1873–1960), the founder of the Liturgical Movement in "its popular and hugely influential form."[31] He realized that the Church comes into being in the Eucharist and that the liturgy is the "very dynamo of ecclesial vitality."[32] He insisted on and stressed the communal nature of the liturgy; it was ecclesial, it was the Church in action and at prayer.[33]

Like de Lubac, he envisaged the Church not in individualistic but in communal terms, i.e., as a mystical union in the body of Christ that is realized in the Liturgy: "From the first centuries to our own day, the Church has ever given to all her prayer a character profoundly and essentially collective. By means of living the liturgy wholeheartedly, Christians become more and more conscious of their supernatural fraternity, of their union in the mystic body of Christ. And this is the most powerful antidote against individualism."[34] Beauduin's insistence on active participation in the liturgy aimed at promoting the awareness of the Church as the body of Christ. McPartlan summarizes the concrete contribution to Roman Catholic ecclesiology made by Beauduin and others as follows: "Beauduin and others in the Liturgical Movement were very conscious that, through the active participation in the Eucharist that they were promoting, the body of Christ, which had seemed abstract to many at Vatican I, was being made a concrete, lived reality."[35]

After his monastic profession, in 1907 Beauduin was appointed to teach ecclesiology. The manuals of ecclesiology that he had at his disposition were not inspiring. However, what did inspire him were the teachings of the Fathers and the councils and particularly the draft text of Vatican I with its opening chapter on the Church as the mystical body of Christ.[36] Beauduin was an ardent advocate of this particular teaching of Vatican I, so that a fuller doctrine of the Church could be elaborated.[37] Vatican I had ended prematurely at the outbreak of the Franco-Prussian War, after having dealt only with the doctrine regarding the papacy out of its original draft constitution on the Church. It was Vatican II that in its Constitution on the Sacred Liturgy followed Beauduin's theological understanding of the liturgy as the Church itself in action and at prayer.[38]

Beauduin's efforts to reform the Church's liturgical life and his insistence on active participation in the Eucharist were remedies for the understanding of the liturgy and the Mass that had prevailed at the start of the twentieth century. At that time liturgy was considered in an individualistic sense, and the Mass was not understood as an action of the whole body of Christ for the very good reason, as McPartlan notes, that the Church itself wasn't understood as the body of Christ, at least not officially.[39] The Church at the turn of the twentieth century was presented in sociological categories as a "perfect society," which does not mean strictly "perfect" in a moral sense, but "complete," in the sense that the Church was juridically endowed with all it needed for its own governance.[40] It was viewed as a juridical pyramid, as described by Gregory XVI (1831–1846) in the nineteenth century: "No one can overlook the fact that the Church is an unequal society in which God has destined some to command and others to obey. The latter are the laity, while the former are the clergy."[41]

During the 1930s and 1940s the historical studies in Emile Mersch's *Le Corps Mystique du Christ* (1933) and Pope Pius XII's Encyclical *Mystici Corporis* (1943), together with the research of Sebastian Tromp, contributed to a return to the biblical and patristic conception of the Church as the mystical body of Christ.[42] Dulles notes that the encyclical was the most comprehensive official teaching on the Church prior to Vatican II, capitalizing on the rich sources of renewal coming from patristic studies and in turn stimulating further studies of the same kind.[43] However, the encyclical seeks to harmonize biblical and patristic teaching on the Church with the juridical ecclesiology that came much later. It states that "Christ and His vicar constitute only one Head," and the bishops, accordingly, are subject to the authority of the Roman Pontiff, from whom they receive jurisdiction.[44] In the encyclical's exposition of the Church as the mystical body, the Eucharist does not occupy a central place, as it does in de Lubac's and Beauduin's expositions of the Church, and the unity that it asserts is a universalistic one with the pope, not one expressed in the form of local churches.[45]

We have seen that the medieval theological dispute over the real presence of Christ in the elements of bread and wine and the subsequent intense focus of Roman Catholic thought on those elements led to a break in the earlier link between the Eucharist and the Church. Within this changed perspective, major changes also occurred in the theology of the episcopate. Being ordained came to mean that a man possessed personally the power to bring about the transubstantiation of the elements. Thus, ordination was understood in the narrow sense of conferring powers for the transformation of the elements; since every priest could do this, it was no longer clear what meaning the sacrament of holy orders had for the bishops. Thus, becoming a bishop was not considered to be an ordination, but rather a consecration to govern the Church.[46]

As McPartlan notes, the Eucharist was the *priest's* job; *bishops* governed the Church, which now was called the mystical body of Christ.[47] As a result of this change, the bishop was seen as somehow floating above the Eucharist. Bishops were priests with added jurisdiction over their local communities and did not constitute a proper rank in the sacrament of orders. Scholastic theologians considered this jurisdiction as flowing from the pope.[48] The scholastic understanding of the episcopate placed the bishop's shepherding tasks of teaching and leadership outside the sacrament of orders. The bishop's pastoral ministry was separated from his sacramental power and was viewed as a power of jurisdiction deriving from the pope.[49] Hence, the emergence of the distinction between power of order and power of jurisdiction, which came to be seen as legitimate by theologians such as Thomas Aquinas and canonists of the Middle Ages.[50] According to this distinction, while the bishops by their *priestly* ordination possess the sacramental power to exercise their ministry (i.e., *potestas ordinis*), it is the pope who subsequently grants to all the bishops the jurisdiction (i.e., *potestas jurisdictionis*) to exercise their pastoral ministry in their own particular churches. The pope assigns to each of the bishops a particular Church in which he exercises his ministry.[51]

William Henn points out the negative consequences of this distinction between order and jurisdiction. First, the Church came to be understood as a single huge diocese (with the Church here structured along the lines of universalistic ecclesiology). The care of individual parts is assigned by the pastor of the whole. The bishops thus came to be considered as vicars to the pope. Also, for Henn, "this view tends to isolate the individual bishop, limiting him to his specific portion of the Church. That the bishops together and even individually have some responsibility for the unity of the church as a whole is at best obscured, at worst lost."[52]

The scholastic view of the episcopate persisted in the Roman Catholic Church into the twentieth century. Not until Bernard Botte (1893–1980), a liturgist, undertook his research into the ancient prayers of ordination was this viewpoint overturned. He was invited to speak to French priests during the worker-priest crisis in the 1950s and says that "they were in search of a theology of the priesthood and they turned to Tradition for an answer."[53] He realized that in their theological studies on the sacrament of orders, there was no place for the episcopate.[54] Ordination and orders applied to priests, giving them the power for transubstantiation of the gifts during the Mass.[55] Botte states: "As a matter of fact, the theological development of Scholasticism on this subject [i.e., the sacraments of orders] took as its point of departure the power to offer sacrifice, that is to say, the priesthood. The episcopate took a back seat. It was no longer an order, at most it was a degree of the priesthood."[56] The scholastic conception of the episcopate had persisted in Roman Catholic theological thought.

By studying the early prayers of ordination, especially in the Apostolic tradition, however, Botte revealed the patristic understanding of the bishop as the high priest of the New Israel.[57] Vatican II bears significant signs of Botte's rediscovery of the bishop as high priest, in its teaching that the episcopate is "the fullness of the sacraments of Orders," which in the liturgical as well as patristic tradition of the Church is called the "high priesthood, the acme of the sacred ministry" (*LG* 21). McPartlan comments that Botte's study of the ordination rites of the early Church showed the bishop to be a high priest in the celebration of the Eucharist and not just a juridical figure as the scholastics had considered him, i.e., as the governor of his Church community.[58] De Lubac followed Botte's work closely, likewise envisaging the bishop as the high priest in the celebration of the Eucharist.[59]

Moreover, Botte notes that the understanding of the priesthood in the 1950s was an individualistic one, with the priest seen "as a man endowed with supernatural power, placed between God and man, halfway between heaven and earth, sent out into the world for the conquest of the souls."[60] In contrast, Botte's studies of the ancient rites of ordination revealed no such understanding. What is revealed in the ordination prayers of the early Church was less a transmission of powers from person to person "than the conferring of the Spirit with a view to the growth of the Body of Christ which is the Church. And in this ecclesial perspective, the episcopate held a central position."[61] Thus, as McPartlan points out, "orders are for the *Church* and *therefore* they immediately relate to the Eucharist."[62] Seen in this perspective, the bishop is the high priest and correspondingly the prime celebrant of the Eucharist.

Vatican II followed Botte's thought in presenting the bishops as the high priests in the offering of the Eucharist: "The bishop, invested with the fullness of the sacraments of Orders, is 'the steward of the grace of the supreme priesthood', above all in the Eucharist, which he himself offers, or ensures that it is offered, from which the Church ever derives its life and on which it thrives" (*LG* 26).

Botte's liturgical research also showed that priests are not to be seen individually; rather, they form a college around the bishop and share in his priesthood. Likewise, individual bishops do not possess their high priesthood self-sufficiently, but they also form a college.[63] The very ordination of the bishop is a clear indication of this. The anointing of a bishop "is a collegial act that incorporates the newly elected into the body of bishops" and for this reason, i.e., the act's collegiality, several bishops conferred episcopal ordination together.[64] Thus, episcopal ordination indicated that it was not something passed from individual to individual, but rather conferred by reception into the episcopal body. McPartlan notes, "*As a member of this order*, which succeeds to the apostles, Botte said that each bishop 'bears with the other bishops the responsibility for the unity and increase of the whole Church'. Thus there was and is no such thing as a freelance bishop, or at lower level, a freelance priest."[65] McPartlan concludes that in this renewed understanding "there is no individualism to be found anywhere, only collegial ministry at the service of the body of Christ."[66]

Furthermore, for Botte, what motivated the bishops in the early Church, when a heresy or a problem of discipline arose, either to convene a council or to write to one another seeking common solutions, was their awareness that, as successors to the apostles, they shared in common a concern for the unity and preservation of the faith.[67] In other words, the historical facts of the early Church point to a visible manifestation and reflection of the collegial character of the episcopate. Ratzinger points out that Botte was the first person who formulated the idea of episcopal collegiality, which was to become one of the pillars of Vatican's II ecclesiology, and that he thus opened the door for the council on this point.[68]

A Brief History of the Constitution *Lumen Gentium*

To determine the concrete program of the council, Pope John XXIII sent out an extensive set of inquiries to bishops all over the world, and to the curia, the cardinals, heads of religious orders, Catholic universities, and ecclesiastical faculties.[69] The answers filled fifteen quarto volumes, and there were in all 8,972 proposals, wishes, and requests. From these the themes of greatest importance were chosen and put before the various commissions for a preliminary investigation.[70] These issues and proposals reflected the situation of the Roman Catholic Church at the time.[71] They also showed that the revival of the Church was one of the principal tasks of the future synod.[72] With regard to the Church, many considered that Vatican II needed to address the issue of the bishops and thus complete the work of Vatican I, which had dealt with papal primacy. More precisely, it was proposed that the council speak about the functions of the bishops and specify the doctrine of their power and authority (the origin of this power, the distinction between the power of jurisdiction and the power of order), and describe the newly recovered aspect of collegiality. It was also proposed that the episcopate be defined as a sacramental order distinct from the presbyterate, and that the offices of teaching, sanctifying, and governing be presented as deriving from episcopal ordination, which confers the fullness of priesthood, the fullness of the sacrament of orders. At the head of his diocese, the bishop represents Christ and is the guarantor of unity.[73]

The curia and the bishops circulated their lists of candidates for membership of the commissions. This membership was a balance between the progressive majority and the curial minority.[74] As Nichols notes, "This contrasts with Vatican I, where the Ultramontanes manoeuvred to screen out all progressive candidates from the conciliar commissions, thus ensuring in advance that the council would not reflect the views of the Gallican minority."[75]

The commission *De doctrina fidei et morum*, which was responsible for matters of doctrine, was under the leadership of Cardinal Ottaviani, with Tromp as secretary, and was divided into a number of subcommissions, one of which was devoted to ecclesiological questions. This subcommission prepared a draft text on the Church (1962) in eleven chapters that was somewhat disjointed.[76]

Many bishops criticized this first curial draft of the Constitution on the Church as being too juridical and clerical in outlook.[77] It was put before them for discussion late in the first session of the council (on December 1, 1962).[78] Many bishops called for an emphasis on new perspectives. Cardinal Lefebvre stated that the nature of the Church as a community should be stressed rather than as a society, without separating the two aspects. Also Bishop Elchinger said:

> Yesterday the Church was considered above all as an institution, today it is experienced as a community. Yesterday it was the Pope who was mainly in view, today the Pope is thought of as united to the bishops. Yesterday the bishop alone was considered, today all the bishops together. Yesterday theology stressed the importance of the hierarchy, today it is discovering the people of God. Yesterday it was chiefly concerned with what divided, today it voices all that unites. Yesterday the theology of the Church was mainly preoccupied with the inward life of the Church, today it sees the Church as orientated to the outside world.[79]

Cardinals Döpfner and Frings pointed out the absence in the draft of the understanding of the Church as mystery and demanded that this mystery not be passed over in silence, as would happen if one clung too exclusively to the juridical aspects.[80] One of the fundamental conflicts of the council became clear, as other speakers stressed the juridical structure of the Church.[81] What became apparent, during this first session of the council, was that the most important section of the draft on the Church would be the one on structure. Further, the issues of episcopal collegiality and the sacramentality of the episcopate would be hotly debated and disputed.[82]

Hopes for a change in the draft in light of the perspectives opened by the debate were not disappointed.[83] The doctrinal commission produced a second draft of the Constitution (1963), which was introduced by Cardinal Otta-viani on the first working day of the second session (September 30, 1963). This second draft contained four chapters, with the following headings: I. The Mystery of the Church; II. The Hierarchy; III. The People of God and the Laity; and IV. The Vocation of all to holiness; Religious.[84] The draft was accepted by a majority (2,231 votes in favor) on the proposition that discus-sion should proceed on each chapter.[85] The titles of the four chapters and the general discussion both indicated that new perspectives had been taken into account in this draft. Thus, for instance, the nature of the Church was described in the draft in communal and sacramental terms.[86]

Before the vote was taken it was suggested that chapter 3 should be divided into two chapters, one on the people of God, which would be inserted between chapters 1 and 2, and the other on the laity. O'Neil describes this suggestion as the principal move that counteracted an excessively juridical approach.[87]

The discussion on chapter 2 was by far the most acrimonious.[88] The chapter was divided into the following sections: Introduction, with allusion to the defi-nition of Vatican I on the primacy; The institution of the Twelve; The bishops as the successors of the Apostles; The sacramental nature of episcopacy; Priests and deacons; The college of bishops in relation to its head; The office of the bishops, and, in particular, their duty of teaching, sanctifying, and governing.[89] Of all the matters treated in the discussion, one of the most controversial was the question of the college of bishops, since it was thought that the authority of the college of bishops might endanger the primacy of the pope.[90]

A minority of bishops found the notion of collegiality problematic, since in their mind collegiality was not in accord with the teaching of Vatican I on papal primacy.[91] This minority feared that the sacramentality and the col-legiality of the episcopate would reduce papal primacy, defined at Vatican I, to a mere title. In this case, the pope would become no more than a *primus inter pares*, answerable to and dependent on the episcopal college of which he was a member.[92]

In order to learn the mind of the assembly on the concept of episcopal collegiality, the moderators posed the following questions:

> The Fathers are asked to say whether they wish the draft to be drawn up in such a way that it declares: 1) that episcopal consecration forms the highest degree of the sacraments of orders; 2) that every bishop legitimately conse-crated, in union with the bishops and the pope, who is the head of and prin-ciple of their unity, is a member of the whole body of bishops; 3) that the body (*corpus*) or college of bishops succeeds to the college of the apostles in the charge of preaching the Gospel, in sanctifying and in governing, and that this body, in union with its head, the pope of Rome, and never without this

head (whose primacy over all pastors and faithful remains whole and intact) possesses full and supreme authority in the universal Church; 4) that this authority belongs to the college of bishops itself in union with its head by divine law (*jure divino*).[93]

The answers to these questions would let the Theological Commission know the assembly's opinions on collegiality. The task of the commission was to examine the bishops' answers and put the amended text to their approval. On October 30, 1963, these propositions were put to a vote and accepted by the majority of the bishops.[94]

All four points on episcopal collegiality appear in the final text of the Constitution. Also, the footnotes appended to questions 3 and 4 are found again word for word in the explanatory note added to the final text of *Lumen Gentium*, which emphasizes the essential role of the pope within the college.[95]

The third draft of the Constitution was completed in March 1964. In this draft the suggested division of chapter 3 was adopted, resulting in the following structure of chapters: I. The Mystery of the Church; II. The People of God; III The hierarchical constitution of the Church, especially the episcopate; IV. The laity; V. The vocation of all to holiness in the Church; Religious; VI. The consummation of holiness in the glory of the saints; and VII. The Blessed Virgin Mary, Mother of God, in the Mystery of Christ and the Church.[96] Placing the chapter on the people of God after the mystery of the Church was a clear indication that Vatican II wanted to move from a juridical-pyramidal approach to the Church to a biblical-patristic one. The phrase "people of God" signifies the patristic notion of the Church as *communion*. It does not consider the Church in terms of democracy and therefore in a manner incompatible with hierarchy.[97]

Finally, a fourth draft was produced, taking into account the observations made by the bishops on the third draft.[98]

On November 21, 1964, the final vote was taken, with 2,151 in favor and only five opposed, and the document was promulgated. The Constitution now consisted of the following eight chapters: I: The Mystery of the Church; II: On The People of God; III: On the hierarchical Structure of the Church and in particular on the Episcopate; IV: The Laity; V: The Universal Call to Holiness in the Church; VI: Religious; VII: The Eschatological nature of the Pilgrim Church and its Union with the Church in Heaven; and VIII: The Blessed Virgin Mary, Mother of God, in the Mystery of Christ and the Church. A note had meanwhile been appended to the text.[99] The *Nota Explicativa Praevia* (Preliminary Note of Explanation) was considered to be "the intervention of the Pope in his efforts to ease the last scruples of the hesitant" and "was intended to meet the persistent difficulties of the minority."[100]

Vatican II's Teaching on Episcopal Collegiality
THE SUCCESSION FROM APOSTLES TO BISHOPS

After stating that the synod is "following in the steps of Vatican I," the Constitution teaches that "Jesus Christ the eternal pastor, set up the holy Church by entrusting the apostles with their mission as he himself had been sent by the Father (cf. Jn. 20:21). He willed that their successors, the bishops, namely, should be the shepherds in his Church until the end of the world" (*LG* 18). The council affirms and "proposes anew" "to be firmly believed by all the faithful," as the text itself states, the teaching of Vatican I on papal primacy and infallibility (*LG*18).

Thus Vatican II supplements teaching on papal primacy with teaching on the office of the bishop. The primacy and the episcopate are traced back to Christ and are of divine origin. Vatican II reaffirms the teaching of Vatican I on the papal primacy, and teaches that Christ endowed Peter and his successor, the Bishop of Rome, with authority *de jure divino* over the universal Church. This teaching points to the line Christ-Peter-Bishops of Rome, in a simple continuity of succession of authority over the universal Church. Here it seems that the Constitution operates with a notion of apostolic succession in terms of linear history. What lies behind this notion of apostolic succession is the idea of transmission of authority and certain powers.[101] We will see that *LG* 19–20 contains the same notion of apostolic succession.

The Constitution teaches that the office of the apostles continues in the order of bishops, which again is a succession understood in terms of linear history: God sends Christ (cf. *LG* 18: where it is stated that Christ entrusted the apostles with their mission as he himself had been sent by the Father), and Christ sends the apostles to preach the Gospel and to designate further ministries. Christ sent the apostles "to the children of Israel and then to all the peoples (cf. Rom. 1:16), so that, sharing in his power, they might make all peoples his disciples and sanctify and govern them (Mt. 28:16–20; Mk. 16:15; Lk. 24:45–48; Jn. 20:21–23) and thus spread the Church and, administering it under the guidance of the Lord, shepherd it all days until the end of the world (cf. Mt. 28:20). They were fully confirmed in this mission on the day of Pentecost (cf. Acts 2:1–26)" (*LG* 19). The Constitution then goes on to say: "That divine mission, which was committed by Christ to the apostles, is destined to last until the end of the world (cf. Mt. 28:20), since the Gospel, which they were charged to hand on, is, for the Church, the principle of all its life for all time. For that very reason the apostles were careful to appoint successors in this hierarchically constituted society"

(*LG* 20). The Constitution assumes that the apostles were sent out by Jesus Christ not as individuals, but as a college (*LG* 19).[102]

Here we find the image of the apostles as persons entrusted with a mission. They are sent by Christ and are dispersed in the world with a message and with authority to preach the Gospel and administer the Church. The Constitution also evokes the classical text of St. Clement, which supports a linear, historical conception of apostolic continuity: "They accordingly designated such men and then made the ruling that likewise on their death other proven men should take over their ministry" (*LG* 20).[103] Thus, the Constitution considers the apostles as missionaries sent by Christ to preach the Gospel, to spread the Church, and to establish ministries.[104]

As Zizioulas explains, in the "historical" approach to apostolic continuity, "the idea of mission and that of historical process go together and lead to a scheme of continuity in a linear movement: God sends Christ—Christ sends the apostles—the apostles transmit the message of Christ by establishing Churches and ministers."[105] Thus for Zizioulas the characteristics of the historical approach are historicity, dispersion, and mission, and a fourth one is the idea of transmission of authority through the notion of *vicariousness* or *representation*. This transmission of authority is organically linked with the Jewish idea of *shaliah*.[106] Zizioulas explains that the apostles are generally understood in this approach as *individuals dispersed* all over the world possessing a message and an authority.[107] He cites 1 Clement as an example of the historical approach to apostolic succession, and draws upon the analysis of *shaliah* by H. Rengstorff and G. Dix that shows that it contains the notion of the "plenipotential," of someone invested with authority to represent another fully in all matters. Zizioulas then finds this idea of *shaliah* in the New Testament sayings of Christ: "As my Father has sent me so do I send you (Jn. 20:21) and he that hears you hears me and he who rejects you rejects me, while he that rejects—or disobeys—me disobeys the one who has sent me (Lk. 10:16)."[108]

LG 20 elaborates this idea of *shaliah* when it says that "the bishops have by divine institution taken the place of the apostles as pastors of the Church, in such wise that whoever listens to them is listening to Christ and whoever despises them despises Christ and him who sent Christ (cf. Lk. 10:16)."

In a purely historical model of continuity, apostolic succession tends to be understood as the transmission of authority from one individual to another; in this case the bishop has received the apostolic authority as an individual, making him *alter Apostolus*. Christ's sending out of the eleven vested them with authority *de jure divino*. By analogy, the bishops, as the successors of the apostles, are the bearers of this divine authority. Thus, the idea of *shaliah* follows a merely linear and historical line and leads to an understanding of the ministry of the bishop as that of an individual possessing the fullness of apostolic authority.

Zizioulas has critiqued this historical approach to apostolic continuity for conceiving of the bishop as being singled out from the Church as an individual possessing in himself the plenitude of apostolicity, which he then transmits to others through ordination.[109] It should be noted, however, that Vatican II did not see the apostles and their successors as individuals, but as a college sent by Christ.

What follows directly from the above conception of apostolic succession is an institutional and juridical view of the Church. In *LG* 20 the linear historical understanding of apostolic succession is accompanied by a juridical view of the Church as a "hierarchically constituted society."[110] Moreover, in the historical approach to apostolic succession, the prime emphasis is Christological.[111] We have seen that the encyclical letter *Satis Cognitum*, like Vatican I, pointed to the line Christ–Peter–Bishop of Rome in a historical continuity of succession of a supreme divine authority and jurisdiction over the Church.[112] More widely, we have now seen from the above analysis that Vatican II understands apostolic succession as a succession in which divine authority is transmitted from Christ through the apostles to the bishops. As indicated above, Vatican II also affirms the teaching of Vatican I concerning the divine authority that is also given to the pope. Overall, the apostolicity of the Church thus seems limited to the papal and episcopal offices. We have noted, however, that while Zizioulas interprets such a historical approach as individualistic, Vatican II shows a desire to see the apostles and then the bishops as a college.

THE DEFINITION OF EPISCOPAL COLLEGIALITY

The historical approach to apostolic continuity leads directly to a conception of episcopal collegiality as existing independently of the local churches. Zizioulas asserts that the linear historical view of apostolic continuity and succession leads to "an understanding of the apostolic college as something standing outside and above the communities" and to "a succession of individuals or of a 'college' of individuals transmitting grace and authority from one another independently of the ecclesial community."[113] By the phrase "college of individuals," Zizioulas means that bishops, even as a college, act individually, that is, independently of their local churches.

Zizioulas maintains that there is also another approach, and he works toward a synthesis between the "historical" approach and the "eschatological" approach, as he calls them. For him both aspects are essential to a full understanding of apostolic succession.[114]

Zizioulas has shown that a Christ-centered image of episcopacy, with the bishop surrounded by the college of presbyters, such as Ignatius and the *Didascalia Apostolorum* describe, has a direct iconic relationship to the apostles, who surround Christ in his eschatological function. In this case, the apostles are gathered as an indivisible college around Christ.[115] As Zizioulas explains:

> Their function is to sit "on the twelve thrones judging the twelve tribes of Israel" (Mt. 19:28) and this they can do only in the context of the *gathered* people of God and under the headship of Christ. Succession in this case has a Christological dimension and requires the community of the Church in order to function. It is a succession of communities and not of individuals. If the bishop is crucial in this kind of succession, it is because he is a head of the community imaging the eschatological gathering of all around Christ and not because he has received apostolic authority as an individual.[116]

Thus, this model of apostolic succession, which is both eschatological and liturgical in nature, passes through the community[117] and is not understood as a transmission of authority through individuals. This approach to apostolic succession also has a concrete consequence for the notion of the episcopal college, since the solely historical approach limits collegiality to the episcopacy, without including the community.[118]

Zizioulas agrees with Congar in rejecting a limited understanding of episcopal collegiality:

> There is, therefore, no apostolic succession which could be limited to the episcopal college as such or to some form of apostolic collegiality. The late Cardinal Yves Congar rightly rejected such a view of episcopal collegiality and asked for its revision. Every bishop participates in the episcopal college *via his community*, not directly. Apostolic succession is a succession of apostolic communities via their heads, i.e. the bishops.[119]

It is important to note in this context that *LG* 22, which contains the teaching of Vatican II on episcopal collegiality, follows *LG* 21, which adopts such a Christ-centered image of bishops, as well as the liturgical designation of the bishop as *High Priest,* which could be taken as a starting point for a synthesis between the eschatological and historical approaches. Such a synthesis would imply for Zizioulas an understanding of episcopal collegiality within the context of the communion of local churches. Vatican II in its Constitution on the Sacred Liturgy, *Sacrosanctum Concilium* (*SC*), n. 41, adopts this liturgical and eucharistic image of the bishop as High Priest, which implies that he is an icon of Christ, as McPartlan notes, surrounded by his college of presbyters in the midst of his faithful.[120]

We have seen, on the other hand, that the historical approach to apostolic succession implies a notion of collegiality that places the bishops above their communities. *LG* 19–20 moves along the line of a historical approach to apostolic continuity and teaches that the apostles are sent by Christ as a college transmitting authority to preach the Gospel, and to administer and shepherd the Church. By analogy the bishops are understood as a college acting independently of their churches. Accordingly, *LG* 22 defines a limited notion of episcopal collegiality: "The order of bishops is the successor to the college of the apostles in their role as teachers and pastors, and in it the apostolic college is perpetuated. Together with their head, the Supreme pontiff and never apart from him, they have supreme and full authority over the universal Church." Moreover, this passage also contains a conception of episcopacy that moves along the line of universalistic ecclesiology. Michael Buckley notes in this regard:

> *Lumen Gentium* no. 22, did not include in its description of the Episcopal college the local Churches of which the bishops were shepherds and representatives. If one fails to place this section within the context of *Lumen Gentium*, no. 23, one would have an understanding of the college of the bishops without the simultaneous and explicit recognition of the communion of churches, indeed, without mention of the local churches at all. The perspective would remain that of a universalistic ecclesiology, and the college of the bishops would be read as if it were primarily a governing board of the whole Church.[121]

Pottmeyer's approach is similar to Buckley's. Pottmeyer indicates that episcopal collegiality derives from the structure of the Church as a communion of local churches.[122] He states:

> Episcopal collegiality, however, is not only in its origin grounded in the college of the apostles, but it is also an expression of the structural character of the universal Church as communion of particular Churches. "It is in these [particular Churches] and formed out of them that the one and unique Catholic Church exists. And for that reason precisely each bishop represents his own Church, whereas all, together with the pope, represent the whole Church in a bond of peace, love and unity" (*LG* 23). Also the relationship between

the particular churches and the whole Church and the connection among the particular churches to each other still require a convincing realization and formation. Not only the pope and the bishops are bearers of *communion*, but the rest of the members of the Church are as well.[123]

Collegiality is also expressed in the mutual relations among the particular churches and their bishops and in the ancient forms of communion among the bishops and with the pope; the holding of regional and ecumenical councils; the emergence of the patriarchates, which are regional structures of communion; and the establishment of the episcopal conferences.[124]

Such an ecclesiology of communion in the form of a communion of local churches flows from a eucharistic ecclesiology. *LG* 26 indicates strongly that the entire Church is formed from local eucharistic assemblies united to their pastors:

> This Church of Christ is really present in all legitimately organized local groups of the faithful, which, in so far as they are united to their pastors, are also quite appropriately called Churches in the New Testament. For these are in fact, in their own localities, the new people called by God, in the power of the Holy Spirit and as a result of full conviction (cf. 1 Thess. 1:5). In them the faithful are gathered together through the preaching of the Gospel of Christ, and the mystery of the Lord's Supper is celebrated "so that, by means of the flesh and blood of the Lord the whole brotherhood of the Body may be welded together." In each altar community, under the sacred ministry of the bishop, a manifest symbol is to be seen of that charity and "unity of the mystical body, without which there can be no salvation." In these communities, though they may be often small and poor or existing in diaspora, Christ is present through whose power and influence the One, Holy, Catholic and Apostolic Church is constituted.

From this it follows that an episcopally structured local Church is not only a part of the universal Church, but also that each local Church is the realization of the universal Church; in other words, the universal Church is constituted by the local churches and is fully present in them. This is an affirmation of the catholicity of the local Church,[125] the latter no longer being understood within the perspective of the universalistic ecclesiology dominant in the West since the Middle Ages, as a part of a universal juridical pyramid, with the pope at its head.

We have seen that Congar, by showing the historical process that led the West to a universalistic ecclesiology, had a prophetic voice, calling the future council to make a historical transition from a universalistic ecclesiology to one of communion. Vatican II made this transition and rediscovered the ancient ecclesiology of communion of local churches. As González de Cardedal puts it: "The rediscovery of the local church is not an isolated discovery. . . . It is the final fruit of the rediscovery of the Church which the First Vatican Council had narrowed down."[126]

Although Pottmeyer and Buckley insist that Vatican II's notion of the episcopal college should be understood as an expression of the nature of the Church as a communion of local churches, *LG* 22 conceives of episcopal collegiality within the context of universalistic ecclesiology, as an administering board with a jurisdiction over the whole Church, in which the communion of local churches is not taken into account. This means that a tension exists regarding the precise meaning of collegiality in *Lumen Gentium*, according to whether it is interpreted in the framework of a universalistic ecclesiology or an ecclesiology of communion.[127]

It should be noted here that Vatican II did not develop systematically an ecclesiology of communion and a theology of the local Church.[128] Legrand asserts that the ecclesiology of communion was not the object of a systematic reflection, as was the case with episcopal collegiality.[129] Also, even though the Constitution on the Church went on to affirm the full catholicity of the local Church by saying that the universal Church is realized in the local Church, the term "universal Church" itself, which seems normally to refer to the present worldwide Church under the leadership of the pope, can also refer to the eschatological fullness of the Church. There is therefore an ambiguity concerning the term "universal Church" in the Constitution on the Church. As McPartlan notes, "An element of ambiguity is therefore attached to the decisive principle stated in *LG* 23, namely that local Churches around their bishops are 'constituted after the model of the universal Church.'"[130] Although the Constitution on the Church does once refer to "the universal Church" in the eschatological sense, what effectively predominates is the worldwide sense of the term (cf. *LG* 23, 25).[131] But if we accept the axiom that the "universal Church" is manifested and edified in the local Eucharist, there cannot be a ministry above the local eucharistic president, i.e., the ministry of the bishop.[132]

However, by reducing the term "universal Church" to the worldwide Church headed by the pope, the Constitution does not guarantee the fullness and the catholicity of each local church, since it keeps simultaneously the idea that the pope has a jurisdiction over and pastoral care for the whole Church.[133] This would imply that each church around its bishop is a microcosm of the worldwide Church led by the bishop of Rome.

THE RELATION BETWEEN THE HEAD AND THE MEMBERS
OF THE COLLEGE

The Preliminary Explanatory Note, *Nota Explicativa Praevia*, attached to
LG, rules out the strictly juridical understanding of the college of bishops
as a college of equals and emphasizes that the college is "a permanent body
whose form and authority is to be ascertained from revelation" (*Nota* 1).

Pottmeyer comments that in Roman canon law, the term "college" is
used in a double sense: in the strictly juridical sense a college is a group of
equals; in a wider sense a college is a permanent group.[134] In the first sense
the chairperson is the representative of the group, who carries out its collective power. In Roman Catholic understanding and tradition this concept
does not apply appropriately to the group of the apostles. St. Peter received
a special mission: the ministry of unity in the group of the apostles and in
the universal Church. Peter's successors have the same mission. Thus, his
successor is not an equal but the head of the college of the successors of the
apostles and the primate of the Church universal. His position as *protos* does
not go back just to the group of the apostles but to Jesus himself. Pottmeyer
immediately adds that the principle of the unity of "the one and the many"
is founded not only in a functional necessity or appropriateness but in the
will of God. Furthermore, Pottmeyer considers that the pope, as head of
the college of bishops, is not above the college but inside it as its head. The
pope is a special member of the college, and his membership is a constitutive
qualification of his primacy. The reason for his inequality within the college is his special mission as Peter's successor.[135] The college is a permanent
group but not a group of equals, since it has a *protos* who has the authority
of primate.[136] The Explanatory Note would therefore exclude the notion
of a college that does not admit a hierarchical structure and order within
itself, i.e., with the primate as preeminent within the college—Peter and
his successor the bishop of Rome—exercising his special ministry of unity.

We saw in chapter 2 Zizioulas's assertion that from a canonical point of
view (cf. Thirty-Fourth Apostolic Canon) the primate exercises a certain
power and authority. For Zizioulas, the Thirty-Fourth Apostolic Canon
teaches a mutual interdependence between the primate and the bishops, and
the authority of the primate is therefore controlled and moderated by the
rest of the bishops.[137] This interdependence is a real communion after the
model of the life of the Holy Trinity.[138]

Pottmeyer admits, however, that the pope can take action—given his special mission and if necessary for the well-being and unity of the college and
the Church—without the participation of the other members of the college.

He points out that there is not perfect reciprocity between the primate and the other members of the episcopal college in the sense of the Thirty-Fourth Apostolic Canon. In quoting the Explanatory Note, note 4, which says: "The Pope, as supreme pastor of the Church, may exercise his power at any time, as he sees fit . . . ," he comments that the pope can act on his own in promulgating laws or other regulations for the universal Church without asking the bishops. For Pottmeyer, this authorization to act alone is not consistent with the ecclesiology of communion. He states that in his opinion and in the opinion of many Roman Catholics, collegiality should be taken more seriously inside the Roman Catholic Church.[139]

The Constitution emphasizes the pope's independence and freedom of action.[140] As Philips has noted in his history of the Constitution, a perusal of the 1964 draft, which was finally adopted by the council, "shows that it is full of additions designed to block at the start every attack on the primacy of the Pope."[141] Thus, the Constitution expressly states that the Roman pontiff, the successor of Peter, and the head of the college, has a power over the whole Church:

> The college or body of bishops has for all that no authority unless united with the Roman Pontiff, Peter's successor, as its head, whose primatial authority, let it be added, over all, whether pastors or faithful remains in its integrity. For the Roman Pontiff, by reason of his office as Vicar of Christ, namely, and as a pastor of the entire Church has full, supreme and universal power over the whole Church, a power which he can always exercise unhindered (*LG* 22).

Also, the Explanatory Note emphasizes the pope's independence and freedom of action when it states that the head of the college preserves his function as pastor of the universal Church as vicar of Christ:

> There is no such thing as the college without its head: it is *"The subject of supreme and entire power* over the whole Church." This much must be acknowledged lest the fullness of the Pope's power be jeopardised. The idea of college necessarily and at all times involves a head and *in the college the head preserves intact his function as Vicar of Christ and pastor of the universal Church.* . . . The Roman Pontiff undertakes the regulation, encouragement, and approval of the exercise of collegiality as he sees fit" (*Nota* 3).

> Likewise, "The Pope, as supreme pastor of the Church, may exercise his power at any time, as he sees fit, by reason of the demands of his office" (*Nota* 4).

Thus the Constitution on the Church and the Explanatory Note affirm the primatial authority of the head of the college over the whole Church.[142]

It is significant, however, from the point of view of the ecclesiology of communion, that the Explanatory Note, while stressing the pope's independence from the college, understands the pope as being included in the college. This it does through its interpretation of the word "*consentiente*" (i.e., consenting).[143] Whereas Nota 4 of the Explanatory Note specifically says that there cannot be any collegial act without the consent of the pope as the head of the college, it explains the meaning of the consent as follows: "The phrase *with the consent of the head* is used in order to exclude the impression of dependence on something *external*: but the word 'consent' entails *communion* between head and members." This particular passage of the Explanatory Note thus seems to demonstrate an interdependence between the head and the other members of the college in the sense of the Thirty-Fourth Apostolic Canon in terms of an ecclesiology of communion. As Pottmeyer explains, the collegial act depends also on the agreement of the majority of the other members of the college.[144]

As the Note indicates it is therefore in this sense that we should understand the following passage from *LG* 22: "The order of bishops is the successor to the college of the apostles in their role as teachers and pastors and in it the apostolic college is perpetuated. Together with their head, the Supreme Pontiff, and never apart from him, they have supreme and full authority over the universal Church. But this power can not be exercised without the agreement of the Roman Pontiff." Thus, a collegial act includes the agreement of the pope and that of the bishops, at least a majority of them, as Pottmeyer explains.[145]

On the other hand, Pottmeyer indicates the reasons for the one-sided emphasis on the pope's freedom of action and independence:

> The first reason was the maximalist interpretation of Vatican I and especially of the statement in the canon directed against Marret. The second reason was the fear that the pope would no longer be free to govern the church if the bishops had a right to share in the government. Since the leading members of the minority of Vatican II were also the members of the Roman Curia, the pragmatic of this argument is obvious. These men were afraid of losing their own shared governance with the pope.[146]

He then concludes:

> The conception of the primacy of jurisdiction as sovereignty was also present and active in the texts of Vatican II with their one-sided emphasis on the

pope's freedom of action. This concept could exist alongside the teaching on the college of bishops, because the exercise of collegial jurisdiction depends entirely on the pope. At the very least, it is striking that nothing is said with comparable clarity about the obligation of the pope to involve the bishops in decisions affecting the universal church.[147]

It follows that Vatican II's universalistic ecclesiology, which develops along the lines of Vatican I and affirms the papal primacy of jurisdiction over the whole Church, exists in tandem with the ancient ecclesiology of communion that Vatican II also adopted, as we have seen.

Nevertheless, as a result of the renewal of liturgical and patristic studies during the first decades of the twentieth century, the Constitution on the Church affirms the sacramental foundation of episcopal ministry.[148] Thus, *LG* 21 affirms the sacramentally based offices (*munera*) of the bishop: "Now, episcopal consecration confers, together with the office of sanctifying, the duty also of teaching and ruling." In rooting the three offices in the sacrament of episcopal ordination, *LG* 21 lessens the distinction between the power of order and the power of jurisdiction.[149] The pastoral ministry of the episcopate was no longer separated from the sacrament of episcopal consecration, but intimately linked to it.[150] Moreover, the possessor is incorporated into the college of bishops (*LG* 22) and therefore, as Pottmeyer points out, "the college of bishops likewise has the office of teaching and ruling the universal Church in communion with the pope as head—due to the episcopal consecration of its members, and thus immediately from Christ."[151] Also, *LG* 21 adds that, of their very nature, the three offices "can be exercised only in hierarchical communion with the head and members of the college." In other words, the exercise of the three offices is understood within the context of the college, comprised of head and members. As Henn puts it, hierarchical communion "situates the exercise of the sacramentally based offices within the context of a college comprised of head and members."[152] As *LG* 22 also states: "One is constituted a member of the episcopal body in virtue of the sacramental consecration and by the hierarchical communion with the head and members of the college."

Henn considers the expression "canonical mission" used in *LG* 24, which preserves the importance and need for granting jurisdiction within Vatican II's vision of episcopal ministry, to be a further specification of the hierarchical communion mentioned in *LG* 21.[153] Henn urges us not to overlook the fact that "the canonical mission of the bishops . . . can be made by legitimate customs that have not been revoked by the supreme and universal authority of the Church, or by laws made or acknowledged by the same authority" (*LG* 24). For Henn, this implies that the granting of jurisdiction can be understood in a variety of ways, including those of the ancient traditions of the first millennium, by which the Roman bishops acknowledged the mission of the bishops of the Eastern patriarchates. Thus, the forms of granting jurisdiction that were developed in the West need not be the only ways in which hierarchical communion is maintained.[154]

Henn notes that, "To the extent that the order-jurisdiction distinction concerned the ability to 'exercise' episcopal ministry, it would appear that the expression 'hierarchical communion' has taken its place."[155] Explanatory Note 2 shows clearly that the phrase "hierarchical communion" expresses the fact that "a *canonical* or *juridical determination* through hierarchical authority is required for such power ordered to action."[156] Here the Explanatory Note makes a distinction between the sacred functions (*munera*)—i.e., teaching, sanctifying, and governing—implied in sacramental ordination and powers (*potestates*), which means the discharge of the functions, given through hierarchical authority. In fact, what we are dealing with here is the relationship between sacramental ordination and the canonical/papal determination and regulation of the exercise of the sacramentally conferred bishop's offices or *munera* as leader, teacher, and priest of a local Church.[157] Thus a directive is given at the end of Explanatory Note 2, which states that the documents of recent popes to the effect that bishops receive their jurisdiction from the pope are to be interpreted as referring to this necessary determination of powers. This directive is indeed a softening of the idea of the pope granting jurisdiction. Vatican II progressed in comparison with the preconciliar Roman Catholic viewpoint, which undervalued the sacramental basis of the episcopacy and overrated the jurisdictional determination by the pope. Moreover, Henn insists that the shift from "jurisdiction" to "hierarchical communion" should not be underestimated. He adds:

> While some have noted that the latter phrase [i.e., hierarchical communion] seems to juxtapose two differing ecclesiological emphases, nevertheless the very word "communion" could open up a more adequate and reciprocal understanding of the conditionedness of the exercise of episcopal ministry in a way that is not possible within the language of jurisdiction and which, moreover, finds roots in the communion ecclesiology of the church from the first millennium.[158]

CHAPTER 4

Orthodox Reactions to Vatican II

This final chapter is divided into three sections, the first of which is divided into two parts. In the first of these sections, we will examine Karmiris's general appreciation of Vatican II's Constitution on the Church, while in the second part the main lines of Karmiris's argumentation against Vatican II's renewed understanding of primacy within the context of its teaching on episcopal collegiality will be analyzed. In arguing against this teaching, Karmiris moves along the same lines that he did with regard to Vatican I. As we saw in chapter 2, this approach was in turn criticized by a second group of Orthodox theologians, represented by Zizioulas and certain Russian theologians. The views of a number of other Greek Orthodox theologians will be indicated in the presentation of Karmiris's position, and a further critique will be provided.

Section 2 briefly presents some Greek Orthodox reactions to Vatican II's understanding of *missio canonica* and of the distinction between *potestas ordinis* and *potestas jurisdictionis*. It will be seen that certain Greek Orthodox theologians believe that for Vatican II the episcopal power that is given through ordination is still dependent on papal power.

Section 3 has three parts. The first is devoted to an examination of Zizioulas's critical assessment of the notion of episcopal collegiality. As we will see, in criticizing the Roman Catholic theory of episcopal collegiality, Zizioulas makes no direct criticism of Vatican II's view on the issue. That said, it will become clear that Zizioulas's general critical assessment of the Roman Catholic concept of episcopal collegiality can also be applied to Vatican II.

The second part of section 3 is concerned with Zizioulas's understanding of the issue of primacy. We will see that he justifies the existence of primacy in the Church on the basis of dogmatic-theological principles that shape the life of the Church and lead directly to the institution of primacy. In other words, Zizioulas bases primacy upon certain theological-ecclesiological principles, such as "the one and the many," which make the existence of primacy in the Church ecclesiologically necessary, i.e., *jure divino*, and which stem from the Church's participation in trinitarian life. As we saw in chapter 2, the first group of Greek Orthodox theologians of the nineteenth and twentieth centuries do not take this view.

Finally, in the third part of section 3, the views of Nicholas Afanassieff, Alexander Schmemann, and John Meyendorff on the issue are reviewed. There are two reasons for bringing these three Russian theologians into the discussion. First, Zizioulas is critical of Afanassieff's eucharistic ecclesiology, in particular because it does not heed the necessary unity between the local churches. By examining his critique of Afanassieff's ecclesiology, we will underscore Zizioulas's view on primacy, which, as we will see, is for Zizioulas a necessary institution for expressing the unity of the churches on the universal level. Secondly, while Zizioulas seems to share the views of the other two Russian theologians with regard to the ecclesiological justification and need for primacy, we will see that he actually differs from them in his justification. Whereas Schmemann and Meyendorff argue from a rather ecclesiological and canonical point of view, Zizioulas justifies the existence of primacy on strictly dogmatic-theological principles, namely from a triadological point of view.

We should note at this point that the Orthodox were invited to attend Vatican II not as members of the council but as observers.[1] As Ware rightly explains, "At the present juncture, for obvious reasons the Orthodox are unable to accept an invitation to an ecumenical council issued by the pope, since they feel that any such acceptance would involve implicitly their acquiescence in the doctrine of papal primacy as defined in 1870."[2]

Karmiris's Critique of Vatican II's Definition of Papal Primacy and Episcopal Collegiality

KARMIRIS'S GENERAL APPRECIATION OF VATICAN II'S CONSTITUTION ON THE CHURCH

In his treatise "The Dogmatic Constitution on the Church of the Second Vatican Council," Karmiris posits that the Constitution is one of the most significant results of Vatican II and that it has a central place in the overall work of the council.[3] For Karmiris the teaching of the Constitution, formulated in the ecumenical spirit that inspired Vatican II, is generally an improvement to be welcomed by the Orthodox. However, he considers that the Constitution is a continuation, completion, and in part a correction of the ecclesiological teaching of Vatican I and that it thus differs on various points from Orthodox ecclesiology. Karmiris stresses that at Vatican II every endeavor was made to safeguard papal primacy and its absolutism, along with ecclesiastical monarchy, and to prevent the limitation of this by the teaching on episcopal collegiality. The power of the bishops, therefore, remains after the Council as it was before: a limited one, coming from the sole and unlimited power of the pope.[4] It is for this reason, Karmiris says, that many additions were made to the text of the Constitution and particularly to the third chapter, describing papal power as full, supreme, and sole, to which is subjected all other legal power of the bishops and their synods, including even the ecumenical councils.[5] For Karmiris, this falsifies the meaning of the synodical institution, abolishing the system from which stemmed the seven ecumenical councils of the ancient Church as well as the equality of all bishops, upon which the synodical institution, handed down from ancient times, is based.[6] Although Karmiris comments negatively on Vatican II's interpretation of the concept of episcopal collegiality, as an Orthodox he nevertheless is pleased with the council's promulgation of this collegiality, however restricted, seeing in it a hopeful sign for ecumenism.

Karmiris notes that the opening of the Constitution, "Christ is the light of humanity" (LG 1), rightly emphasizes the Christocentric character of ecclesiology, making the latter subordinate to Christology and inconceivable without and outside it.[7] For Karmiris, the Orthodox reader is in accord with this, as he too believes that Christ "is the light of the world, from whom we go forth, through whom we live, and toward whom our whole life is directed" (LG 2). Karmiris then adds that the Church is also the "fullness of Christ" and has Christ as her center and head. The Church participates in the life of Christ, and this must be reflected in her faith, preaching, worship, and polity.[8]

Moreover, for Karmiris, Orthodox readers would also agree with the heading of the first chapter of the Constitution, "The Mystery of the Church"; he affirms that the Church is a mystery linked with the mystery of the incarnation. Karmiris says that the Church is a mysterious and inexplicable unity of the divine and the human, of the incarnate Logos with the saved members of his body, and of the heavenly and invisible Church with the earthly and visible.[9] The Church is not only a visible institution, as presented in the one-sided emphasis of Bellarmine's earlier Roman Catholic theology, in opposition to the one-sided belief of the Protestants in the invisible Church.[10] For Karmiris, the Constitution on the Church now rightly teaches that the invisible and visible Church "are not to be thought of as two realities. On the contrary, they form one complex reality which comes together from a human and a divine element"(LG 8).[11]

On the other hand, Karmiris considers as unacceptable to the Orthodox the Latin ecclesiological view also found in *LG* 8, namely:[12]

> This is the sole Church of Christ which in the Creed we profess to be one, holy, catholic and apostolic, which our Saviour, after his resurrection, entrusted to Peter's pastoral care. . . . This Church, constituted and organised as a society in the present world, subsists in the Catholic Church, which is governed by the successor of Peter and by the bishops in communion with him. Nevertheless many elements of sanctification and of truth are found outside its visible confines. Since these are gifts belonging to the Church of Christ, they are forces impelling toward Catholic unity.

For Karmiris this identification of the confines of the true Church solely with those of the Roman Catholic Church governed by the successor of Peter and by bishops in communion with him is unacceptable to the Orthodox Catholic Church. It is not grounded in Scripture and in the ancient and pure sacred Tradition. It is not in accord with other, correct teachings of the same chapter (chapter 1) on the Church as a "mystery" and as the "body of Christ" governed by her head, according to the teaching of St. Paul and the Fathers of the Church. Finally, it excludes the preexisting and heavenly Church.[13] Nevertheless, Karmiris appears to express considerable agreement with the content of the first chapter and particularly with its mysteriological and Christological approach to ecclesiology.

Stylianos Harkianakis also expresses the satisfaction of the Orthodox with the description of the Church as a "mystery" and as a "sign." He says:

> Let us examine how the Church, according to Vatican Council II, is described. Firstly, the basic characteristic of the Church in the text on the Church and on Ecumenism as a "sign" placed by God in the midst of His people and as a "mystery" is totally in harmony with Orthodox ecclesiology as well as in the other points of these texts that describe the Church in images from the Old and New Testament. Also not a few Protestant theologians were satisfied by this characterisation of the Church.[14]

Karmiris claims, ironically, that the redactors of *LG* 8 did not forget their Roman origins and therefore were tempted, even when speaking of the Church as a mystery, to insert inopportunely the purely human new papal teachings and objectives, which were not in accord with the truth revealed in the Holy Scriptures and with the divine teaching witnessed in the ancient and pure Holy Tradition.[15] In citing this particular criticism by Karmiris,

Harkianakis considers that the two positions about primacy in *LG* 8, namely that Christ "after his resurrection, entrusted to Peter the pastoral care of the Church" and that "this Church, constituted and organised as a society in the present world, subsists in the Catholic Church, which is governed by the successor of Peter and by the bishops in communion with him" are in contrast with the spiritual atmosphere of this fundamental chapter.[16]

Karmiris also considers that the statement in *LG 8* that "many elements of sanctification and of truth are found outside [the Catholic Church's] visible confines" cannot be applied to the Orthodox Catholic Church. The reason for this is that the Orthodox Church believes that she possesses not only some elements of sanctification and truth, but the fullness of sanctifying and saving grace and of revealed truth. She has kept the faith, which "was once for all delivered to the saints" (Jude 3), and the policy of the ancient Church and Tradition unaltered; she is the true and the One Holy Catholic and Apostolic Church, etc.[17] Thus, for Karmiris, the Constitution on the Church sees in the Orthodox Church nothing but a collection of elements of the true Church. However, we should recall in this context that Cardinal Johannes Willebrands's nuanced assessment on this matter does not agree with that of Karmiris. In interpreting the expression "subsists" in *LG* 8, Willebrands claims that:

> It would nevertheless be a mistake to think that the expression aims to concentrate all ecclesiality solely in the Catholic Church and considers the *elementa* present elsewhere as detached and drifting fragments. The insistence of the text on the role of the Holy Spirit in non Catholic communities where, also in them, "he works through his sanctifying power, his gifts and his graces" [*LG* 15] prompting them to unity "in one flock under one shepherd" forbids denying to those communities *as such* all properly ecclesial reality. Moreover, what I have said about the traditional attitude toward the eastern Churches—though they too are detached "from communion under the succession of Peter"–shows that instinctively the Catholic Church has refused to see in the Orthodox communities nothing but a collection of elements of the Church. She has seen them as authentic Churches. Perhaps this case is regarded as an exception? It would surely be a significant one, which deserves full attention. Moreover, No. 15 of the constitution includes the traits proper to these Churches in a long list directed at *all* the "Churches and ecclesial communities" cut off from full communion with the bishop of Rome.[18]

Karmiris welcomes the representation of the Church promoted by the second chapter of the Constitution as the "People of God," which includes the hierarchy and the laity.[19] For Karmiris, in this chapter, the laity, which in the past was ignored by the hierarchical autocracy of the Roman Catholic Church, is emphasized, and the common priesthood of the laity and its right to participate in the Church's affairs are affirmed, while on the other hand the old Latin clericalism is tempered and the character of the clergy in terms of service is generally recognized.[20] This, for Karmiris, is without doubt an improvement for the Roman Catholic Church and, in a way, a point of meeting with the Orthodox Church, which has always recognized the laity's place in ecclesiastical organization and the rights of the laity, as members of the body of Christ, to participate in ecclesiastical services, which derive from their participation in the priestly, prophetic, and kingly office of Christ.[21]

On the other hand, Karmiris considers article 15 of chapter 2, directed "to the baptized who are honored by the name of Christian, but who do not however profess the Catholic faith in its entirety or have not preserved unity or communion under the successor of Peter," as groundless and unacceptable to the Orthodox. While the Orthodox Church does not preserve unity or communion with the Roman Catholic Church under the "successor of Peter" as understood by the latter, given that Holy Scripture and genuine Tradition are ignorant of the Roman view of Peter's successor, Karmiris affirms that the Orthodox Church keeps the faith transmitted by the apostles, maintaining the apostolic and synodical traditions, with apostolic succession and the polity of the Church entire and unchanged.[22] Karmiris then concludes that the Orthodox faithful, with their canonical bishops, who possess uninterruptedly the apostolic succession and, as was the case in the ancient Church, are not subject to the pope, form the one, holy, catholic, and apostolic Church. They reject the later Latin innovations and new teachings, such as those of the two Vatican councils.[23]

Karmiris refuses the notion of unity and communion with the pope because such a union and communion equals submission to the pope and is a recognition of the papal primacy of jurisdiction. The text of LG 15 does make a reference to the encyclical letter Satis Cognitum of Pope Leo XIII, which, as we have seen above, understands unity and communion with the pope in terms of submission to him.[24]

KARMIRIS'S CRITICISM OF VATICAN II'S TEACHING ON PAPAL PRIMACY

Karmiris saves his most vigorous criticism of the Constitution for the third chapter, which he views as the core and center of the whole Constitution. For Karmiris, this chapter addresses the hierarchical structure of the

Church and for the most part picks up where the proceedings of Vatican I left off, defining the position of the episcopal office in the Church, although for him not fully successfully and not clearly. Karmiris asserts that an Orthodox reader will find both a positive element, namely the collegiality of the bishops (although not to the extent that this term was understood and operative in the ancient Church), and a negative one, namely, a strengthened and completed double dogma on primacy and infallibility, even though this dogma was not discussed anew at the council.[25] Here, for Karmiris, Vatican II made no changes to the definitions of Vatican I.

Further, in his view, the Orthodox reader gains two impressions: first, that the authority and power of the bishops is under the supreme, full, and universal authority of the head of the episcopal college, and secondly, that while an attempt is made to harmonize these two powers, the danger of diarchy is not in fact avoided. Two authorities now exist in the Roman Catholic Church: that of the pope and that of the college of bishops, according to the following schemes, which are unknown in the New Testament or the ancient Tradition of the Church: (1) Christ–Peter–pope; and (2) Christ–the eleven apostles–the college of bishops.[26] In Karmiris's view this new teaching was characterized by the Roman Catholic side as a necessary completion of Vatican I's decision on primacy and infallibility, while from the Orthodox viewpoint, it is a new and untraditional invention of the twentieth century. In particular, Karmiris considers the idea of collegiality, with the pope as the head and member of the college, as a new idea.[27] He is one of several Greek Orthodox theologians who oppose the Roman Catholic concept of episcopal collegiality.[28]

As we have seen, Karmiris singles out the eleven as the college of the apostles, which is succeeded by the college of bishops. At this point it should be remembered that Vatican II's doctrine of collegiality essentially includes the pope in the college, which does not exist without him. The diarchy that Roman Catholic theology actually recognizes is now the following: (1) the pope as the head of the college, and (2) the pope as the head of the college together with the college of the bishops. Following Vatican II a debate continues within Catholic ecclesiology about who holds supreme authority in the Church, but the two alternatives are not the same as in conciliarism (i.e., the pope or the bishops); they are first the pope himself, and second, the pope together with the college of bishops. The two alternatives are therefore not fully distinguished (as they were in conciliarism) since both include the pope.[29]

For Karmiris, what follows from *LG* 22 and from the teaching of Vatican I and II on infallibility is that the source of the administrative and teaching authority of the bishops, and of the college, is the pope. As vicar of Christ and successor of Peter, the pope possesses the plenitude of authority over the Church, while episcopal authority springs from papal authority and is exercised in union with the pope and under the pope, with the exercise of such authority depending on the pope's consent (*et nonnisi consentiente capite*—and only with the consent of its head) (*Nota*, 4).[30]

Karmiris considers, therefore, that the requirement of "communion" and "unity" in the activity of the college and the pope binds only the episcopal college and not the pope, who, according to the Preliminary Explanatory Note, can exercise his supreme administrative authority outside of and independently of the college—"*seorsim*" (outside), "*ipse solus*" (he alone), and "*ad placitum*" (as he sees fit).[31] As evidence of this, Karmiris cites certain passages from the Explanatory Note: "There is no such thing as the college without its head . . . and in the college the head preserves intact his function as Vicar of Christ and pastor of the universal Church" (*Nota* 3); "in fact it is only occasionally that it engages in strictly collegiate activity and that only with the consent of the head. The pope, as supreme pastor of the Church, may exercise his power at any time, as he sees fit, by reason of the demands of the office" (*Nota* 4). Karmiris asserts that the pope, in exercising his absolute primacy of power, is not obliged to rely on the college or to be in communion and in union with the college or with his synod. On the other hand, the college cannot act except in communion and in union with the pope, even when the college is assembled in council, including an ecumenical council, as pointed out at Vatican II. For Karmiris, this implies a corruption of the ancient synodical institution and of the power of the episcopal college in the intervals between synods.[32] Karmiris agrees with Afanassieff's similar appraisal of Vatican II's idea of collegiality. Afanassieff asserts that between the councils the collegiality of the bishops finds itself in a state of "anabiosis," from which it cannot emerge save at the pope's desire. He doubts, therefore, that it is possible to speak of the supreme authority of the bishops, for according to the Explanatory Note the pope as the pastor of the Church can exercise his power at any time and as he sees fit.[33]

Based on all of the above, Karmiris believes it is clear that for the Roman Catholic Church, despite the enactment of episcopal collegiality, the absolute monarchy of the pope remains unaffected: he concentrates in himself all authority and power over the bishops, and over the faithful, and even over the ecumenical councils, which become simply advisory bodies to him, while the episcopal college and the bishops are deprived of their *jure divino* power, which is only activated by papal approval. Thus, for Karmiris, the papal institution emerged from Vatican II stronger than it did from Vatican I.[34]

Karmiris is quite right in criticizing the pope's independence from the college because, as noted earlier, both the Constitution and the Explanatory Note do emphasize the supracollegial position of the pope and his freedom of action.[35] There is, therefore, a lack of reciprocity, which allows the pope, the head of the college, to act without the consent of the other members of the college while the college cannot act without its head.

In line with Karmiris, Harkianakis also criticizes the lack of reciprocity in the Constitution on the Church between the episcopal college and its head as well as the pope's right to act independently and without the bishops. After praising Vatican II's teaching on episcopal collegiality and its emphasis on the importance of the local churches, Harkianakis says:

> The key phrase that is the guiding principle in these problems is expressed in the Constitution on the Church (ch. 3.22) as follows: For our Lord made Simon Peter alone the rock and keybearer of the Church (cf. Mt. 16:18–19), and appointed him shepherd of the whole flock (cf. Jn. 21:15ff). It is definite, however, that the power of binding and loosing, which was given to Peter (Mt. 16:19), was granted also to the college of apostles, joined with their head (Mt. 18:18; 28:16–20). The exact meaning of this double ecclesiological position becomes completely clear in all of the texts of the Council where there is a question of the collegial relation of Peter to the rest of the apostles and analogously of the pope to the college of the rest of the bishops. But correctly and with absolute scientific deduction the famous Catholic dogmatic professor, Father Joseph Ratzinger, explains the above phrase by saying that between the two parts he sees a relationship expressed precisely in this way as, "This college cannot function without its head (the pope), while the head can quite well function without the college."[36]

Harkianakis considers that the Constitution on the Church affirms such an explanation given by Ratzinger:

> We need not listen to any other explanation from other Catholic theologians since we have this analytically expressed again in the same Constitution on the Church in a passage that precedes the above citation, even though normally it should follow it as its logical explanation: "But the college of the body of bishops has no authority unless it is simultaneously conceived of in terms of its head, the Roman Pontiff, Peter's successor, and without any lessening of his power of primacy over all, pastors as well as the general faithful. For in

virtue of his office, that is, as Vicar of Christ and pastor of the whole Church, the Roman Pontiff has full, supreme and universal power over the Church and he can always exercise this power freely (cf. 3.22)."[37]

Harkianakis then asks,

In what way is there any progress in the idea of collegiality of bishops and the representation of local churches since theoretically the pope remains, even according to Vatican II, the absolute monarch of the Church? What meaning is there in the other new initiatives and freedom which Vatican II has guaranteed to the bishops if the dogmatic positions in an official text show such centralization? Of what worth are the praises and hymns of Vatican II exalting the ancient traditions and individual customs, the liturgical, theological, ethnic and, in general, the ecclesiastical structure of the individual local churches if the bishop of Rome guards categorically for himself his God-given (as is affirmed in the text) rights to act at any moment in history independently and without the bishops?[38]

Karmiris stresses that with Vatican II's decision on collegiality, the episcopal institution and the ancient institution of the ecumenical councils with supremacy over the bishops, including the bishop of Rome, are not restored to their fullness and authenticity. Instead, the supremacy of the pope is categorically emphasized, as is his "prerogative to convoke such councils, to preside them and to confirm them," because only thus a "truly collegiate act may result" (cf. *LG* 22). Karmiris asserts, therefore, that for *LG*, the ecumenical council is not above the pope, as was the case in the ancient Church and is still in the Orthodox Church. On the contrary, for Karmiris the pope is above the ecumenical council because he has the prerogative to convoke it, to direct it, and to confirm its decisions. These decisions are valid if the pope convokes the council, directs its decisions, and freely approves them.[39] Thus, for Karmiris, in the Constitution on the Church the ecumenical councils are under the absolute power of the Roman pontiff and have no validity without his approval and confirmation.

It would appear that, according to the definition of Vatican II, the supreme power of the college exercised in an ecumenical council is placed under the absolute power of the pope. As noted earlier, for Roman Catholic ecclesiology, the pope's acceptance of a council as ecumenical is clearly an indispensable, and indeed decisive, criterion. The Orthodox, on the other hand, have always been reluctant to isolate the pope from his brother bishops and from the whole body of the Church, and therefore, for them the pope cannot act in isolation as final arbiter of conciliar ecumenicity.[40] It is being presumed at this point that were the two Churches to reunite, the Orthodox Church would certainly agree that the bishop of Rome, with the agreement of all the bishops, would be the one to convoke an ecumenical council and preside over it.[41]

Karmiris asserts that in *LG* the power of the bishops, even when they are gathered at ecumenical councils, is limited, subject to, and dependent on the "full, supreme and universal power over the whole Church" of the "successor of Peter, Vicar of Christ and visible head of the Church, who is the foundation and the holder of the keys of the Church and the shepherd of his (i.e., Christ's) whole flock" (cf. *LG* 22). For Karmiris, this is unacceptable from an Orthodox point of view and can only be intended for pastoral and catechetical purposes with regard to Roman Catholics. It cannot be counted among the revealed "dogmas of God."[42] Karmiris concludes that Vatican II attempted in vain to reconcile the irreconcilable powers in the Church—namely the *jure divino* power of the bishops, gathered at ecumenical councils and existing in the ancient Church as well as in the present Orthodox Church, with the absolute power of the pope, which virtually encompasses episcopal and synodical power.[43]

Similarly, Harkianakis asserts:

> Since even according to Vatican II the pope stands above the rank of bishop and above the college of bishops . . . it follows that even this office and the sacramentally [sic] coming together of the Episcopal body in ecumenical councils is in the absolute power of the Roman Pontiff and such gatherings have no validity without at least tacit approval. Connected with this and quite explicitly the Constitution on the Church gives the following: "A council is never ecumenical unless it is confirmed or at least accepted as such by the successor of Peter. It is the prerogative of the Roman Pontiff to convoke these councils, to preside over them, and to confirm them. The same collegiate power can be exercised in union with the Pope by the bishops living in all parts of the world, provided that the head of the college calls them to collegiate action, or at least so approves or freely accepts the united action of the dispersed bishops that it is made a true collegiate act" (ch. 3.22).[44]

In asserting that the power of the episcopal college totally depends on papal power, Karmiris refers to the opinion of another Greek Orthodox theologian, Athanasius Delikostopoulos, who voices the suspicion that the Roman Catholic theory of collegiality, in stressing the body of the bishops as an entity, i.e., the *corpus episcoporum*, naturally leads to the need for a head, namely Peter and the pope.[45] Karmiris rejects this Roman Catholic idea, which leads to a universalistic view and particularly to the idea of a universal head, the pope, with authority and power over the college of bishops. As we shall see, Zizioulas also considers this as a universalistic conception of episcopal collegiality.

However, in criticizing Vatican II's teaching on collegiality, Karmiris invokes the same arguments that he used against Vatican I's teaching on primacy. As was seen above, a second group of Orthodox theologians criticized these particular arguments and showed their incoherence and weaknesses. Let us briefly review the main points of Karmiris's argumentation within the context of Vatican II:

(1) In arguing against the definition of papal primacy at both Vatican I and Vatican II, Karmiris sides with conciliarism. He argues against papal primacy on this basis, affirming that an ecumenical council is above the bishops and the pope, as was the case in the ancient Church and is still the case in the Orthodox Church. This position implies that a council is above any primate, which for Zizioulas, as we have seen, makes primacy incompatible with synodality.[46]

(2) In his appreciation of the Constitution on the Church, Karmiris repeats the argument that only Christ, and not the pope, is the head of the whole Church.[47] Afanassieff, as we have seen, implies that this particular argument against universal primacy is inconsistent.[48]

(3) Karmiris asks how the bishops can reconcile their own power as exercised in their own dioceses with the full, immediate, and ordinary power of the pope over the universal Church, granted to him by Vatican I and affirmed and increased by Vatican II. Karmiris states that, according to the teaching of the ancient Church as well as the present Orthodox Church, the bishops are fully bishops of their own local churches and of the universal Church, exercising *eo ipso* the fullness of their episcopal power. The bishops have received and possess this power *jure divino*, without any dependence on the bishop of Rome. Finally, Karmiris categorically states that the Orthodox Church has rejected the *jure divino* supreme, immediate power and monarchy of the pope over the whole Church, instead recognizing him as *primus inter pares honoris causa*. This primacy is given by the synods, i.e., *jure humano*, and not by divine right.[49]

We saw that for Zizioulas such a description of primacy in terms of *primus inter pares honoris causa* contradicts canonical facts. Karmiris's conception of primacy in terms of simple honor and of *primus inter pares* is in fact incoherent and is not found in the ancient Church or in the Orthodox Church today. In spite of his arguments, Karmiris himself seems implicitly to accept these sources, which actually prove that primacy is not just of simple honor.[50]

We saw also that Zizioulas is critical of understanding primacy as a matter of purely human order since this implies that the Church could exist without primacy. Karmiris nevertheless accepts that synods exist *jure divino* and as part of the Church's *esse*, but Zizioulas points out the weakness of such a position, noting that it overlooks the simple and obvious fact that *synodality* cannot exist without *primacy* and that therefore, if synodality exists *jure divino*, primacy also must exist by the same right.[51]

Missio Canonica and the Distinction between *Potestas Ordinis* and *Potestas Jurisdictionis*

Harkianakis notes that in Roman Catholic teaching the canonical election and installation of a bishop depends directly on the pope, as shown by the following text from the Constitution on the Church: "The canonical mission of the bishops, on the other hand, can be made by legitimate customs that have not been revoked by the supreme and universal authority of the Church, or by laws made or acknowledged by the same authority, or directly by Peter's successor himself. Should he object or refuse the apostolic communion, then bishops cannot be admitted to office (*LG* 24)."[52]

Nevertheless, Harkianakis appreciates the fact that in the third chapter of the Constitution on the Church the medieval distinction between *potestas ordinis* and *potestas jurisdictionis* is abandoned. There is now reference to three offices (*munera*), based on one sacred power.[53] He asserts that although the three offices of the bishops—sanctifying, teaching, and ruling—are conferred by Christ through the sacrament of ordination and therefore independently of the pope, Vatican II adds another presupposition to the existing mysteriological presupposition of these offices when it says that these three offices can only be exercised "in hierarchical communion with the head and the members of the college" (*LG* 21). Harkianakis points out that this additional presupposition strictly refers only to the two offices of teaching and ruling (*docendi* and *regendi*) since, in order to be canonically exercised in the Church according to its nature, they require the presupposition of hierarchical communion. The pope wanted this presupposition to be added.[54] He then asserts that in this way, although the common source of the three offices of the bishop is the sacrament of ordination, the so called *missio canonica* still remains valid in Roman Catholic ecclesiology and is necessary in order for the bishop to exercise canonically all three offices. This additional presupposition is given by the pope just as it used to be.[55]

Harkianakis considers therefore that *LG* 21 and the expression "hierarchical communion" contained therein imply that the bishop's three powers are totally dependent on the pope through the *missio canonica* (i.e., the granting of power of jurisdiction granted by him). We recall that Henn considers that the expression "canonical mission," which preserves within Vatican II's vision of episcopal ministry the importance of and need for the granting of jurisdiction, is a further specification of the hierarchical communion in *LG* 21.[56] Harkianakis notes that Explanatory Note 2 underlines the point that, although episcopal ordination ensures an ontological share (*ontologica participatio*) in the three offices, this should be clearly distinguished from power ordered to action (*potestas actu expedita*). He then asks whether, given such a condition, it is possible for the bishops to be regarded as being free from the absolute power of the pope, as long as such power ordered to action is granted by his *missio canonica*.[57]

Rodopoulos considers that, although the Constitution on the Church does not refer clearly to the distinction between *potestas ordinis* and *potestas jurisdictionis*, neither does it deny this distinction.[58] For Rodopoulos, such a distinction would be in contradiction with Vatican II's Decree on the Catholic Eastern Churches, *Orientalium Ecclesiarum* (article 27), which accepts the validity of the sacraments performed by Orthodox priests. Rodopoulos asks, therefore, how the sacraments performed by Orthodox bishops and priests could be valid if Orthodox clergy do not possess the *potestas jurisdictionis*, since they are not appointed by the pope? These sacraments are valid because, according to this decree, the ordination of Orthodox bishops and priests is a valid sacrament.[59]

Rodopoulos asserts that the distinction found in Explanatory Note 2 between the sacred functions given by consecration and power ordered to action given through hierarchical authority clearly implies a distinction between *potestas ordinis* and *potestas jurisdictionis*. This distinction is made in order to strengthen papal power and to place its juridical aspect above the sacramental aspect of ordination, through which the body of the bishops is exalted.[60] Speaking as an Orthodox, Rodopoulos says that the episcopal office and power are given to the bishop after his canonical election and by the ordination performed by canonical bishops.[61] Harkianakis states that the Orthodox cannot deny that for the canonical exercise of the episcopal office, the coexistence of the sacramental element and the canonical one is necessary and that when the ordination is canonically performed, these aspects cannot be sharply and chronologically separated from each other, nor can the organs that grant these two aspects. This is because the synod of the bishops, which elects the candidate, is the source of his ordination, while by these two acts (i.e., election and ordination) both of the above aspects are obtained.[62] Harkianakis says specifically that the canonical aspect is covered by the election of the candidate bishop and is not simply an administrative act but is performed under the direct supervision of the Holy Spirit and is valid after the ordination, when it is thus unbreakably bound with the sacramental aspect.[63]

It is clear that the above-mentioned Orthodox theologians should criticize the notion of *missio canonica*, for it does indeed imply a dependence of the sacramental powers of the bishops on papal power. Pierre Duprey asserts similarly:

> In order to safeguard the principle of there being no powers other than sacramental ones, Orthodox theologians state that in the Church there is no power greater than that of a bishop over his diocese. This is in fact one of the basic reasons for rejecting papal primacy. Another important result, as regards the ordination of a bishop, is that canonical election and consecration is enough to constitute him as a bishop of the Church for which he is consecrated. He has, by his very ordination, the three powers necessary for his function, so that there is no need, or even room, for a "canonical mission" which would be added to the election-and-ordination performed in the communion of the Church so as to complete the latter for the sake of the exercise of the function. Thus the Orthodox remain most perplexed by the "*missio canonica*" and the texts in which it appears. On the other hand, they appreciate very much the statement of the sacramental nature of the episcopate and of the ordination which, of itself, confers the three *munera*.[64]

The Position of John Zizioulas
ZIZIOULAS'S CRITIQUE OF THE ROMAN CATHOLIC CONCEPT OF EPISCOPAL COLLEGIALITY

In a general appreciation of Vatican II, Zizioulas praises the council for the introduction of the idea of communion into ecclesiology. He says notably:

> Vatican II has given hope and promise to many people that something can be done. I am not an expert on the theology of the council, but I feel that one of the directions in which it has pointed can be particularly important,

namely the introduction of the notion of communion into ecclesiology. This, combined with the rediscovery of the importance of the λαός of God and the local Church, can help even the Orthodox themselves to be faithful to their identity.[65]

Zizioulas is also happy with the representation of the Church as a *Mystery* in *Lumen Gentium*, as he shows when he speaks of the significance of the theology of the Church underlying Vatican II's Decree on Ecumenism. He notes with appreciation:

> The Decree on Ecumenism presupposes a concept of the Church which is different from the traditional Roman Catholic identification of the ecclesial reality solely and exclusively within the canonical limits of the Roman Catholic Church. In *Lumen Gentium* the Church is presented as a *Mystery*. This implies that the Church in her essence is a divine reality implanted in history and therefore greater than its actual historical and institutional form. As Pope Paul VI put it in his opening address at the second session on September 29, 1963, "The Church is a mystery. It is a reality imbued with the hidden presence of God. It lies, therefore, within the very nature of the Church to be always open to new and greater exploration."[66]

On the other hand, Zizioulas has questions regarding the Roman Catholic concept of episcopal collegiality. He asserts that "this concept raises some problems for the Orthodox, and perhaps also for many Roman Catholics."[67] Zizioulas argues as follows:

> The way in which the idea was formulated and presented around the time of Vatican II by Roman Catholic theology gives the impression that what is meant by "collegiality" is a structure of an episcopal body standing above the local churches and overseeing them with the pope as its head. The idea seems to be founded upon the college of the Twelve with Saint Peter as the head of the college.[68]

He further explains:

> At first sight the notion of collegiality seems to be a welcome correction to monarchical conceptions of primacy and authority in the Church. But the decisive point appears when the question of the local church is raised. Thus with regard to the college of the Apostles the question is whether the Twelve form the foundations for *each* local church or for the Church universal. If the

answer is the former, then each bishop is successor of Peter (cf. Saint Cyprian) while the apostolic college seems in this case to be transferred to the presbyterium. This was in fact the case with the ecclesiology of Saint Ignatius of Antioch. If on the other hand the answer is that collegiality refers to the universal Church, then the picture is entirely different. Each bishop is part of this universal college and each local church is part of the universal Church. In this case we are dealing with universalistic ecclesiology.[69]

At the time of Vatican II, in his doctoral dissertation Zizioulas was already critical of the notion of collegiality described by Roman Catholic theologians; he considered it in disaccord with the ecclesiology of the first three centuries.[70] In his systematic study of this particular period of the Church, Zizioulas asserts that, while it is correct to speak of the collegiality of bishops, at least from Cyprian's time, the notion of collegiality as expounded by Roman Catholic theology appears in many respects questionable.[71] He explains:

> The central point at issue in this case is the very notion of "collegiality," which presupposes the idea that Churches in various places and their Bishops are *parts* of a *collective organism*, complementing one another in a unity formed by *addition*. For modern exponents of the theory of "collegiality," the Bishops throughout the world constitute as a whole a "college" which is the antitype and successor of the college of the Twelve.[72]

Hence, for Zizioulas "it is not difficult, but is on the contrary imperative, for this college to have a head corresponding to that of the college of the Twelve, and this is the Bishop of Rome who occupies the place of Peter."[73] He then says that "although this theory of 'collegiality' stresses the importance of the Council as institution, far from diminishing the position of the Bishop of Rome, it actually gives it ecclesiological support because he is now regarded as the indispensable figure who expresses the unity of the episcopate."[74] Zizioulas here suspects that the Roman Catholic conception of episcopal collegiality is a universalistic one, leading inevitably to the idea of a universal head and bishop.

LG 22 demonstrates just such a universalistic conception of episcopal collegiality, of which Zizioulas is critical on the ground that it sees local churches and bishops as parts of a whole. It explicitly declares, for example, that the pope—Peter's successor—and the bishops are the *jure divino* successors to the apostolic college: "Just as, in accordance with the Lord's decree, St. Peter and the rest of the apostles constitute a unique apostolic college, so in like fashion the Roman Pontiff, Peter's successor, and the bishops, the successors of the apostles, are related with and united to one another." Likewise, "the order of bishops is the successor to the college of the apostles in their role as teachers and pastors, and in it the apostolic college is perpetuated."

Such a universalistic conception, which considers the pope as standing among the bishops as Peter among the apostles, implies inevitably that the pope is the universal bishop of the whole Church. *LG* 22 expresses this universalistic view, namely of the pope as standing inside the college as Peter at its head and in this sense exercising a jurisdiction over the whole Church. It says expressly that the college of the bishops has no authority unless united with the Roman pontiff, Peter's successor, as its head, whose primatial authority over all, whether pastors or faithful, remains in its integrity. The Roman bishop, by reason of his office as Vicar of Christ and as pastor of the universal Church, has full, supreme, and universal power over the whole Church. Also, the Explanatory Note stresses in this regard that in the college the head preserves intact his function as Vicar of Christ and pastor of the universal Church (nota 3).

For Zizioulas, the principal question is whether or not, in the consciousness of the early Church in the first three centuries, the correspondence between the college of the Twelve and that of the bishops was such as to make each of the bishops a successor of only a part of the college of the twelve and all of them collectively successors of the twelve as a whole. After his investigation of this crucial and formative period of the Church, Zizioulas answers categorically that "the college of the Twelve and the 'throne of Peter' which was pre-eminent within it formed the foundation, not of one Church, but of *every* episcopal Church because *every* bishop was understood as being a successor to *all* the apostles—and to Peter."[75] Zizioulas explains that "the unity of the bishops in consequence was not 'collective' or 'collegial' in the sense of bringing together by addition an apostolic succession which was divided up among the various Bishops. Every one of the Bishops sat on the throne of Peter; his Church being regarded as fully apostolic and based on the foundation of *all* the Apostles."[76]

Zizioulas refers here particularly to St. Cyprian, who considered each bishop to be a successor of Peter and to sit on the *cathedra Petri*. Thus, Zizioulas concludes that Cyprian is not proclaiming a universalistic ecclesiology, as Afanassieff asserted, but "understands the *cathedra Petri* not in relation to the Church universal, but *to every local church headed by a bishop*."[77] Given that, for Cyprian, Peter was the head of the apostolic college, this implies that each bishop, being a successor to Peter, is also a successor to all the apostles.[78]

Furthermore, for Zizioulas, from this flows the essential equality of all bishops, since each bishop is successor of the entire college headed by St. Peter. Most importantly this means that each bishop is directly responsible to God for his community, as Cyprian says.[79] In other words, each bishop is Peter in his own diocese, and we cannot therefore speak of *unus episcopatus* as being dispersed over the earth with Peter as its head. Zizioulas refers to the latter view when he says, "This leads to the concept of episcopal collegiality, as it has been expounded today in Roman Catholic theology."[80]

Here it is relevant to point out Meyendorff's similar judgement—with which Zizioulas seems to agree—that the Roman Catholic view of episcopal collegiality is a universalistic one. In particular, Meyendorff complains that Vatican II applies the image of the local community to the universal Church, that is, a single "universal bishop" surrounded by a college of presbyters-bishops. For Meyendorff, "such, in fact, was the picture evolved by Vatican I, and, alas, it remains basically the same after Vatican II."[81]

In conclusion, Zizioulas asks whether Vatican II is in fact operating with two ecclesiologies, one universalistic and one local:

> It is difficult for an outsider to decide what in fact the Roman Catholic position is in this case. Is the idea of episcopal collegiality identical with a universalist ecclesiology or not? How is it to be understood so that it can be reconciled with the recognition of the fullness and catholicity of the local diocese by Vatican II? Or is it perhaps true that the council operated with two ecclesiologies at the same time, one universalist and the other local?[82]

Also, Zizioulas asserts that episcopal collegiality seems here to be a structure of an episcopal body standing above the local churches and overseeing them with the pope as its head. In this case, "the bishops meet by virtue of their authority as members of the apostolic or episcopal college in order to dictate to the churches what to do or to believe."[83]

Zizioulas's appraisal seems fully justified, for as we have seen, *LG* 22 approaches the notion of collegiality from the context of universalistic ecclesiology, seeing it as an administrative board existing above the local churches, whereas certain Roman Catholic theologians insist that episcopal collegiality should be approached from the context of *LG* 23 and 26, which both place it in the perspective of a eucharistic ecclesiology of communion, a communion of local churches fully catholic in themselves.[84] However, the fact remains that the parallel existence of these approaches introduces a tension with regard to Vatican II's exact and precise notion of episcopal collegiality.[85]

Olivier Clement points implicitly to such a tension between the two understandings of episcopal collegiality. He considers that the passage from *LG* 22 that states that the college of bishops has supreme and full authority over the universal Church understands episcopal collegiality within the frame of universalistic ecclesiology, namely as a power, similar to the papal one, over the Church and not as a universal expression of an ecclesiology of communion. However, for Clement the phrase from the same passage in *LG* 22 that says that, "this college, in so far as it is composed of many members, is the expression of the multifariousness and universality of the People of God" indicates the emergence of the diversity of local churches.[86]

We have seen that this particular understanding of episcopal collegiality along the lines of universalistic ecclesiology arises from a purely historical approach to apostolic continuity.[87] For Zizioulas, the prime factor in such a historical conception of apostolic succession is Christology. He explains:

> In this historical approach, Christology is inevitably the primary thing that provides the structure of continuity. The Holy Spirit is the one that is *transmitted* and He is transmitted *by Christ*. He is the divine power which enables the apostles in their mission. He is also the one who creates the response to their mission. He is the animator of the *pre-conceived structure*. In such an approach Pneumatology indicates an *agency*; the Spirit is the *agent of Christ* and is dependent on Him.[88]

LG 19 and 21 provide us with such a picture regarding apostolic succession and the office of the bishop. In these passages, the Spirit is seen as being transmitted by Christ and as enabling the apostles and their successors, the bishops, in their mission and their performance of the functions given to them by Christ: "They [the apostles] were fully confirmed in this mission on the day of Pentecost according to the promise of the Lord" (*LG* 19), and "in order to fulfil such exalted functions, the apostles were endowed by Christ with a special outpouring of the Holy Spirit coming upon them (cf. Acts 1:8; 2:4; Jn. 20:22–23), and, by the imposition of hands (cf. 1 Tim. 4:14; 2 Tim. 1:6–7), they passed on to their auxiliaries the gift of the Spirit, which is transmitted down to our day through episcopal consecration" (*LG* 21).[89] In this case the Holy Spirit indeed sustains and animates a structure established by Christ on the basis of the authority and mission given by Christ to the apostles as a college and through them to the bishops.

Zizioulas asserts that "the ecclesiology of Vatican II gives the impression that pneumatology is used *after* the structure of the Church is established with the help of Christology."[90] Moreover, Zizioulas expresses with other Orthodox theologians the following criticism:

> In general, it was felt that in comparison with Christology, Pneumatology did not play an important role in the council's teaching on the Church. More particularly, it was observed that the Holy Spirit was brought into

ecclesiology *after* the edifice of the Church was constructed with Christological material alone. This, of course, had important consequences for the teaching of the council on such matters as the sacraments, ministry and ecclesial institutions in general.[91]

It is evident that *LG* 22, in dealing with the collegiality of bishops, moves along the Christological line: it implies that Christ sends out the apostles who form a college with authority and the power of preaching, teaching, and governing the Church and that by analogy the order of the bishops, as successors to the college of the apostles in their role as teachers and pastors, has supreme and full authority over the universal Church.[92]

TOWARD A THEOLOGY OF PRIMACY: JUSTIFICATION OF PRIMACY ON ECCLESIOLOGICAL AND DOGMATIC PRINCIPLES AND ZIZIOULAS'S CONTRIBUTION

The Priority of the Theological over the Historical Method. Zizioulas has spoken of the necessity of universal primacy as an expression of the unity of the Church at the universal level: "Can there be unity of the Church without primacy on the local, the regional and the universal level in an ecclesiology of communion? We believe not. For it is through a 'head,' some kind of 'primus,' that the many, be it individual Christians or local Churches, can speak with one voice."[93]

Let us consider how he develops his view on the issue of universal primacy. First, it must be noted that Zizioulas distinguishes two ways of approaching the issue of primacy in general: historical and theological. Zizioulas considers that the historical method, which has been used in the past extensively, "has led to no fruitful result." In regard to the primacy of the bishop of Rome, Zizioulas considers that "biblical and Patristic evidence cannot decide the issue."[94]

Although Zizioulas admits that "there is undoubtedly a petrine primacy in the college of the Twelve," on the other hand, he considers it difficult to "establish on biblical grounds the link between the ministry of St. Peter and that of the bishop of Rome."[95] In a foundational address during a symposium on the petrine primacy in 2003, Zizioulas went on to explain that "although Peter's position among the Twelve is recognized more and more also by the Orthodox, the particular importance attached to him by the Roman Catholics is strongly disputed by them."[96] He then pointed to the impasse caused by disagreement with regard to Peter's position in the New Testament: "If we wait until biblical scholars come to an agreement on this issue, we may have to postpone the unity of the Church for another millennium if not infinitely."[97] In this context we earlier noted the examples of such a disagreement between the classical Roman Catholic view and the Greek Orthodox one on Peter's position in the New Testament.[98]

Furthermore, Zizioulas says that Oscar Culmann's point "that in fact the ministry of the Twelve is unique and unrepeatable continues to be valid as long as continuity is understood strictly in historical terms, i.e. as a matter of linear historical succession."[99] He doubts that the link between the petrine and the papal primacy can be based on the fact that Peter died and was buried in Rome; he considers that this fact "can hardly convince the historian that such a link can follow by logical necessity."[100]

Zizioulas further contests the link by drawing upon the following facts, namely (1) "Paul also died in Rome and so did many other martyrs of the Church, but there has been no claim of their succession by the bishop of Rome," (2) "as it is indicated by the controversy concerning the celebration of Easter in the second century, other churches in Asia Minor boasted for having hosted the tombs and relics of apostles in their territory, but none of them thought of using this as a justification for a claim of apostolic succession," and (3) "as the late Francis Dvornik demonstrated in his work, *The Idea of Apostolicity in Byzantium and the Legend of the Apostle Andrew*, it was only much later that the argument of apostolicity on the basis of a Church's foundation by an apostle began to be used widely."[101]

Thus, history, for Zizioulas, is an unsafe ground for rapprochement between Roman Catholics and Orthodox with regard to papal primacy. Zizioulas quotes in this regard Yves Congar, who points out the difference between East and West on the authority of the see of Rome, as follows:

> In the East, the authority of the see of Rome was never that of a monarchical prince. The history of the Sixth Ecumenical Council (680–681) is eloquent on this point. Pope Agathon was acclaimed not because his authority would be obeyed but because the expression of the authentic faith was recognised in his words. The theory of Pentarchy . . . was a way of structuring communication between the Churches and ensuring unity. . . . The Pentarchy was, in its way, an expression of the collegial sense of the synodal East in so far as it was a form of communion of the Churches in homophony. . . . The Body of Christ has no Head other than Christ himself. . . . The Byzantine theologians very rarely relate the primacy of the see of Rome to the Apostle Peter, although authors of prestige like Maximus the Confessor or Theodore the Studite do, at times, say something to this effect.[102]

We saw in chapter 2 that after Vatican I Roman Catholics appealed to the history of the ancient Church and to the Fathers in order to find incontrovertible evidence in favor of a papal primacy of jurisdiction over the Church, while on the other hand, the Orthodox regarded such evidence as not implying such a primacy at all. Zizioulas says that "historians may disagree as to the extent to which the authority of Rome was recognised in the East, but no one can dispute the divergence between East and West on this matter long before the schism of the eleventh century."[103] He concludes:

> Thus the study of history offers to help us in the present, ecumenically, only in two ways—both of them unrealistic. One is for Roman Catholics and Orthodox to return to the situation of the first millennium. This is unrealistic mainly because the Roman Catholic Church would not be prepared to eliminate her second millennium from history in order to unite with the Orthodox. The other way is to regard the differences between the Orthodox and the Roman Catholics on the subject of primacy as two parallel or complementary traditions that can exist side by side. This would also prove to be unrealistic, since it would in fact mean that the Pope would have to renounce *in practice* his claim of universal jurisdiction, limiting it only to the West (or to his own flock). As a matter of fact this was proposed as a solution by Roman Catholic theologians several years ago, but nothing came out of it.[104]

Zizioulas regards *theology* as the only way of coming out of the impasse caused by the historical method. His conviction is that if we approach the problem of universal primacy "with the help of an ecclesiology of communion we may manage to bring the two traditions closer to each other on a subject as crucial for the unity of the Church as that of primacy."[105]

This does not imply that Zizioulas ignores history or considers it as antithetical to theology but rather that he prefers to establish the theological and ecclesiological basis upon which the whole issue of universal primacy must rest, namely, an ecclesiology of communion, which he says was experienced historically by both East and West until the sixteenth century, when a monarchical understanding of papal primacy became dominant in the West. Zizioulas draws on Congar for such an approach:

> Father Congar, one of the pioneers of the ecclesiology of communion on the Roman Catholic side, believed that the papal primacy, in spite of monarchical tendencies prevailing at that time, was exercised within an ecclesiology of communion also in the West until about the sixteenth century, when the

papacy succeeded in imposing monarchical primacy on the whole of the West. If that is the case, the return to such an ecclesiology of communion may not be so unrealistic a proposition.[106]

Addressing the Roman Catholic side, Zizioulas emphasizes an ecclesiology of communion as common ground for a theological and ecclesiological justification of universal primacy, the very ecclesiology that was adopted by Vatican II. For Zizioulas, a eucharistic ecclesiology of communion of local churches involves a balance and a relationship expressed by the principle of "the one and the many," i.e., the many churches and the one Church. Primacy in such an ecclesiology of communion of local churches is theologically sound and justified for it is the means of realizing and guaranteeing the balance between the many local churches in the one Church and thereby of securing the catholicity of each local Church:

> If, therefore, we cannot meet on the ground of either biblical exegesis or history, we may ask ourselves whether we can meet on the basis of certain fundamental theological principles in order to give a common answer to the question raised above, namely, whether and for what *theological* reasons we need a universal *primus*, and how we can understand his nature and function. Such theological reasons can emerge from an *ecclesiology of communion*, which is beginning to establish itself in our time as a result of the theological insights of Vatican II and the overcoming of Scholasticism in both Roman Catholic and Orthodox theology in our time. This would mean that the justification of the Roman primacy would depend on whether we agree that the Church consists of *full local Churches* united into *one Church* without losing their ecclesial fullness, and that primacy at all levels is a necessary means to realize and guarantee this balance between the many and the one.[107]

The Justification of Primacy upon the Ecclesiological Principle of "The One and the Many." Zizioulas points out that if history and the Bible cannot provide common ground for achieving an agreement on the issue of primacy, theology and certain fundamental theological-ecclesiological principles may do so. In fact, Zizioulas prefers to base the whole issue of primacy on ecclesiological and theological grounds and not on history. Speaking of the issue of Roman primacy, he states: "Is such a primacy necessary ecclesiologically, and if it is in what sense should it be understood and applied? . . . The question for me is not an historical but a theological one."[108]

What, for Zizioulas, are the theological-ecclesiological principles that make necessary the existence of primacy in the Church? He explains, in his important paper, "Primacy in the Church," that the fundamental theological principle is that of the "one and the many." This principle, as Zizioulas says, stems from trinitarian theology as well as from Christology in its relation to pneumatology, and it is also supported by the eucharistic nature of ecclesiology.[109] Let us see in detail how Zizioulas applies this fundamental ecclesiological principle in his eucharistic ecclesiology, how for him this principle, institutionally speaking, leads to the synod and to primacy, and how it is reflected in both these institutions.

Zizioulas criticizes Afanassieff's eucharistic ecclesiology for failing

> to take into account the fact that the eucharist involves a universal communion: there is only one Eucharist, even if it is celebrated in different places, just as there is one body of Christ. As is made clear in the Orthodox Liturgy, every Eucharist is offered on behalf of the One, Holy, Catholic and Apostolic Church. The whole Catholic Church throughout the world is involved in each Eucharistic celebration, and therefore the nature of the Eucharist itself points to the need for communion among the local Churches. . . . So this "eucharistic ecclesiology" which is in the centre of Orthodox ecclesiology involves a proper balance between the local and the universal Church. One must not absorb the other.[110]

What Zizioulas here implies is that in a eucharistic ecclesiology of communion the local church cannot be isolated from the rest of the local churches, but rather that each is in communion with the other, united in one Church in the world. So there is one Church in the world, i.e., the universal Church, which is at the same time many. There is, therefore, no dichotomy between the local and the universal Church, for the nature of the Eucharist does not allow such a separation. The nature of eucharistic ecclesiology points rather to a simultaneity between the universal Church and the local churches. In other words, the nature of such a eucharistic ecclesiology of communion supports the fundamental principle of "the one and the many."[111]

Zizioulas explains that the principle of the "one and the many" arises from a eucharistic ecclesiology of communion:

> One community isolated from the rest of the communities cannot claim any ecclesial status. There is *one* Church in the world, although there are *many* churches at the same time. This paradox lies at the heart of an ecclesiology of communion. The proper relationship between the "one" and the "many" is at stake once again. How is it to be worked out both in theory and in practice?[112]

An answer to this question lies in a synthesis between Christology and pneumatology, through which a proper relationship between the one Church and the many churches could be worked out: "From the viewpoint of theology, we have here to do with a proper synthesis between Christology and Pneumatology (or even a proper understanding of the 'one' and the 'many'—the Three—in the Holy Trinity). The Holy Spirit particularises the one body of Christ by making each local Church a full and 'catholic' Church."[113] He goes on to explain the consequences of the lack of a proper balance in ecclesiology: "Whenever Pneumatology is weak or dependent in relation to Christology (a sort of 'Filioquism' in ecclesiology), there is bound to be a submission of the local Church to a universal Church structure. The 'koinonia of the Holy Spirit' suffers in this case."[114]

Zizioulas criticizes Western theology for taking the position that the universal Church has priority over the local churches. He explains that this took a particular form in Western ecclesiology, in which the universal Church was considered to be something with its own structure and its own existence, above the local churches. This structure is expressed through the ministry of the pope, who is not simply the bishop of a local church, but a universal bishop, i.e., bishop and head of the whole Church, of the one Church throughout the world. Zizioulas argues that if there is a priority of substance over persons in Triadological theology, so in a corresponding manner there will be a priority of the one universal Church over the local churches. For Zizioulas, Western theology affirms such a priority.[115] He goes on to say that this logical priority of the universal Church in Western ecclesiology took a concrete form at Vatican I, in the dogma of the infallibility of the pope and the principle that the bishops must agree with the pope. In his opinion, this is not just a juridical-legal matter; its origins are to be found in the precedence of the one and of the essence over the many and the persons. This priority of the one over the many was confirmed by Vatican I and then modified by Vatican II. Zizioulas implies that, although thanks to the Orthodox influence Vatican II affirms the catholicity of each local church, there is still not a proper balance between the many local churches and the one universal church.[116]

On the other hand, Zizioulas asserts that "equally, if the local Church is not related to the one Church of God in the world, this is a sign of submission of Christology to Pneumatology (a sort of 'Spirituquism' in Triadology as well as in ecclesiology)."[117]

He then points to the results of a proper synthesis in eucharistic ecclesiology: "If we attach to Christology and Pneumatology an equal importance, we are bound to attribute full catholicity to each local Church (the *totus*

Christus) and at the same time seek ways of safeguarding the oneness of the Church on the universal level. How can this be done?"[118]

> In response, he says that "the answer to this question is to be found in the right understanding of two things: the synodal system and the ministry of primacy." Zizioulas then emphasizes that both of these institutions express the unity of the universal church—the one Church in the world (the aspect of "the one")—and must not be understood as structures above the local churches. They are realities expressing the communion of the local churches (the aspect of the "many") without undermining their catholicity and leading therefore to universalistic ecclesiology. The first thing that must be emphasised is that, in an ecclesiology of communion, neither synodality nor primacy can be understood as implying structures or ministries standing *above* the ecclesial communities. Only by a structure or a ministry that would involve the community of each local Church can synodality and primacy be realities of communion. . . . Without synodality unity risks being sacrificed in favour of the local Church. But a synodality which expresses the catholicity and integrity of the local Church can lead to ecclesiastical universalism. The same must be said about primacy. Can there be unity of the Church without primacy on the local, the regional and the universal level in an ecclesiology of communion? We believe not. For it is through a "head," some kind of "primus," that the "many," be it individual Christians or local Churches, can speak with one voice. But a "primus" must be part of a community; not a self-defined, but a truly relational ministry. Such a ministry can only act together with the heads of the rest of the local Churches whose consensus it would express. A primacy of this kind is both desirable and harmless in an ecclesiology of communion.[119]

Thus from the above follows his statement that a eucharistic ecclesiology of communion, which by its nature supports the principle of the one and the many, leads directly to and requires an institution of unity, i.e., a primate—"the one"—who expresses and safeguards the unity and the oneness of the Church as the communion of many local churches. In other words, this pattern of "the one and the many" is applicable on the universal level, i.e., between the local churches and their bishops in the world.[120]

Moreover, Zizioulas associates this eucharistic ecclesiology of communion, which includes an institution of unity on the universal level that expresses the communion of the local churches, with a patristic understanding of the Trinity, and in particular with St. Basil's teaching on God:

Instead of speaking of the unity of God in terms of His one nature, he [i.e., St. Basil] prefers to speak of it in terms of the *communion of persons*: communion is for Basil an ontological category. The *nature* of God is communion. This does not mean that the persons have an ontological priority over the one substance of God, but that the one substance of God coincides with the communion of the three persons. In ecclesiology all this can be applied to the relationship between local and universal Church. There is one Church as there is one God. But the expression of this one Church is the communion of the many local churches. Communion and oneness coincide in ecclesiology. Now, when we look at the institutional aspect of ecclesiology it follows that the institution that is supposed to express the unity of the Church must be an institution which expresses *communion*. . . . The institution of universal unity cannot be self-sufficient or self-explicable or prior to the event of communion. . . . Equally, however, there is no communion which can be prior to the oneness of the Church: the institution which expresses this communion must be accompanied by an indication that there is a ministry safeguarding the oneness of the Church.[121]

Nevertheless, Zizioulas is careful to emphasize that although the Cappadocians do speak of the one substance of God with reference to the divine unity, for them it is in fact the person of the Father that remains the ground of unity of the Holy Trinity. The one God is the Father. The one ontological *arche* in the Trinity is the Father, which means that the One, the Father, causes the other two persons.[122] We are dealing here with the concept of corporate personality, which is a key point of Zizioulas's theology and ecclesiology. McPartlan explains that "the 'one' in God is the Father, thus 'the one' in corporate personality is not the total, overall unity, but the specific person at the heart of 'the many'. Moreover, 'the many' include 'the one'; 'the one' is one of 'the many' and does not stand outside them."[123] The Father is therefore a relational being, who, as Zizioulas strongly emphasizes, has his identity, his personhood, from his relations to the Son and the Spirit.[124] Zizioulas also emphasizes the point that the Cappadocian teaching on the Father as the personal cause of the Son and the Holy Spirit implies an asymmetry or hierarchical *taxis* and structure within the Trinity, with the Father being the first in this hierarchical ordering.[125]

Such a hierarchical order existing within the Trinity has implications in the realm of ecclesiology, which Zizioulas discusses.[126] Just as there is a hierarchical order and structure existing within the Trinity, i.e., the Father as the first in the Trinity, the principle and the expression of its unity, in an analogous way there is a hierarchical order between the local churches, with a local church and its local bishop being first in order among the others, expressing the unity of the local churches.[127] Zizioulas notes another important implication, namely that this trinitarian model results in an ecclesiology in which each local church is conceived as a fully catholic Church and as equal to the others without implying any subjection of one to another: "The Trinitarian model involves a *taxis*, a hierarchy, which brings forth 'others' of full ontological integrity and, therefore, equality of nature, dignity, and so on. This suggests an ecclesiology in which the one Church is constituted as many local Churches of full 'catholic' ecclesial integrity, with no one of them being subject to another as 'part' of another or of a whole, but each being 'whole of the whole.'"[128]

Zizioulas explains how the theological principle of "the one and the many," which, as we have seen, flows from the dogma of the Holy Trinity, applies on the regional level of the Church. By appealing to the early structures of the Church and concretely to the Thirty-Fourth Apostolic Canon, Zizioulas offers a coherent understanding of the synodical institution in Orthodox theology, in which the primate finds his proper place:

> The true significance of the synod in Orthodox Tradition, however, seems to me to be given in the canon 34 of the so-called *Apostolic Canons*; and its meaning is based on two fundamental principles put forth by this canon. The first principle is that in every province there must be *one* head—an institution of unity (i.e. the first one). There is no possibility of rotation or of collective ministry to replace this one head. The local bishops-Churches can do nothing without the presence of the "one."[129]

Here it should be pointed out that, for Zizioulas, in the early period of the Church the bishops commemorated the whole episcopate in the Liturgy. Later, with the creation of centers of unity—i.e., the primacies—which formed the metropolitan system and the Pentarchy, the bishops commemorated the name of their own primates. However, for Zizioulas, the commemoration of one's own primate in the practice of the Orthodox Liturgy does not imply that the local bishop is administratively subject to his own primate, but rather indicates that each of the local bishops has to recognize one among them as the primate—i.e., an institution of unity—in the sense of the Thirty-Fourth Apostolic Canon, and that he is in communion with that primate. These regional centers of unity are not understood as having administrative jurisdiction over the local churches. The commemoration of the primate by the bishops does not imply that the Eucharist is dependent on the primate and therefore celebrated in his name, which would imply a universalistic ecclesiology.[130] On the other hand, if the local churches and their bishops throughout the world do not recognize a primate, this nonrecognition affects the Eucharist of each local church, because it prevents the local Eucharist from realizing its full ecclesiological content, which is also the unity of the Church on the universal level, manifested through the ministry and the institution of unity, i.e., the primate.[131]

Zizioulas then points to the other fundamental principle from canon 34: "On the other hand the same canon provides a second fundamental principle, namely that the one cannot do anything without the many [i.e., the heads of the local churches]. There is no ministry or institution of unity which is not expressed in the form of communion."[132] For Zizioulas, the ministry of unity, i.e., the primate, should be placed within the context of an ecclesiology of communion that derives from a pneumatologically conditioned Christology and ecclesiology, making the one simultaneously recognized as many: "There is no 'one' which is not at the same time 'many'—is this not the same as the pneumatologically conditioned Christology?"[133]

Zizioulas emphasizes that both aspects are present in the Church, thanks to a proper synthesis between pneumatology and Christology, as implied in the following:

> The "many" always need the "one" in order to express themselves. . . . This mystery of the "one" and the "many" is deeply rooted in the theology of the Church, in its Christological (the "one" aspect) and pneumatological (the aspect of the "many") nature. Institutionally speaking, this involves a ministry of primacy inherent in all forms of conciliarity. An ecclesiology of communion, an ecclesiology which gives to the many the right to be themselves, risks being pneumatomonistic if it is not conditioned by the ministry of the "one", just as an ecclesiology of a pyramidal, hierarchical structure involves a Christomonistic tendency, which undermines the decisive role of the holy Spirit in the life and structure of the Church.[134]

Zizioulas analyzes how the primate looks in the context of the reality of communion, i.e., in a synodical context, and how this is explicitly stated in the Thirty-Fourth Apostolic Canon. Zizioulas insists that primacy in its regional and universal form should be exercised in a synodical context, and this means that the spirit and provisions of the Thirty-Fourth Apostolic Canon have to be respected.[135] After underlining the fact that primacy is attached to a particular office or ministry and to a particular person, Zizioulas explains that the primate should be situated in a reality of communion, reflecting in this way the communal life of the Holy Trinity as the canon implies by its concluding doxology.

Since, however, this office or ministry finds its *raison d'être* in the synodical institution of which it is part, it can only function *in relation to those who comprise the synod*, and never in isolation. Primacy, like everything else in the Church, even in God's being (the Trinity) is *relational*. There is no such thing as individual ministry, understood and functioning outside a reality of communion. This is precisely what the well-known thirty-fourth Canon of the Apostles clearly and explicitly states. This canon can be the golden rule of the theology of primacy. It requires that the *protos* is a *sine qua non conditio* for the synodical institution, hence an ecclesiological necessity, and that the synod is equally a prerequisite for the exercise of primacy. And all this, as the canon culminates, because God himself is Trinity.[136]

Most importantly, Zizioulas explores the profound theological and ecclesiological implications of the reciprocal conditioning between primacy and synodality defined in the Thirty-Fourth Apostolic Canon. These implications, as we shall see immediately, are crucial to a proper understanding of primacy in the Church.

First, the reciprocity between the primate and the synod "means that primacy is not a legalistic notion implying the investment of a certain individual with power, but a form of *diakonia*, that is, of ministry in the strict sense of the term."[137] Second, this reciprocity implies also that "this ministry reaches the entire community through the communion of the local churches manifested through the bishops that constitute the council or synod."[138] It is for this reason, in Zizioulas's view, that the primate should be the head of a local Church, i.e., a bishop. This will allow each local Church to be part of a conciliar reality as a full and catholic Church.[139] For Zizioulas, such a primacy does not undermine the ecclesiological integrity of a local Church; rather, "the primate, as the head of a local Church and not as an individual, will serve the unity of the Church as a *Koinonia* of full churches and not as a 'collage' of incomplete parts of a universal Church." He thus stresses the following:

It is of crucial importance that this primacy be given to a bishop, that is, to the head of a local church. In Orthodox canon law the primates of each region are tied to certain *sees* and not to individuals. A "see" means a local church with its own historical traits. It is, therefore, impossible to move outside the context of local churches in dealing with the idea of primacy. The primate has no right to intervene in the affairs of another diocese, not even to celebrate the liturgy there without the permission of the local bishop. The principle of catholicity is thus maintained in all the aspects of the synodal system.[140]

For Zizioulas, a universal primacy of the Bishop of Rome would not be exercised directly over the entire Church, but would express the communion of local churches.

> Given the established structure of the Church the universal primacy of the Church of Rome would mean in the first instance that the Bishop of Rome will be in cooperation on all matters pertaining to the Church as a whole with the existing patriarchs and other heads of autocephalous churches. His primacy would be exercised *in communion*, not in isolation or directly over the entire Church. He would be the president of all heads of churches and the spokesman of the entire Church once the decisions announced are the result of consensus. But communion should not be exhausted at the level of heads of the churches; it should penetrate deeply all levels of church life, reaching all bishops and all the clergy and all the people.[141]

The Function and the Role of the Primate. Zizioulas's description of the role and ministry of the primate within the Church can be summarized in the following points:

(1) A primate, as head of a local Church, exercises his primacy within a communional-synodical context, being a spokesman for the unity of the Church, so that the Church may speak with one voice. Within a synod the primate expresses the communion of local churches on matters pertaining to the whole Church, provided that the decisions on these are the result of consensus. The Thirty-Fourth Apostolic Canon provides for such a communional understanding of the institution of unity (primate) and for reciprocity between the primate and the synod (i.e., "the one" and "the many"), which for Zizioulas, as we have seen, implies that the ministry of unity reaches the entire community through the communion of the local churches manifested through the bishops that constitute the council or synod.

Zizioulas emphatically states that the existence and presence of the primate within the synod is so fundamental that the Thirty-Fourth Apostolic Canon categorically makes the provision that the synod cannot do anything without him. For Zizioulas, the meaning of this principle for the convocation and presidency of a synod can be summarized in the following:

i. The person who convokes a synod and presides over it must be the same. The Nineteenth Canon of the Council of Antioch makes specific provision for this. Not to do so would be contrary to the spirit and reason of the canons, which are ruled by the principle that the local churches must act in a council as united and not divided. With this in mind, it is possible to understand the Thirty-Fourth Apostolic Canon's insistence that none of the bishops can act synodically without the primate: the function of the primate is related to the expression of the unity of the churches and consequently is inseparable from the act of convoking the synod.[142]

ii. On the other hand, the primate's convocation of a synod is inconceivable without the agreement of the other bishops. This clearly derives from the Thirty-Fourth Apostolic Canon as well. It is the primate who convokes the council, but in fact all the local churches through their bishops participate in the event of the convocation. The primate who convokes the council is the mouthpiece of all the bishops; there is no mention of any monarchical rights of the primate or of an authority which is based on his office, to be exercised *ipso jure* and automatically, namely without the agreement and the will of the other bishops. The ecclesiological character of the primate's ministry expresses the communion of the churches, not only a legal authority.[143]

iii. Any discussion of co-presidency of the synod is to be rejected because it is contrary to the very existence of the synod, which is the formation and unity of the local churches into one body. None of the early canons made provision for a co-presidency of the synod, because in the mentality of the early Church there prevailed the principle that, while everything in the Church takes place as communion, this communion is expressed through one person, the bishop. It is on this principle that the development and formation of the episcopal ministry is based (the local church is a communion that is expressed through one person, the bishop). It is also profoundly linked to the meaning of the Triadological life of God, where communion becomes unity through one person, the hypostasis of the Father.[144] For Zizioulas, the Thirty-Fourth Apostolic Canon shows clearly that the issue of the ministry of the primate and the synodical institution is linked to these profound theological presuppositions because the canon justifies the relation between the primate and the synod by a reference to the communion and the glory of the Holy Trinity.[145] Zizioulas then concludes that no institution in the Church could be understood as ecclesiologically or canonically indispensable if it is not somehow linked with the profound dogmatic (i.e., doctrinal) faith of the Church.[146]

The overall context in which the relation between the primate and the synod should be placed is a trinitarian one, i.e., the communional life of the Holy Trinity. The very existence of the ministry of the primate is also a reflection of the life of the Holy Trinity, for, as we have just seen, Zizioulas says that the person through whom the communion of the Holy Trinity becomes unity is the Father. Thus, the communional configuration of the "one and the many" in the Trinity is invoked.

(2) "The authority of a council or synod is limited to the affairs pertaining to the communion of local churches with one another." "Through the synodical system we do not arrive at a universal church; we rather arrive at a *communion of churches. Universality becomes in this way identical with communion.*"[147]

(3) Both the institution of the synod and that of the primate are therefore visible ways of manifesting the communion of the local churches without arriving at a universal Church or universal ecclesiology, since neither of them can intervene directly in the affairs of the local churches.[148]

(4) Zizioulas excludes any understanding of the Church as a confederation of local churches, and he insists that the Orthodox view of the Church, in his understanding, "requires an institution which expresses the oneness of the Church and not simply its multiplicity."[149]

In an unpublished paper read at an Orthodox conference on the topic of contemporary Orthodox ecclesiastical legislation, held in Belgrade in 2003, Zizioulas was insistent that a canonical structure and indeed a primacy, as an expression of the unity of the Orthodox Church on the universal level, appear today to be necessary in the Orthodox Church:

> The question whether the Church needs a *protos* at the universal level is becoming crucial not only with regard to the Roman Catholic claims, but also as an internal matter within the Orthodox Church. In fact the existing canonical order which has been established by Ecumenical Councils is not doubted by any Orthodox Church. . . . According to it there is an order among the Autocephalous Orthodox Churches, with Constantinople as the *primus*, i.e., as the one which should co-ordinate the Orthodox Churches and express after

consultation convergence on matters pertaining to the whole of the Orthodox Church both *ad intra* and *ad extra*, so that the Orthodox Church may appear as the one Church in spite of being many Autocephalous Churches. I believe that such a provision of inter-Orthodox unity must find its place in the constitutions of each Orthodox Church because, unlike the past, today appears to be necessary a canonical structure of pan-Orthodox unity.[150]

We conclude that for Zizioulas councils cannot replace the oneness of the Church manifested through a universal ministry of unity, i.e., a primus. That he excludes such a possibility can be seen from the following statement: "The council is not present in Orthodox theology as a substitute for the Roman Catholic Pope, and this for the simple reason that the council cannot play the role of the Pope or replace his ministry."[151]

Thus, addressing the Orthodox, Zizioulas implies that the synodical institution cannot itself manifest the oneness of the Church on the universal level. This must be expressed through a universal primacy: "Is there a primacy, a universal ministry of unity, or is such a thing not necessary? The Orthodox have to make up their minds about this, because while on the one hand we stress unity at the universal level through the synods, on the other hand we also recognise a certain primacy in certain sees."[152]

It should however be noted that at an earlier stage, as McPartlan observes, a tension existed in Zizioulas's thought. Thus, McPartlan asserts that "whereas Zizioulas recognises the unity of persons in the local church as the many forming a differentiated unity-of-complementarity around the one in their midst who holds them apart in unity, he describes the unity of local churches as a coincident, or overlapping, unity-of-identity. This latter description dates from 1969."[153] In his 1965 doctoral dissertation, Zizioulas said that this unity of identity, i.e., a unity of the local churches in the one Church throughout the world, was manifested in time through identity with what the Lord and the apostles taught (apostolic succession of bishops) and in space through identity with what the other churches taught (institutions of councils).[154]

McPartlan shows clearly that "Zizioulas has gradually moved toward resolving this tension in the direction of recognizing a need for the local churches throughout the world to be configured as a one-many unity around a genuinely primatial local church."[155] By presenting in precise terms this movement in Zizioulas's thought, McPartlan asserts that the Thirty-Fourth Apostolic Canon is the evidence that Zizioulas finds to confirm that the unity of the local churches is found in a "one-many" configuration, i.e., the one primatial community–bishop and the many local churches–bishops that are mutually constitutive as required by the concept of corporate personality. Further, for Zizioulas, the "one-many" configuration is also applied among the local churches throughout the world.[156] This implies that for Zizioulas, the Thirty-Fourth Apostolic Canon and the principle of "the one and the many" that it espouses are applicable not only at the regional level but also at the universal level.

ZIZIOULAS'S CONCEPTION OF PRIMACY IN COMPARISON WITH THAT OF SEVERAL CONTEMPORARY RUSSIAN OR-THODOX THEOLOGIANS

Nicholas Afanassieff. We saw that Afanassieff poses a logical question—if the Church has Christ as head, why does a local Church have a (single) visible head in the person of its bishop and why does an autocephalous Church have a primacy and a visible head as a manifestation of its unity? He also goes a step further and asks how the unity of the whole Orthodox Church can be given empirical expression in the absence of a universal primacy.[157]

In attributing to St. Cyprian the idea of universal ecclesiology, Afanassieff asserts:

> S. Cyprian did not succeed in constructing his system without some idea of primacy and this shows that if a universal theory of the Church is adhered to, the doctrine of primacy will somehow be a necessary concomitant. A single body must be crowned by a single head, showing in his own person the unity of the whole system.[158]

It appears that he does not accept universal primacy as an expression of the overall unity of the local churches since he alleges, as seen from the above quotation, that the whole concept of primacy is logically linked with universal ecclesiology. We may then conclude that for Afanassieff the idea of a primate as head—which empirically expresses the unity of an autocephalous Church or of the whole Church in the world—is also excluded, for such an idea is part and parcel of universal ecclesiology. In other words, it seems that Afanassieff in fact does not accept the primate's role of expressing visibly and empirically the unity of the Church on the universal level since such a function is attached to a universalistic view of the Church.

Afanassieff distinguishes between eucharistic ecclesiology and universal ecclesiology, excluding the possibility of any place for primacy in his eucharistic ecclesiology since primacy implies a universalistic conception of the

Church. Instead, he introduces the term "priority" as the only one that fits with eucharistic ecclesiology:

> We may now return to a former enquiry: does the eucharistic type of eccle-siology include the idea of primacy, or not? After all we have said about it, clearly the only answer is negative: eucharistic ecclesiology excludes the idea of primacy by its very nature. As we already know, primacy means the power of one bishop over the whole universal Church. . . . Primacy is a legalistic expression, whereas priority is founded on authority of witness, and that is a gift God grants to the church-in-priority. . . . Finally, we should note that the two concepts imply different doctrines of Church unity: the "primacy" school attributes the unity to the Church universal. . . . The difference between the concepts (primacy and priority) is very important: if you accept the idea of primacy you must ban eucharistic ecclesiology; conversely, accept the notion of priority and there is no room for universal ecclesiology.[159]

Afanassieff considers that in the ancient Church the local churches were equal in value because each one of them possessed the fullness of the Church of God and therefore their unity was not the result of adding separate parts but the unity of one and the same church. This equality created a hierarchy of churches grounded in the authority of witness belonging to the several local churches.[160] "If there is a hierarchy of churches, there must be a church to head the hierarchy—therefore, a church that takes the first place."[161] Thus, Afanassieff accepts that within the communion of the local churches there is a local church that possesses a priority of witness.

In comparing Afanassieff's eucharistic ecclesiology with that of Ziziou-las, McPartlan brings out the crucial difference between them with regard to the issue of primacy. With regard to Zizioulas's own criticisms of Afa-nassieff, McPartlan asserts that "Zizioulas does not bring fully to light the real issue, which is that of whether being equally answerable vertically to God for their own churches precludes the bishops from having in their midst one whose horizontal role is truly unique and personal."[162] McPart-lan makes the following important remark: "Afanassieff cannot conceive of a way in which these two realities might be compatible; for him there can be no primacy with a unique and personal role within a communion of full local churches, there can only be a priority."[163]

On the other hand, as McPartlan observes, the compatibility of these two realities is an extremely important insight on the part of Zizioulas, who con-siders that the "one-many" configuration applies not only within but also among the local churches in the world. McPartlan continues: "Each church is equally full in itself but they all depend upon this configuration in order to be fully themselves. Their unity derives not from their sameness but from their existence in this differentiated configuration."[164]

This penetrating remark implies that in Afanassieff's eucharistic ecclesiology there is no place for a primate—"the one" among the many local churches, he who would manifest the unity and communion of the local churches on the universal level—but rather simply a unity based on the sameness of the local churches. We have already seen that Afanassieff does not accept the primate's role of expressing visibly and empirically the unity of the Church since such a function is concomitant with universal ecclesiology.

Zizioulas criticized Afanassieff's eucharistic ecclesiology for not stressing the necessary unity between the local churches but rather implying their independence.[165] Nevertheless, Afanassieff admits that, though in the early Church a local Church possessed the fullness of the Church of God, "it could not live apart from the other churches and could not shut itself in or refuse to be acquainted with the happenings in other local churches."[166] But as McPartlan makes quite clear, Zizioulas's real objection to Afanassieff is that the necessary unity between the churches is a differentiated one and therefore depends on the "one and many" configuration and is not just one of sameness, as Afanassieff asserts.[167]

We have seen that Zizioulas envisages the unity of the Church, on the universal as well as on the regional level, as deriving from "the one and the many" configuration, as the Thirty-Fourth Canon of the Apostles teaches. The unity of the local churches not just regionally but throughout the world must be configured as a "one and many" unity, which implies primacy as an institution of unity, i.e., "the one." The Thirty-Fourth Apostolic Canon therefore applies also to the universal level.[168]

Zizioulas believes that in a eucharistic ecclesiology of communion, which results from a proper relationship between Christology and pneumatology, a proper relationship between the one Church in the world and the many churches can be worked out. Zizioulas asserts that, by giving equal importance to Christology and pneumatology, we simultaneously attribute full catholicity to each local Church and seek ways of safeguarding the oneness and the unity of the Church on the universal level. This unity is expressed in the ministry of primacy—the ministry of "the one."[169] There is then for Zizioulas a simultaneity between the local and the universal Church, not a priority of the one over the other. Zizioulas finds that Afanassieff's ecclesiology lacks a proper synthesis between Christology and pneumatology and that this has an effect on his ecclesiology. He believes that Afanassieff gives priority to pneumatology over Christology and that this leads to a priority of the local Church over the universal.[170]

Zizioulas criticizes Afanassieff's eucharistic ecclesiology for not taking into account the need for universal unity and for not recognizing the unity of the universal Church. He charges Afanassieff with a one-sided emphasis on the local church and with "localism."[171] From an ecumenical point of view, Zizioulas says with regard to Roman Catholic reactions to Afanassieff's ecclesiology:

> The Roman Catholics especially found it easy to think of unity with the Orthodox on the basis of the fact that they, too, celebrate the Eucharist, and therefore there is automatically a basis for unity. Now, the interesting and paradoxical thing is that later, on reflection, the Roman Catholic theologians themselves found his theory extremely inconvenient, since it does not take into account the need for universal unity.[172]

He goes on to note:

> If one says that each Eucharistic celebration constitutes the Church, one does not need anything further than the local Eucharistic community in order to realize the concept of the Church; and indeed many people have understood Orthodox ecclesiology in these terms, as being basically an ecclesiology of the local Church which does not recognize the unity of the universal Church. But the latter is essential to the Roman Catholics because it involves the primacy of the pope. Even without the pope, the notion of the universal Church is very important for a Roman Catholic, so the original enthusiasm was lost. Now everybody sees that there are defects in this form of ecclesiology as it was presented by Fr. Afanasiev.[173]

In criticizing Afanassieff, Zizioulas does not stress the additional fact that the latter, apart from not recognizing the unity of the universal Church, also does not recognize the importance of a universal primate—"the one" among the many bishops and local churches—who manifests that unity. Zizioulas himself, of course, does recognize such a universal ministry and institution of unity that expresses the unity of the Church on the universal level.

Afanassieff also asserts that there is no pan-Orthodox head or universal primate in the Orthodox Church capable of convoking a council. He says in this regard:

> All attempts to convoke a pan-Orthodox council in our own age have not succeeded, and it is rather unlikely that such a council could ever be convoked. This is due to the absence of a primacy capable of commanding recognition by all

the Orthodox churches. There is no pan-Orthodox Head of the Church, consequently any convocation of a council is a practical impossibility. Supposing that the leaders of the autocephalous churches should all agree to allow a patriarch to convoke an ecumenical council, their action would imply that this patriarch was recognised as primate of the Orthodox Church. I shall put off any attempt to decide whether the Patriarch of Constantinople has the right to convoke a council, and confine myself to a single remark: ever since the ninth century the *de facto* position of the Patriarch of Constantinople has favored his claim to this right, and yet the Patriarch is well known never to have convoked an ecumenical council: he has never explored the possibilities of planning such a convocation. One thing is clear: if the autocephalous churches had recognised the right of the Patriarch of Constantinople to convoke, they would simultaneously have recognised his primacy in the Orthodox Church.[174]

Since primacy for Afanassieff is a necessary concomitant of universal ecclesiology and implies a power and authority over the Church, an act of convocation by the patriarch of Constantinople would therefore be universalistic since it would be, in his view, a manifestation of universal primacy in the Orthodox Church. Actually, his claim that the patriarch of Constantinople has not convoked an ecumenical or a pan-Orthodox council since the ninth century contradicts historical facts since the Ecumenical Patriarch has indeed convoked numerous pan-Orthodox councils.

Drawing upon Metropolitan Maximos of Sardes, Zizioulas asserts that since the schism, the primate in the Orthodox Church has been the patriarch of Constantinople. Consequently, this patriarch has without doubt the canonical right of convocation of a pan-Orthodox council and of presidency over it.[175] Zizioulas is not speaking here of monarchical rights; the primate convoking a council must be acting with the agreement of all bishops and expressing the communion of the local churches.[176]

While Afanassieff denies the universal primacy of the Ecumenical Patriarch and his right to convoke a council, he does accept the canonical fact that a regional primate as head of an autocephalous Church has the right to convoke councils: "The councils cannot be gathered together automatically; they must be convoked by the head of the diocese. If there had been no single heads in the autocephalous churches, councils could never have existed; otherwise, anarchy would have reigned, with every bishop thinking he had a right to convoke councils."[177]

Afanassieff emphasizes that synodality cannot exist without primacy but actually presupposes it; in this way, he highlights the error of basing arguments against primacy on the conciliar principle. Nevertheless, he appears to be speaking of the regional primate, namely the patriarch of each autocephalous Church, as we may conclude from his following statement:

> I must once more point out the error of basing arguments against primacy on the conciliar principle. . . . The conciliar principle serves to limit the power of the primate-bishop, but we must not think that this is a hard and fast limitation in legal terms. There is another way to describe it. The bishop possessing primacy acts with the agreement of the whole body of bishops: this agreement is manifest in the council in which the primate-bishop participates as its president. In Orthodox theology, the patriarch is conceived of as being *primus inter pares* among the bishops. This formula, though generally allowed, is misleading, and it would be difficult to find justification in the history of the Orthodox Church. It is indeed doubtful that the bishops ever thought themselves the equals of the patriarch in every respect, or that he thought himself their equal. Equality is really a difficult claim, when the patriarch possesses rights of which the other bishops are deprived. . . . The patriarch as a member of the episcopate of the autocephalous church is not above it, but as its leader he is the first in the episcopal body.[178]

From the above, it follows that Afanassieff accepts the existence of primacy within each autocephalous Church, while refusing the existence of a universal primacy. In general, he dislikes the term "primacy" and considers it as universalistic, namely as implying power over the Church. He says in this regard: "Orthodox theology indeed rejects the idea of primacy on the universal scale, but it recognises a partial primacy at the centre of every autocephalous church, a primacy belonging to the head of that church. We are concerned here with primacy, not priority, for priority implies that every local church has fullness of ecclesiastical *esse*."[179]

We have seen that Afanassieff criticizes Orthodox theology for conceiving primacy in terms of *primus inter pares*; he finds that there is an inequality between the primate and the other bishops because the patriarch as a primate has special rights in relation to other bishops.

In presenting the Orthodox view on the issue of primacy, Duprey notes:

> Theoretically it was stressed that all bishops were equal and that the relation of patriarch to patriarchs was that of *primus inter pares*. This received special emphasis whenever polemics with Rome were in the air. The expression "*primus inter pares*" is generally accepted, although Nicholas Afanassieff does not hesitate to call it mistaken on the grounds that "it is very

difficult to speak of equality when the patriarch possesses rights which are denied to other bishops." Granted, even, that these rights are balanced by the duty of doing nothing without the agreement of all, this still does not give equality.[180]

Zizioulas is also critical of his fellow Greek Orthodox who consider the primacy in terms of *primus inter pares*—an honorific primacy, implying no rights or authority at all.[181] For Zizioulas, the description of primacy in terms of *primus inter pares* is in contradiction with basic canonical principles such as those contained in the Thirty-Fourth Apostolic Canon that there must be a primate without whom the bishops of the district cannot do anything while he himself can do nothing without the others. This implies that the primate can even block the deliberations of the synod. We recall that Zizioulas emphasizes the canonical provision in the Orthodox Church that, in the absence of the patriarch or during the vacancy of his throne, there cannot be episcopal elections or performance of any canonical act.[182] Thus, canonically speaking, a primate has real authority and rights. Elsewhere Zizioulas stresses that the primacy of a patriarch is certainly more than a primacy of honor. He then refers to the right of the patriarch to convoke the synod and set its agenda. His presence is a *sine qua non* condition for all canonical deliberations such as the election of bishops. This means that the synod cannot function without its head. For Zizioulas, the Thirty-Fourth Apostolic Canon underlies Orthodox ecclesiology in this respect. He asserts that "this is definitely a true primacy, although not an absolute one, since it is controlled and moderated by the rest of the bishops."[183]

Afanassieff explains that, in the hierarchy that existed in the ancient Church, the church that possessed priority had no power over the other local churches or special rights but possessed the highest authority of witness. Its acts of bearing witness to the events in other local churches had a sovereign value and its act of reception was of decisive importance.[184] He then concludes that the basis of priority is neither power nor honor but only the authority that flows from love.[185]

On the one hand, Afanassieff recognizes the canonical right of the regional primate to convoke a council and considers the term *primus inter pares* as misleading since the primate has special rights of which the other bishops are deprived. Yet on the other hand, he seems implicitly to reject a primacy with real power and rights because he maintains that the only acceptable form of primacy in the ancient Church was simply a priority of witness and love, which would exclude a primacy of power and rights. His rejection of the term *primus inter pares* would then also be a criticism of the historical position of the patriarch, namely his rights and power, which he does not appear to accept. We have seen that from a historical and canonical point of view the primate possesses rights and power. We have also seen that primacy in the ancient Church contained a real power and authority, which consisted, for example, in the right and the power of the primates to ordain all the bishops and to approve their ordinations.[186]

While Afanassieff correctly asserts that primacy should not be understood in terms of universal ecclesiology, as a power over the other churches, nevertheless, the primate's power and rights are real from a canonical point of view, as Zizioulas says, and cannot simply be conceived only in terms of love and witnessing.

For Zizioulas, the distinction made by Afanassieff between primacy and priority remains an ambiguous one, and he asks himself: "Why should priority mean necessarily 'grace' and primacy 'legalism'?"[187] For Zizioulas, the power of the primate must be placed in the context of an ecclesiology of communion. In this sense it is not an absolute power since it is moderated and controlled by the other bishops. Neither should primacy be understood as a jurisdictional power over the Church. Thus, Zizioulas rejects a primacy that he maintains is understood as being *over* the Church, but an interesting feature of his distinctive approach to the issue of primacy is that there can be a primacy *within* the communion of the local churches, on all levels, regional and universal, and that this is much more than mere *priority*.

Alexander Schmemann and John Meyendorff. In this subsection we will review the points of convergence between Zizioulas and two other important Russian Orthodox theologians—namely Alexander Schmemann and John Meyendorff—with regard to the issue of primacy.

In his paper "Recent Discussions on Primacy in Orthodox Theology," Zizioulas indicates his agreement with the above Russian theologians on the issue of primacy. In fact, Zizioulas acknowledges that the paper, a brief survey of the discussion on primacy in the twentieth century, shows that Orthodox theology is ready to accept primacy at all levels of Church structure, including the universal one, as ecclesiologically justifiable.[188] He cites both Russian theologians in support of this point.

Zizioulas notes that Afanassieff's view about primacy does not seem to be fully shared by other émigré Russian theologians such as Florovsky, Meyendorff, and Schmemann. Zizioulas considers Schmemann—who does not adopt the term "priority" that was used by Afanassieff—as the most outspoken. He agrees with Schmemann in considering primacy as being of the

Church's *esse*. Zizioulas says in this respect:

> He [Schmemann] appeals to the Orthodox to free themselves from the "age-long anti-roman prejudice [that] led some Orthodox canonists simply to deny the existence of such [universal] primacy in the past or the need for it in the present." For him "an objective study of the canonical tradition cannot fail to establish beyond any doubt that, along with local 'centres of agreement' or primacies, the Church had also known a universal primacy." Primacy for Schmemann is of the Church's *esse* (contrast this with Karmiris and the other theologians who deny any *jure divino* character to primacy). "A local Church," he writes, "cut from the universal *koinonia* is indeed a *contradictio in adjecto*, for this *koinonia* is the very essence of the Church. And it has, therefore, its *form* and *expression*: primacy. Primacy is the necessary expression of the unity in faith and life of all local Churches, of their living and efficient *koinonia*." Schmemann has for this reason a critical view of certain Orthodox positions concerning autocephaly.[189]

Zizioulas goes on to cite these views:

> At a relatively recent date there arose among the Orthodox Churches the opinion that the Church is based in her life on the principle of autocephaly. . . . According to this opinion, the principle of autocephaly is not only one of the historical "expressions" by the Church of her universal structure, but precisely the ecclesiological foundation of the Church and her life. In other words, the unique universal organism of Roman ecclesiology is opposed here to autocephalous organisms, each one constituted by several dioceses. . . . All these "autocephalies" are absolutely equal among themselves, and this equality excludes any universal centre or primacy.[190]

It is clear from the above that for Schmemann the particular theory of autocephaly, which denies the existence of a universal primacy, is contrary to the canonical tradition of the Church. Thus, both Zizioulas and Schmemann believe that primacy, including universal primacy, is part of the Church's *esse* and an ecclesiological necessity for expressing unity and communion among the local churches—the unity of the Church.

Nevertheless, although Schmemann emphasizes the ecclesiological necessity of primacy in the church, he justifies this necessity of primacy by practical and utilitarian reasons—in terms of efficiency. Thus, in speaking of the primate, he says that the primate must speak for all because this very unity of the church requires in order to be *efficient* a special organ of expression, a mouth, a voice (i.e., the primate).[191] For Zizioulas such practical and utilitarian reasons are insufficient to make the existence of primacy necessary.[192]

Zizioulas, citing Meyendorff's view on the issue of primacy, points out that the latter's views are similar to those of Schmemann. Zizioulas quotes from Meyendorff's book *The Byzantine Legacy in the Orthodox Church*:

> The very *idea* of the primacy was very much a part of ecclesiology itself: the provisional Episcopal Synods needed a president, without whose sanction no decision was valid. Such is indeed an inevitable requirement of the very existence of the Church in the world. . . . It is a fact, however, that there has never been a time when the Church did not recognize a certain "order" among first the apostles, then the bishops, and that, in this order, one apostle, St. Peter, and later, one bishop, heading a particular church, occupied the place of a "primate." . . . I would venture to affirm here that the universal primacy of one Bishop . . . was not simply a historical accident, reflecting pragmatic requirements. . . . The function of the one bishop is to serve that unity on the world scale, just as the function of a regional primate is to be agent of unity on a regional scale.[193]

Zizioulas seems to agree with Meyendorff in regarding primacy, including universal primacy, as *ecclesiologically necessary* for serving the unity of the Church. However, as noted above, Zizioulas justifies the existence of the primate from a rigorous dogmatical point of view, namely from a trinitarian viewpoint, while both Meyendorff and Schmemann tend to justify primacy from a pragmatic, canonical, and ecclesiological point of view.

General Conclusions

We have examined the reactions of Greek Orthodox theologians of the nineteenth and twentieth centuries to papal primacy as defined at Vatican I and II. In considering the arguments invoked by official patriarchal letters and by certain Greek Orthodox theologians directly or indirectly against the teaching on the papal primacy expressed at the two councils, we have identified two distinct groups of theologians, and we saw that the critique offered by one group lacked coherence and authenticity, as was noted by the second group. As has been shown, the second group, in criticizing the first, actually provides a coherent and authentic understanding of the issue of primacy. Another important finding is that there was, in fact, a transition within Greek Orthodox ecclesiology in the period between the two councils from an inauthentic and unclear description of primacy in terms of honor or as *primus inter pares* to an authentic and coherent understanding and description of primacy based upon Orthodox canon law and unable to be described in terms of simple honor. It has finally been shown that, with the second group of theologians, represented principally by Metropolitan John Zizioulas, Greek Orthodox theology has moved in the direction of viewing primacy mainly from a dogmatic perspective.

The first group is represented by the letters issued by the Ecumenical Patriarchate after Vatican I, certain selected theologians and authors of that same period of time, like Grigorius Zigavinos, John Messoloras, Anastasios Kyriakos, and Spiridon Papageorgiou, as well as John Karmiris, a modern Greek Orthodox theologian of the twentieth century. The second group is represented primarily by John Zizioulas and by various Russian Orthodox theologians such as John Meyendorff, Alexander Schmemann, and Nicholas Afanassieff.

The arguments of the first group against papal primacy have been seen to be the focus of criticism by the second group. In other words, we have seen an Orthodox critique of the Orthodox arguments used by the first group of Orthodox theologians against papal primacy. Zizioulas also criticizes

Karmiris's more recent argumentation against the papal primacy, and because Karmiris follows the same line of argumentation as the Greek Orthodox theologians of the nineteenth century, Zizioulas's critique of Karmiris is implicitly directed against those theologians as well. In light of the above, I will briefly review the argumentation of the first group in the nineteenth century.

The Period after Vatican I—The Nineteenth Century

This particular time was characterized by polemics. Uniatism contributed to this polemical climate, since it has never been accepted by the Orthodox as a method of unity and was strongly condemned by the Orthodox Church of the time (cf. the Orthodox patriarchal letter of 1895). In such an atmosphere of polemics, Pope Leo XIII issued his encyclical letters, inviting the Orthodox churches to union with the Church of Rome on condition that the Orthodox accept the papal primacy of jurisdiction over the whole Church.

In our examination of the encyclical letters of Leo XIII, *Praeclara Gratulationis* and *Satis Cognitum*, together with the writings of some Roman Catholic authors from that period who wrote against the patriarchal letter, we saw that they all used a historical method in order to prove biblically and historically the papal primacy of jurisdiction. Thus, none of them go beyond what Vatican I taught on the issue. Since we do not have a direct and immediate official Greek Orthodox reaction to the definition of Vatican I on the papal primacy, Orthodox responses to the above papal encyclicals can be taken as an indirect reaction to Vatican I's teachings on papal primacy and to its universalistic and pyramidal view of the Church. As noted above, the Orthodox did not accept the papal invitation to Vatican I since they felt that to do so would imply their acceptance of the pope's primacy of jurisdiction.

What may be concluded from our study of the nineteenth century with regard to the main Roman Catholic arguments in favor of a papal primacy of jurisdiction and the principal Greek Orthodox arguments against it is reviewed briefly below.

(1) While the Roman Catholic Church maintained that an exclusive petrine primacy of jurisdiction over the whole Church could be proved from the Bible, as Vatican I taught, the Greek Orthodox, on the other hand, contended that it could not. Both sides engaged in polemics, trying to

prove that the petrine texts in the Bible did or did not imply a monarchical primacy of jurisdiction and power over the whole Church.

(2) The first group of Greek Orthodox theologians of the nineteenth century opposed to the above classical Roman teaching invoked the classical Orthodox argument that only Christ is the head of the Church and that the pope therefore cannot be considered as the visible head of the Church with a *jure divino* power over her, as taught by Vatican I. Mesoloras, among others, argued in this way. The patriarchal letter likewise taught that only Christ is the head of the Church and that the pope cannot be the infallible head of the Church. This argument was directed against a juridical and pyramidal view of the unity of the Church under the power of a visible head and universal center, i.e., the pope. Mesoloras, by reacting polemically against such a juridical conception of the Church, went to the other extreme, denying the existence of any visible center of the Church on the universal level. The unity of the churches was seen therefore in purely invisible and spiritual terms, namely, as a spiritual unity of independent churches in faith, in dogma, in love, in worship, etc., or as a unity understood in terms of a confederation of national autocephalous churches, but not as a unity under the pope, which would imply their submission to him. It was a model of unity opposed to the papal primacy of jurisdiction.

(3) In its argumentation against papal primacy, the patriarchal letter of the nineteenth century (1895) sided with the Western theory of conciliarism, which declares the supremacy of councils of bishops, rather than that of the pope.

(4) Further refuting the claim that the bishop of Rome has jurisdiction over the whole Church, certain Greek Orthodox theologians (e.g., Zigavinos) and the patriarchal letter of 1895 assigned to the bishop of Rome only an honorary primacy, as *primus inter pares*. Although Zigavinos seems to accept a primacy that implicitly involves power, he nevertheless adopts the term of "first among equals" in speaking of the universal primacy of the bishop of Rome.

(5) In another polemical reaction against the Roman Catholic claim to a *jure divino* justification of the Roman primacy of jurisdiction, some Greek Orthodox theologians and the patriarchal letter considered primacy in the Church, including the Roman primacy, to be *jure humano*.

The Critique of the Critique

As already noted, the second group of Orthodox theologians, represented principally by Zizioulas and several Russian Orthodox theologians, criticized the argumentation used by the first group. A summary of the main lines of the second group's critique, which highlights the inconsistencies and weaknesses of the first group's arguments, is given below.

(1) Meyendorff, the Russian Orthodox theologian, found that the arguments of the first group against a petrine primacy of jurisdiction were polemical and contradicted the traditional recognition of Peter's personal role acknowledged in the patristic tradition. Moreover, for Meyendorff, certain Orthodox ecclesiastical writers, even after the schism, maintained the patristic tradition and recognized Peter's personal function in the foundation of the Church but did not consider this recognition as implying the jurisdiction of the Roman bishop over the whole Church. For them the ministry of each bishop originates from the function and the ministry of Peter.

(2) Regarding another polemical argument against papal primacy of jurisdiction, namely that only Christ is the head of the Church, Afanassieff points implicitly to the logical incoherence and inconsistency of that argument since it accepts the existence of a visible head of the Church at some levels but not at the universal level.

(3) Some Greek Orthodox theologians, Mesoloras among them, in a polemical response to the monarchical unity of the Church under the pope, denied the very idea of a visible ecclesial center of the Church, somehow forgetting the obvious fact that the Church always had an ecumenical center in the person of a universal primate. Schmemann notes that the Church, from the first days of her existence, always had an ecumenical center of unity. He is, therefore, critical of an ecclesiology that renders a universal center unnecessary in the Church. Some of the Greeks (such as the Metropolitan of Stavroupolis, Constantine Tipaldos), however, did recognize from a canonical point of view a visible universal center in the Orthodox Church itself: there was a certain hierarchical order and structure of unity, with the patriarch of Constantinople being the first center of that unity.

Institutionally speaking, the unity of the Orthodox churches was also visibly expressed through synods. What some Greek Orthodox theologians failed to acknowledge, however, was the existence of a universal center and primacy in the universal Church and in their own Orthodox church that could express the oneness of the Church. Some others considered the Orthodox church as a confederation of local churches. For Zizioulas this view of confederation fails to recognize the institution that expresses the unity of the Church on the universal level.

(4) To claim that an ecumenical council is the highest authority in the Church, above pope and patriarch, is an argument that is both mistaken and incoherent. It contradicts the canonical fact that in the Orthodox Church a synod cannot function without a primate (cf. Thirty-Fourth Apostolic Canon). Zizioulas criticizes the first group of Greek Orthodox theologians for invoking such an argument against the papal primacy of jurisdiction. Moreover, the patriarchal encyclical letter issued in 1895, as well as some of the Greek Orthodox theologians of the nineteenth century, considered conciliarism as being in accord with the constitution of the ancient Church, a view that is by no means true. In fact, for Zizioulas, this argument implies that the synod can function without the primate. For Zizioulas, the primate and the synod coexist, without either one being above the other. Through a careful interpretation of the Thirty-Fourth Apostolic Canon, Zizioulas avoids having to place one above the other. Zizioulas also considers the axiom that an ecumenical council is the highest authority to be juridical and to present an institutionalist view of conciliarity.

(5) Zizioulas considers that the description of primacy in terms of simple honor or as *primus inter pares* excludes the right of the primate to exercise jurisdiction, whereas, canonically speaking, the primate does possess a real authority. By appealing to the canonical principles of the Orthodox Church and to the Thirty-Fourth Apostolic Canon, Zizioulas presents a coherent and authentic understanding of the nature of primacy in the Orthodox Church that is neither a primacy of jurisdiction nor a primacy of simple honor. For Zizioulas, canonical principles and the Thirty-Fourth Apostolic Canon in particular implicitly assign a real authority to the *primus,* but this authority is not absolute and monarchical since it is moderated by the other bishops; it is understood within an ecclesiology of communion.

(6) Zizioulas is also critical of the argument invoked by the first group that primacy is simply a matter of order and is justified *jure humano.* Such a view implies that primacy is not truly a matter of ecclesiology and therefore that the Church could exist without primacy. Zizioulas notes that this view rests upon a scholastic distinction between the human and the divine aspects of the Church such that whatever belongs to order in the Church is understood to exist *jure humano*. For Zizioulas this distinction is based on a curious ecclesiology and Christology. He does not accept such a distinction, arguing that there is in ecclesiology, as in Christology, an *antidosis idiomatum* between the divine and the human. In sharp contrast not only with most of the Greek Orthodox theologians of the nineteenth century but also with his contemporaries who consider the primacy as being simply *jure humano*, Zizioulas holds that primacy is *jure divino*, a matter of ecclesiology and a necessary element of the Church's *esse* and therefore a matter of dogma. As has been shown, Zizioulas bases his understanding of primacy upon dogmatic and ecclesiological principles, namely, upon the principle of "the one and the many," which stems from the life of the Trinity. We see, therefore, that with Zizioulas Greek Orthodox ecclesiology moves from a view of primacy as being *jure humano* to an understanding of it as being *jure divino*.

(7) By directly criticizing Vatican I's definition of papal primacy, Karmiris and other Greek Orthodox theologians of the twentieth century followed the same line of argument as their predecessors, which was criticized by Zizioulas and various Russian theologians of the twentieth century. Zizioulas also criticizes directly some of the main lines of Karmiris's argument and points out its weaknesses, along with those of the nineteenth-century theologians. Like his predecessors, Karmiris is of the opinion that primacy in the Church is a primacy of honor and that it exists *jure humano* and in no way *jure divino*, as the Roman Catholic Church asserts. He also criticizes the papal primacy of jurisdiction on the basis of the argument of Western conciliarism, which, as we have noted, makes primacy incompatible with conciliarity.

(8) In examining Zizioulas's criticism of Karmiris's arguments, we come to the following conclusions:

i.   Karmiris's ecclesiology presents an incoherent view of primacy in terms of simple honor that is in contradiction with the canonical principles of the Orthodox Church, and also in terms of conciliarism, which is likewise incoherent since it abolishes the role of the primate and fails to incorporate the primate into synodality, thus ignoring the canonical fact that a synod cannot function without a primate. While Karmiris allows the primate to preside over a council, he argues on the basis of conciliarism that an ecumenical council is the highest authority and thus above any primate. It must be emphasized here that the council is not above the pope or patriarch, nor is the pope or patriarch above the council. Trying to place one above the other is an unnecessary dilemma because the primate, be he pope or patriarch, is *within* the synod, not above or below it. In this context we recall that Zizioulas incorporates the ministry of the primate into conciliarity by drawing upon the Thirty-Fourth Apostolic Canon: the synod cannot function without the primate, nor can the primate function without the synod. They work together in common, as the Thirty-Fourth Apostolic Canon implies.

ii.   Karmiris's conception of primacy in terms of simple honor or of *primus inter pares* does not exist in the ancient Church or in the present Orthodox Church. Both these descriptions of primacy contradict canonical and historical facts that Karmiris himself nevertheless seems to accept implicitly, facts that prove that the primacy contains rights and power, duties and responsibilities. In contrast with Zizioulas, who asserts from a canonical point of view that a real power and rights are assigned to the primate, Karmiris is content to view the primacy simply in terms of honor, failing to see the incoherence of this view—that it is in contradiction with the canonical principles of the Orthodox Church and misleading if taken literally.

iii.   Karmiris sees no connection between primacy and ecclesiology and dogma since for him primacy is *jure humano* and not *jure divino*. Yet, to view the primacy from a purely human aspect would tend to make it unnecessary. As we have pointed out, primacy in the Church is necessary from a canonical point of view. Zizioulas justifies primacy from a dogmatic point of view upon the principle of "the one and the many," a principle that, for Zizioulas, stems from the Holy Trinity and is also reflected in the Thirty-Fourth Apostolic Canon, which contains a triadological doxology indicating that primacy is more than a purely human matter. Karmiris's ecclesiology excludes any theological or dogmatic justification of primacy. Zizioulas disagrees with Karmiris's view that only synods and bishops are justified *jure divino* and that primacy is not. He points to the weakness and incoherence of this position by noting that there has never been a synod or council without a primate. If synodality exists *jure divino*, then primacy also must exist *jure divino*. Zizioulas's eucharistic ecclesiology regards primacy from a strictly dogmatical viewpoint; he implies therefore that primacy is *jure divino* since it is grounded in the dogma of the Holy Trinity, namely upon the principle of "the one and the many" that shapes the life of the Church. It seems that Zizioulas is the first Greek Orthodox theologian to move the discussion of primacy from a purely human-pragmatic realm into a strictly dogmatic one.

iv. For Karmiris, councils, whether regional or ecumenical, are the center and the means of unity of the churches; through them the unity of the local churches in one body is expressed. He therefore does not believe, as Roman Catholics do, that the unity of the Church is a unity in one bishop but instead considers that it is manifested through the synods. In fact, Karmiris rejects a monarchical and juridical unity under the pope and instead proposes a unity manifested though the councils. However, as we have noted, Karmiris's view of the councils is not free from juridical conceptions. In taking this position, Karmiris fails to see the primate as also expressing the oneness of the Church on the regional and universal level. It is, of course, true that synods express the unity of the Church, and Zizioulas would agree with that position. However, Karmiris also maintains that the Orthodox Church is simply a confederation of local churches, while Zizioulas implies that this view fails to see the necessity of an institution—the primacy—that expresses the unity of the Orthodox Church on the universal level. As noted above, Zizioulas insists on the necessity of the institution of primacy, which expresses the oneness of the Church *within the synodical context*. As he states emphatically, the Church must speak with one voice, and the primate in this case is the spokesman of the whole Church.

Vatican II and the Greek Orthodox Theologians of the Twentieth Century

(1) In the twentieth century an enormous development took place in Roman Catholic ecclesiology. The ninety years between Vatican I and Vatican II are part of what has been called the century of the Church. Vatican I was a radical council that provoked an equally radical

reaction, either prolonging emphases on the themes that the council adopted or directing attention toward those it did not address.
Pope Leo XIII, aware of the partiality and ecclesiological deficiencies of Vatican I, directed the attention of Roman Catholics to the
interior and constitutive elements of the Church. Certain theological
movements before Vatican II, namely the patristic and the liturgical
movements, influenced the doctrinal definitions of Vatican II on the
Church, including those on primacy and collegiality. The patristic
movement contributed to the rise of a eucharistic ecclesiology, also
called an ecclesiology of communion, that influenced Vatican II's
teaching on the Church. Afanassieff's eucharistic ecclesiology contributed to the renewed patristic understanding of the Church, in
the light of which the local church also came into view. Afanassieff
was very influential in Vatican II's teaching on the link between the
Eucharist and the fullness and catholicity of the local church. In the
period between the councils, a theology of the local church was also
developing. By showing the transition from an earlier ecclesiology
of communion to a universalistic ecclesiology that took place in the
Middle Ages, Congar acted as a prophet, calling the future council to
make a historical transition back to an ecclesiology of communion
among the local churches. Meanwhile, the liturgical movement formulated the idea of episcopal collegiality, which was one of the most
fundamental teachings of *Lumen Gentium*, that had not had a chance
to be expressed at Vatican I partly because of the premature suspension of the council and partly because of then-prevailing views.

In the context of this renewed patristic understanding of the
Church as a communion of local churches, Vatican II formulated
its teaching on episcopal collegiality. Some Roman Catholic theologians, such as Pottmeyer, insist on approaching this teaching from
the context of an ecclesiology of communion of local churches. In
their view, it was in order to highlight the communal understanding of episcopal collegiality that the council placed the chapter on
the hierarchical structure of the Church in *Lumen Gentium* after and
within the context of the chapters on the Mystery of the Church and
the People of God.

(2) While Karmiris welcomes Vatican II's teaching on episcopal collegiality, he believes nevertheless that despite the endorsement of episcopal collegiality by Vatican II, the pope still has an absolute and monarchical authority over the Church and over the councils. It seems

to Karmiris that the papal institution emerged from Vatican II even stronger than it was after Vatican I. Karmiris is correct in asserting that the Dogmatic Constitution on the Church affirms the pope's independence and freedom of action. As noted above, *Lumen Gentium* and the Explanatory Note affirm the possibility of a supracollegial act of the pope and his complete freedom of action.

Karmiris complains that the ecumenical council is not above the pope, in the teaching of Vatican II, as was the case in the ancient Church and is still the case in the Orthodox Church. On the contrary, for Karmiris, the pope is above the ecumenical council, because he has the prerogative to convoke it, to direct it, and to confirm its decisions. Its decisions are valid if the pope convokes the council, directs its decisions, and freely approves them. As noted above, for the Roman Catholic Church, the pope's acceptance of a council as ecumenical is clearly an indispensable and indeed decisive criterion, whereas the Eastern Orthodox, on the other hand, have always been reluctant to isolate the pope from his brother bishops and from the whole body of the Church. It should be pointed out that in the case of reunion between the two Churches, the Orthodox Church would agree that the bishop of Rome, with the agreement of all the bishops, would convoke an ecumenical council and would preside over it. But the pope cannot act in isolation as the final arbiter of conciliar ecumenicity.

Karmiris's argument against Vatican II's teaching on papal primacy sides with Western conciliarism. This is a weakness in his argument, for conciliarism renders primacy incompatible with conciliarity. Also, Karmiris repeats the same arguments against papal primacy at Vatican II as he did against Vatican I's definition. Zizioulas, of course, criticizes this argument. Thus, within his critique of Vatican II, Karmiris argues that the Orthodox Church has always recognized the pope only as *primus inter pares honoris causa* and that this primacy is given by the synods and not *jure divino*—which implies that primacy is purely of human origin. Also, Karmiris argues that Christ, and not the pope, is the head of the Church, a previously invoked but still incoherent argument, as we have seen.

(3) Zizioulas considers that the Roman Catholic theory of episcopal collegiality is a universalistic one, in two ways: a) as leading to the idea of a universal head-bishop; and b) as an administrative board above the local churches. Zizioulas's view can be applied specifi-

cally to Vatican II's teaching on episcopal collegiality and, indeed, is confirmed by the fact that *LG* 22 presents both universalistic understandings. For Zizioulas, the understanding of episcopal collegiality as an episcopal structure standing above the local churches stems from a purely historical approach to apostolic continuity, the prime influence being Christology. In this view, as Zizioulas asserts, the Holy Spirit is transmitted by Christ and is the divine power that enables the apostles in their mission and animates a preconceived structure of the Church. Zizioulas believes that in Vatican II pneumatology is invoked once the structure of the Church is established with Christology.

We have seen that *LG* 19–20 has a historical approach to apostolic continuity, teaching that the apostles are sent by Christ as a college, transmitting authority to preach the Gospel and to administer and shepherd the Church. By analogy the bishops are understood as a college transmitting authority. *LG* 22 defines such a limited notion of episcopal collegiality: "The order of bishops is the successor to the college of the apostles in their role as teachers and pastors, and in it the apostolic college is perpetuated. Together with their head, the Supreme pontiff, and never apart from him, they have supreme and full authority over the universal Church." We have noted above that *LG* 19–20 deals with apostolic continuity from a historical point of view and that certain passages from *LG* 19 and 21 present a picture in which the Spirit enables the apostles and by analogy the bishops in their mission and in performing the functions given to them by Christ. What follows is a universalistic conception of episcopal collegiality, with the episcopal college being understood as an administrative body above the local churches, with an authority over the whole Church, as *LG* 22 teaches.

Zizioulas believes that the eschatological model of apostolic continuity, which is liturgical in context, requires the community of the Church in order to function. It is a succession of communities and not of individuals. In such a case, the bishop, surrounded by the college of the presbyters in the midst of his faithful, is an icon of Christ surrounded by the apostles. For Zizioulas, a synthesis between an eschatological view of apostolic continuity and a historical one implies a communal understanding of apostolic succession that is not limited to the episcopal college but includes the bishops with their local communities. There is in the Constitution on the Church a historical approach to apostolic continuity; however, *LG* 21 and *SC* 41 adopt a Christ-centered image of the bishop, which could be taken as a starting point for a synthesis between the eschatological view of apostolic continuity and the historical view, a synthesis which for Zizioulas would have implications for episcopal collegiality, as it would move toward an understanding of episcopal collegiality within the context of communion ecclesiology.

Although *LG* 22 presents a universalistic conception of episcopal collegiality, at the same time the Constitution also approaches episcopal collegiality from the perspective of an ecclesiology of communion of local churches: *LG* 23 and 26 both place the notion of episcopal collegiality in the perspective of a eucharistic ecclesiology of communion as a communion of local churches—all fully catholic in themselves.

John Zizioulas: A Unique Theology of Primacy

(1) Zizioulas distinguishes two methods of approaching the issue of primacy in general—one historical and the other theological. Zizioulas considers that the historical method, which has been used extensively in the past, has not been fruitful. For example, Orthodox and Roman Catholics disagree with regard to Peter's position in the New Testament. Zizioulas himself doubts that there is a link between the petrine and the papal primacy. Thus, history cannot be the ground for a rapprochement between Roman Catholics and Orthodox with regard to primacy. For one, there is the disagreement on Peter's position in the New Testament. For another, as we have seen, nineteenth-century Roman Catholics appealed to the history of the ancient Church and to the Fathers to find incontrovertible evidence in favor of papal primacy, whereas the Orthodox considered such evidence as refuting the idea of a papal primacy of jurisdiction over the whole Church.

Zizioulas, however, cannot be accused of ignoring history and making it antithetical to theology. He prefers rather to establish the theological and ecclesiological basis upon which the whole issue of primacy, including universal primacy, can be grounded, namely an ecclesiology of communion, experienced historically by both East and West. Within the context of the dialogue between the Orthodox and the Roman Catholic churches, Zizioulas offers a way of breaking the impasse caused by reliance on the historical method.

(2) For Zizioulas, the fundamental ecclesiological principle lying at the heart of a eucharistic ecclesiology of communion is that of "the one

and the many," which flows from a correct synthesis between Christology and pneumatology. We have seen that this fundamental principle in Zizioulas's ecclesiology leads institutionally speaking to a ministry of primacy that expresses the unity of the Church on the universal level of the communion of local churches (the aspect of "the many").

(3) Zizioulas associates this eucharistic ecclesiology of communion, which includes an institution of unity, with the Cappadocians' understanding of the Holy Trinity. Specifically, Zizioulas states that as there is in the Holy Trinity a hierarchical order, i.e., the Father is the first—the cause—"the one" in the Holy Trinity, so by analogy there exists a hierarchical ordering in the local churches, with a local church and its local bishop expressing the unity of the other local churches. Thus, the ministry of the primate is a reflection of the life of the Holy Trinity, for as we have seen, in commenting from a theological point of view on the Thirty-Fourth Apostolic Canon, Zizioulas states that the communal life of the Holy Trinity has a unity in the person of the Father. In other words the fundamental principle of "the one and the many" applies here. Thus we may conclude that for Zizioulas the trinitarian life, which is structured in the form of "the one and the many," is analogously reflected in ecclesiology. In sharp contrast with Karmiris and other Greek Orthodox theologians, Zizioulas makes primacy a matter of dogma—a matter of faith—and not simply a matter of *jus humanum* and of mere organization. Zizioulas's thought goes beyond pragmatic and historical realities, which obviously played a significant role in the emergence and establishment of primacies in the Church, and bases primacy on dogma and faith, making it thus a necessary thing for the Church's *esse*. The canonical provisions that necessitate the presence and existence of primates in the Church (cf. Thirty-Fourth Apostolic Canon) are therefore related to dogmatic and ecclesiological principles and to the faith of the Church.

(4) The Thirty-Fourth Apostolic Canon is for Zizioulas an application of the principle of "the one and the many" at the regional level. We have seen how Zizioulas moved toward recognizing the need for local churches throughout the world to be configured as "the one and the many," thus applying this principle also on the universal level.

(5) In discussing the role and the ministry of the primate, Zizioulas states that the ministry of unity—the "one"—should be placed in

the context of an ecclesiology of communion, which is shaped by a pneumatologically conditioned Christology, allowing the one to be simultaneously many, as the Thirty-Fourth Apostolic Canon implies. By taking this canon as an example, Zizioulas shows how the primate looks within such an ecclesiology of communion. The reciprocity that exists in the Thirty-Fourth Apostolic Canon implies that the ministry of the primate reaches the entire community through the communion of the local churches, manifested through the bishops that constitute the council. In other words, "the one" expresses the communion of the local churches through the institution of the synod.

(6) Although the unity of the Church is expressed through the synodical institution, the oneness of the Church at the regional and the universal levels is manifested through the primate, the ministry of "the one." In this case, the primate is the voice and spokesman of the Church, which speaks with one voice. Zizioulas believes that the existence of the primate is based on dogma and is dogmatically necessary in the Church. For the Orthodox, Zizioulas believes that a canonical structure of pan-Orthodox unity through a primate, in this case the patriarch of Constantinople, is proving even more necessary today than in the past. He urges the Orthodox to make more visible the unity of their own Church at the universal level. We have seen that in the past this unity has been obscured both by nationalistic tendencies, still prevailing today, and by the polemical reactions of the Orthodox to papal primacy.

(7) Afanassieff excludes the idea of a universal primate as head, who visibly and empirically manifests the unity of the Church. For him, this is part and parcel of universal ecclesiology, whereas in his eucharistic ecclesiology there is no place for a primate—"the one"—who would express the unity of the Church on the universal level. For Afanassieff, the unity of the local churches worldwide is to be described as one of utter sameness. For Zizioulas, on the other hand, this unity is configured as "the one and the many," which necessarily implies an institution of unity, "the one," who expresses and manifests the unity of the Church on the universal level.

Afanassieff implies that the right of the patriarch of Constantinople to convoke a pan-Orthodox or ecumenical council would automatically constitute a manifestation of his universal primacy in the Orthodox Church, again a characteristic of universalistic ecclesiology. Afanassieff's assertion that the patriarch of Constantinople has not convoked an ecumenical or a pan-Orthodox council since the ninth century is in fact not historically true, since the Ecumenical Patriarch has convoked pan-Orthodox councils at various times in the second millennium. Zizioulas, on the other hand, recognizes the right of the patriarch of Constantinople to convoke a pan-Orthodox council.

Afanassieff accepts the existence of primacy within each autocephalous Church, but not a universal primacy. In principle, he is not happy with the term "primacy" at all, whether universal or regional, because for him primacy is a universalistic term. He does recognize the canonical right of the regional primate to convoke a council and considers the term *primus inter pares* as misleading since there is no equality of a primate in relation to the other bishops. The primate has special rights of which the other bishops are deprived. On the other hand, he does not come to terms with a primacy implying real power and rights because, as we have seen, he maintains that the only acceptable form of primacy in the ancient Church was a priority of witness and love, thus excluding such power or special rights. It seems therefore that when Afanassieff rejects the term *"primus inter pares,"* saying that it does not do justice to the historical position of the patriarch among the bishops, he is implicitly criticizing his rights and power because in principle he does not accept such a form of primacy.

For Zizioulas, the power and rights of the primate are real from a canonical point of view, and the primacy cannot be conceived only in terms of love and witnessing. The authority of the primate must be placed in the context of an ecclesiology of communion. In that case, such authority is not absolute since it is moderated and controlled by the other bishops. We may conclude that for Zizioulas primacy is not considered to imply a jurisdictional power *over* the Church; instead, supported by the canons, he maintains that there is a primacy *within* the communion of the local churches, on all levels, regional and universal, and that this view of primacy means much more than mere *priority* in terms of love and witnessing.

(8) Zizioulas agrees with Schmemann in considering the primacy as an ecclesiological necessity to express and manifest the unity of the Church at the regional and universal levels. Zizioulas also appears to agree with Meyendorff in regarding primacy, including universal primacy, as ecclesiologically necessary to serve the unity of the Church. Where they differ is in their approach: both Schmemann and Meyendorff tend to justify primacy from an ecclesiological and

canonical point of view, whereas Zizioulas justifies and necessitates the existence of primacy in the Church from a rigorously dogmatic point of view, namely through Triadology—the "one and the many" in the life of the Trinity—which is reflected in the life of the Church.

Zizioulas seems to be the only Greek Orthodox theologian who views the issue of primacy from a dogmatic point of view. In fact, he has made an important contribution to Greek Orthodox ecclesiology by facilitating the transition from a problematic view of primacy in terms of simple honor or of *primus inter pares* to a coherent view of primacy that contains a real power and to an understanding of primacy as being *jure divino* rather than *jure humano*. The arguments of the first group of theologians have been successfully countered and corrected by those of the second group, represented principally by Zizioulas, who provides us with a sound view of primacy, grounded in the context of an ecclesiology of communion.

Overall, then, we have seen that the reaction of many Greek Orthodox theologians against the definition of papal primacy at Vatican I manifested a true Orthodox instinct but was actually expressed in a rather incoherent and inauthentic way. The inadequacies of the arguments of these theologians belonging to the first group have been identified and criticized by the theologians of the second group, with the result that the Orthodox critique of the teaching both of Vatican I and of Vatican II on this topic has been progressively refined, and a coherent and authentic Orthodox account of primacy in the Church has gradually taken shape.

Notes

All English translations of Vatican II documents are taken from A. Flannery, ed., *Vatican Council II: The Conciliar and Post Conciliar Documents*, revised edition. Dublin: Costello Publishing, 1988.

Abbreviations

CD: *Christus Dominus*, Vatican II, Decree on the Pastoral Office of Bishops in the Church
LG: *Lumen Gentium*, Vatican II, Dogmatic Constitution on the Church
SC: *Sacrosanctum Concilium*, Vatican II, Constitution on the Sacred Liturgy
PG: *Patrologia Graeca*

Introduction

1. See Clement, *You Are Peter*, 87.
2. Ibid., 69–70.
3. For the background to the theological dialogue between the two churches, see Fortino, "Theological Dialogue," 15–36; for further background and for the texts produced by the dialogue, see *Documents of the Joint International Commission*. Mgr. Fortino, the Roman Catholic co-secretary of the theological dialogue, says that Vatican II and the Pan-Orthodox Conferences opened the way for the dialogue between the two churches ("Background to the Theological Dialogue between the Catholic Church and the Orthodox Church" in *Documents of the Joint International Commission*, 2–3).
4. See the communiqué of the tenth meeting of the Joint International Commission for the Theological Dialogue between the Orthodox Church and the Roman Catholic Church on the website of the Ecumenical Patriarchate: www.patriarchate.org.
5. See Kasper, *Petrine Ministry*, 11.

6. For the papers read at this symposium and a summary of the discussion that followed, see ibid.

7. Pottmeyer, *Towards a Papacy*, 118.

8. Translation from Ratzinger, "Il Concetto della Chiesa nel Pensiero Patristico," in *I Grandi Temi del Concilio* (Rome: Paoline, 1965), 154–55.

9. See chapter 4.

10. Kasper, *Theology and the Church*, 157.

11. Kasper, *Petrine Ministry*, 17.

12. Pottmeyer, *Towards a Papacy*, 130.

13. Tillard, *Bishop of Rome*, 160.

14. Ibid., 160–61; see also David Pietropaoli, *Visible Ecclesial Communion*, 286. In this book Pietropaoli compares views of certain Orthodox and Roman Catholic theologians, like Congar, Tillard, Meyendorff, and Zizioulas, on authority primacy and conciliarity in the light of published documents of the Roman Catholic–Orthodox dialogue.

15. McPartlan, "Local Church," 26.

16. Ibid., 27n13.

17. See Volf, *After Our Likeness*, 67–72.

18. McPartlan, "Local Church," 27.

19. http://www.pcf.va/roman_curia/pontifical_councils/chrstuni/ch_orthodox_docs/rc_pc_chrstuni_doc_20071013_documento-ravenna_en.html

20. See chapter 4; "Primacy in the Church," 122.

21. Bermejo, *Church, Conciliarity*, 9–12.

22. Ibid., 12.

23. Kasper, *Petrine Ministry*, 229.

24. De Ville, *Orthodoxy and the Roman Papacy*.

25. Ibid., 17–46.

26. Ibid., 117–59.

27. Ibid., 14.

28. Ibid., 150–55.

29. Ibid., 157.

30. See chapter 4.

31. De Ville, *Orthodoxy and the Roman Papacy*, 158.

32. Mavrichi, "Rev. Dr. Dumitru Staniloae," 6.

33. We will see that certain Greek Orthodox theologians, like John Karmiris, consider the ecumenical council as the highest authority in the Church.

34. For a further discussion on the debate of eucharistic ecclesiology within the Orthodox Church, see, for example, Papanikolaou, "Integrating the Ascetical"; Mavrichi, "Rev. Dr. Dumitru Staniloae"; Berger, "Does the Eucharist?"; Ware, "*Sobornost*"; Bordeianu, "Orthodox-Catholic Dialogue."

35. Papanikolaou, "Integrating the Ascetical," 173.

36. Zizioulas, "Ἡ Εὐχαριστιακή Ἐκκλησιολογία στήν Ὀρθόδοξη Παράδοση," 8. This is a Greek translation of the article "Eucharistic Ecclesiology."

37. See Zizioulas's collective volume of articles *Εὐχαριστίας Ἐξεμπλάριον* [*Manifestation of Gratitude*], 38–39.

38. For Zizioulas's criticism of Afanassieff's ecclesiology, see *Eucharist, Bishop, Church* and "Η Εὐχαριστιακή Ἐκκλησιολογία," 5–7.

39. See below.

40. See Zizioulas, "Eucharistic Ecclesiology." I totally agree with Metropolitan Kallistos Ware's opinion that Zizioulas gives to his ecclesiology a firm patristic basis (Ware, "*Sobornost*," 225).

41. *Εὐχαριστίας Ἐξεμπλάριον*, 43.

42. See Papanikolaou, "Integrating the Ascetical," 179–82.

43. Ibid., 180.

44. See Zizioulas, "Father as Cause"; cf. below, n640.

45. Ware, "*Sobornost*," 231.

46. See chapter 4. Metropolitan Kallistos ignores the fact that Zizioulas makes significant modifications in H. Wheeler Robinson's presentation of corporate personality, as Paul McPartlan showed in his book *Eucharist Makes the Church*, 170–80.

47. See Berger, "Does the Eucharist?" 50–57.

48. Ibid., 46, 68.

49. See Zizioulas, *Εὐχαριστίας Ἐξεμπλάριον*, 89–106, where he appeals to biblical, liturgical, and patristic testimonies on the unbreakable relationship of baptism to the eucharist.

50. For Stăniloae, see Bordeianu, "Orthodox-Catholic Dialogue," 253. While Bordeianu acknowledges that Zizioulas began the exploration of the issue of primacy, on the other hand he makes some criticisms of Zizioulas's eucharistic ecclesiology which are relevant to our study. His first critical point, namely that Zizioulas overemphasizes the hierarchical character of the Church, is rather vague (*Dumitru Staniloae*, 209–10). For Zizioulas, communion ecclesiology applies not only to the bishops, but equally to the faithful. Zizioulas's eucharistic understanding of the Church leads him to believe that the laypeople are essential to the constitution of the Church and can express their opinion on every ecclesiastical matter, trusting the bishops, who are accountable to God, with the final responsibility. Also, Zizioulas claims that baptized laypeople may take part in Church administration (*Εὐχαριστίας Ἐξεμπλάριον*, 48–49).

Bordeianu's critical claim that Zizioulas repeatedly gives priority to the "many," to "persons," and to the "local," and that this brings Zizioulas closer to Afanassieff than Zizioulas would probably want to be (ibid., 199), is not convincing in my estimation. In criticizing Zizioulas on this particular point, Bordeianu omits to say that Zizioulas roots the ecclesiological principle of the "one" and the many in the life of the Holy Trinity. For Zizioulas, the divine essence is simultaneous with the Trinitarian existence of God initiated by the Father (*Communion and Otherness*, 140). This shows how fundamental the one is to the many. In an analogous way there is a simultaneity of the local Churches and the universal Church.

Because of external factors such as persecution, Bordeianu questions the absoluteness of the principle that the Eucharist makes the Church, and he asks if the fullness of the Church might be accomplished other than directly in the Liturgy (*Dumitru Staniloae*, 101). In such abnormal circumstances, it seems to me that we can only entrust to God those Christians who are not able to participate in the Holy Eucharist.

Finally, Bordeianu asserts that if eucharistic communion between the Orthodox and Roman Catholic Churches is quite distant there may be a possibility of communion in other sacraments (*Dumitru Staniloae*, 213–14). I think it would be good to acknowledge some merit in Bordeianu's desire to acknowledge some degree of communion among separated Christians, even though the lack of a shared Eucharist is a massive problem.

51. See Berger, "Does the Eucharist?"; also see Papanikolaou, "Integrating the Ascetical," 181.

52. Papanikolaou, "Integrating the Ascetical," 181.

53. See Zizioulas, Εὐχαριστίας Ἐξεμπλάριον, 53, 58–59.

54. Ibid., 139–40. In order to further support his view, Zizioulas refers to the fact that in the ancient Church all the mysteries were performed within the eucharist (ibid., 140).

55. Ware, "*Sobornost*," 231. Metropolitan Ware refers to certain criticisms of Zizioulas's eucharistic ecclesiology. However, in light of the restricted focus of this book, the critique by Ware, as well as that by Berger in his above-mentioned article, will not be developed here.

56. Zizioulas, "Ortodossia," 2. Zizioulas comments that this principle is "an authentically Orthodox theological principle."

1—Vatican I

1. See Butler, *Vatican Council*, 11.

2. Pottmeyer, *Towards a Papacy*, 37.

3. Ibid., 38. The Council of Trent issued an important decree that strengthened the authority of the bishops in their own sees. But, as Hubert Jedin points out, this authority was given to them "in their quality as delegates of the Holy See" (quoted by Terence L. Nichols, *That All May Be One*, 205).

4. Cf. Schatz, *Papal Primacy*, 130–33.

5. The close relationship among conciliarism and Gallicanism and German episcopalism is indicated in Schatz, ibid., 135–38, 139–40, and Pottmeyer, *Towards a Papacy*, 39.

6. Schatz, *Papal Primacy*, 139.

7. Ibid., 142.

8. Ibid., 140.

9. Pottmeyer, *Towards a Papacy*, 40. The very first of the four "Gallican articles" denied the temporal power of the Pope and insisted on the independence of secular authority (cf. Schatz, *Papal Primacy*, 137). Schatz speaks on the same lines

concerning Gallicanism: "To begin with it [i.e., Gallicanism] was the form in which conciliarism lived on in combination with the politico-ecclesial definition of the French monarchy" (*Papal Primacy*, 135).

10. Pottmeyer, *Towards a Papacy*, 44.

11. Schatz, *Papal Primacy*, 144–45.

12. Ibid.

13. Pottmeyer, *Towards a Papacy*, 43–44.

14. Ibid., 45–46.

15. Butler, *Vatican Council*, 54.

16. For the movement of Ultramontanism, see Butler, *Vatican Council*, 44–62; Terence Nichols, *That All May Be One*, 221–26; Schatz, *Papal Primacy*, 147–55; and Tillard, *Bishop Of Rome*, 18–25. Nichols points out that in part the Ultramontane ecclesiology was politically motivated. At least in France, Ultramontanism had a practical and political character in comparison with Ultramontanism in England, which was more theological in character (Terence Nichols, *That All May Be One*, 224; Butler, *Vatican Council*, 56–57).

17. Schatz is of the opinion that one can understand Ultramontanism in the nineteenth century if one realizes that it started from the periphery (*Papal Primacy*, 151). In 1856 the French historian Alexis de Tocqueville wrote that "the Pope is driven more by the faithful to become absolute ruler of the Church than they are impelled by him to submit to his rule" (*Papal Primacy*, 151).

18. Pottmeyer, *Towards a Papacy*, 47; see Congar, *L'Eglise de Saint Augustin*, 424–25.

19. Pottmeyer, *Towards a Papacy*, 43.

20. Ibid., 42.

21. Mauro Cappellari, *Il trionfo della Sancta Sede e della Chiese contro gli assalti de' novatori reprinti e combattuti colle stesse armi* (Roma, 1799).

22. P. Tamburini, *Vera idea de la Santa Sede* (Pavia, 1784).

23. Pottmeyer, *Towards a Papacy*, 51.

24. Ibid., 51–52; Schatz, *Papal Primacy*, 142.

25. Pottmeyer, *Towards a Papacy*, 52.

26. Ibid., 53

27. Ibid., 54.

28. Ibid., 52.

29. Ibid., 52.

30. Ibid., 54–55

31. Ibid., 51.

32. Ibid., 43–44, 53. Nevertheless, this undifferentiated and authoritarian notion of the primacy laid itself open to the criticism of many bishops and theologians, even within the Ultramontane movement in the nineteenth century (ibid., 55).

33. For de Maistre and Lamennais, see Terence Nichols, *That All May Be One*, 222–24; Schatz, *Papal Primacy*, 148–50; Pottmeyer, *Towards a Papacy*, 53–54; Congar, *L'Eglise de Saint Augustin*, 414–15. Lamennais's ideas about the freedom of the Church

from national control, separation of Church and state, freedom of the press, freedom of education, freedom of conscience, and religion, equal rights, universal suffrage, and democracy were condemned by Gregory XVI's encyclical *Mirari Vos* (1832). The more Gregory XVI and Pius IX turned in an antiliberal direction, the more Lamennais became an opponent of the Church, for he considered that the Church's freedom could be secured only within a society based on freedom (Terence Nichols, *That All May Be One*, 223; Pottmeyer, *Towards a Papacy*, 54). Maistre's book *Du Pape* was weak in its analysis of history and scripture, and its theological treatment of papal authority has no ground, either in the episcopal college, or in the *ius divinum*. For this reason it was received coolly in Rome (Terence Nichols, *That All May Be One*, 222).

34. Congar, *L'Eglise de Saint Augustin*, 416.

35. Ibid.

36. Butler, *Vatican Council*, 98–99; Pottmeyer, *Towards a Papacy*, 56. However, Maret declared his adherence after the council to its decrees and withdrew the book from circulation (Butler, *Vatican Council*, 99).

37. Pottmeyer, *Towards a Papacy*, 56.

38. Maret, *Du concile général*, 437: "Il faut remarqer, en troisième lieu, que l'unité collective de Pierre et des autres Apôtres forme le tribunal suprême de l'Eglise. Remarquons encore que c'est *l'Eglise*, ou l'unité collective de Pierre et des autres Apôtres, *qui est la colonne et le soutien de la vérité*."

39. Maret, *Du concile général*, 336–38, 341.

40. Tanner, *Decrees*, 2: 814–15; cf. Dewan, "Vatican Council's Schema," 42, 56.

41. Terence Nichols, *That All May Be One*, 222; Pottmeyer, *Towards a Papacy*, 54.

42. Terence Nichols, *That All May Be One*, 224; Tillard, *Bishop of Rome*, 19, and Schatz, *Papal Primacy*, 153.

43. Tillard, *Bishop of Rome*, 20.

44. Thomas Aquinas also had no doctrine of episcopal collegiality (Congar, *L'Eglise de Saint Augustin*, 237). Episcopal-jurisdictional authority derives from the pope, who is the head of the Church on earth. According to Aquinas, institutional unity in the Church derives from submission to the pope, so that every schism is caused by separation from the pope, not from Christ (Terence Nichols, *That All May Be One*, 162–63, and Congar, *L'Eglise du Saint Augustin*, 237).

45. Bellarmine held that the pope as head of the Church represented Christ in relation to the Church, and only the pope held the fullness of power. The bishops held a fullness of power over their dioceses, which, after all, derived from the pope. Accordingly, he laid down that the pope is above the Ecumenical Councils (Congar, *L'Eglise de Saint Augustin*, 373–74; Terence Nichols, *That All May Be One*, 208–9, and Butler, *Vatican Council*, 40–41).

46. Terence Nichols, *That All May Be One*, 224–25.

47. Pottmeyer, *Towards a Papacy*, 55.

48. Ibid., 47–48.

49. For an excellent treatment of this period, see Chadwick, *A History of the Popes*. With the issuing of the dogmatic constitution on the Catholic Faith, *Dei Fi-*

lius, which opposed the modern "errors," this defensive stance found its chief expression.

50. Pottmeyer, *Towards a Papacy*, 47–50.

51. Dewan, "Vatican Council's Schema," 25.

52. Quoted from Dewan, "Vatican Council's Schema," 25–26. As we shall see, this was a statement that was endorsed by Vatican I and repeated.

53. Dewan, "Vatican Council's Schema," 28–31; Butler, *Vatican Council*, 64–65. For the bishops' opinion on the current errors that the council should address, see Butler, *Vatican Council*, 65. Some of the bishops, like F. Doupanloup of Orleans, did not consider it possible to hold a council in the existing disturbed state of the world. But the majority was favorable (Butler, *Vatican Council*, 64).

54. Dewan, "Vatican Council's Schema," 31.

55. Ibid.

56. Ibid.; Butler, *Vatican Council*, 193–95.

57. Dewan, "Vatican Council's Schema," 43; McPartlan, "Vatican I," 737; Thils, *Primauté Pontificale*, 86, 108. For the original draft, see Martin, *Omnium Concilii*, 32–54; Mansi, *Sacrorum Conciliorum*, 53: 308–17.

58. Dewan, "Vatican Council's Schema," 31–37.

59. Ibid., 37. Dewan gives a brief account of their positions on the Roman Primacy, 31–36.

60. Ibid., 37–38.

61. Ibid., 40.

62. Ibid., 40–41. For the text of the schema, see ibid., 43–46.

63. See the text in ibid., 44–45.

64. Ibid., 48.

65. Eybel's pamphlet *Was ist der Papst?* was a critique of the historical development of the papacy (Congar, *L'Eglise du Saint Augustin*, 408).

66. Cited in Dewan, "Vatican Council's Schema," 48.

67. Ibid., 48–49. Though, for Pottmeyer, in the preparatory commission that composed the draft text on the Church, the Ultramontanist idea of an absolute papacy prevailed, there was a determination not to deny or to weaken the rights of the bishops (*Towards a Papacy*, 62).

68. See the text in Dewan, "Vatican Council's Schema," 45.

69. Ibid., 49.

70. The text of the draft states categorically that "we reject the opinions of those who, straying from the faith and heeding the spirit of error, deny that Christ the Lord instituted the primacy in Peter . . . or who also maintain that it is licit to appeal from a General Council, as to an authority superior to the Roman Pontiff" (Dewan, "Vatican Council's Schema," 46).

71. Pottmeyer, *Towards a Papacy*, 62; cf. Butler, *Vatican Council*, 330.

72. Pottmeyer, *Towards a Papacy*, 63; cf. George Dejaifve, "Primauté et collegialité," 642–47; Butler, *Vatican Council*, 332–34. In this context Butler's statement is significant: "It is of first importance for the understanding of the attitude of the

Minority to make it clear beyond possibility of doubt that there was no disposition on their part to question or to minimize the nature and the extent of the jurisdiction and powers inherent to Primacy." Nevertheless, the minority were critical of the fact that the bishops' rights were passed over in complete silence and that the ordinary, immediate, and episcopal jurisdiction of the pope would interfere with the bishop's immediate and ordinary jurisdiction over his diocese (*Vatican Council*, 333–34).

73. Pottmeyer, *Towards a Papacy*, 63; Dejaifve, "Primauté et collégialité," 643, 644–45.

74. Küng, *Structures of the Church*, 212; Mansi, *Sacrorum Conciliorum*, 52: 1109–10; Pottmeyer, *Towards a Papacy*, 67; Butler, *Vatican Council*, 405.

75. Butler, *Vatican Council*, 478.

76. Thils, *Primauté Pontificale*, 88–89; Pottmeyer, *Towards a Papacy*, 63.

77. Thils, *Primauté Pontificale*, 88–89.

78. Butler, *Vatican Council*, 334.

79. Pottmeyer, *Towards a Papacy*, 64–65.

80. Mansi, *Sacrorum Conciliorum*, 52: 1105; Küng, *Structures of the Church*, 213; Pottmeyer, *Towards a Papacy*, 66; Thils, "Potestas Ordinaria," 699–700.

81. Cited in Küng, *Structures of the Church*, 213; Mansi, *Sacrorum Conciliorum*, 52: 1105.

82. Cf. Küng, *Structures of the Church*, 211.

83. Pottmeyer, *Towards a Papacy*, 66; Küng, *Structures of the Church*, 211.

84. Cited in Pottmeyer, *Towards a Papacy*, 66; Mansi, *Sacrorum Conciliorum*, 52: 1115.

85. Küng, *Structures of the Church*, 211; Dewan, "Potestas vere episcopalis," 683–84.

86. Küng, *Structures of the Church*, 214.

87. Pottmeyer, *Towards a Papacy*, 66.

88. Tillard, *Bishop of Rome*, 28; Küng, *Structures of the Church*, 206–22.

89. Pottmeyer, *Towards a Papacy*, 65; Mansi, *Sacrorum Conciliorum*, 52: 311, 592, 682.

90. Tanner, *Decrees*, 814.

91. Tillard, *Bishop of Rome*, 28.

92. Pottmeyer, *Towards a Papacy*, 67. The Bishop of Grosswardein in Hungary of the Greco-Romanian rite, Mgr. Joseph, and the Bishop of Gap, Mgr. Aimé, made the two requests. The first believed that an omission of episcopal collegiality would shut the door on the Eastern Churches separated from Rome (see Hamer, *Church Is a Communion*, 220; Mansi, *Sacrorum Conciliorum*, 52: 601–5, 620).

93. Mansi, *Sacrorum Conciliorum* 52: 1109–10; Hamer, *Church Is a Communion*, 222–23.

94. Küng, *Structures of the Church*, 222–23.

95. Hamer, *Church Is a Communion*, 224; for the text, see in Mansi, *Sacrorum Conciliorum*, 53: 308–17.

96. The original text is given with an English translation in Tanner, *Decrees*,

813–16.

97. Tanner, *Decrees*, 811–12.

98. Ibid., 813.

99. Quoted in Bermejo, *Toward Christian Reunion*, 98; cf. Mansi, *Sacrorum Conciliorum*, 52: 714D–715A.

100. Bermejo, *Toward Christian Reunion*, 99; Mansi, *Sacrorum Conciliorum*, 52: 715B–C.

101. Bermejo, *Toward Christian Reunion*, 103. D'Avanzo considers Mt. 18:18, quoted by Cardinal Schwarzenberg as a counterbalance to Mt. 16:18f, as a clear confirmation of the apostles' total and absolute dependence on Peter (cf. Bermejo, *Toward Christian Reunion*, 99n14; Mansi, *Sacrorum Conciliorum*, 52: 717B). D'Avanzo seems to have been obsessed with the idea of this dependence. He claimed that such a complete dependence is found in Mt. 16:18; Lk. 22:32; and Jn. 21:15–19 (Bermejo, *Toward Christian Reunion*, 99n14).

102. Bermejo, *Toward Christian Reunion*, 105.

103. Ibid.

104. Ibid., 106.

105. Ibid.

106. Ibid.

107. Tanner, *Decrees*, 813.

108. Ibid.

109. Bermejo, *Toward Christian Reunion*, 100. Schatz mentions a number of problems surrounding the text of Irenaeus (*Papal Primacy*, 9–10).

110. Bermejo, *Toward Christian Reunion*, 100. Wessel in her book *Leo the Great* treats Leo's understanding of Peter's continual presence in his successors with admirable detail.

111. Ibid., 106–7.

112. Tanner, *Decrees*, 813.

113. Bermejo, *Toward Christian Reunion*, 107.

114. Ibid., 108.

115. Ibid.

116. Ibid., 108n40.

117. Ibid., 107–22.

118. Ibid., 108n40.

119. Ibid., 118–19.

120. Ibid., 108n40.

121. Ibid.

122. Cf. Meyendorff, *Orthodoxy and Catholicity*, 55; Bermejo, *Toward Christian Reunion*, 110.

123. Bermejo, *Toward Christian Reunion*, 117.

124. Tanner, *Decrees*, 815.

125. Pottmeyer, *Towards a Papacy*, 69, 73.

126. Aubert, *Le Saint Siège*, 31; O'Donnell, *Ecclesia*, 259: "He was apparently

the first pope to speak of separated brothers."

127. Encyclical Letter, *Praeclara Gratulationis*, in Leo, *Great Encyclical Letters*, 303–19.

128. Aubert, *Le Saint Siège*, 33.

129. Leo, *Great Encyclical Letters*, 306.

130. Ibid., 307.

131. Ibid.

132. The encyclical letter, *Satis Cognitum*, in Leo, *Great Encyclical Letters*, 351–91. Germain Trinadtzatsky considers *Satis Cognitum* as an attempt to answer the Orthodox position on the papal primacy found in the letter of the Patriarch of Constantinople issued in 1895 (*L'Eglise Russe*, 180).

133. Leo, *Great Encyclical Letters*, 371. For the perfect society view of the Church, see O'Donnell, *Ecclesia*, 359; this theory was found frequently in the encyclicals of Pope Leo XIII (p. 359); see also Congar, "Pilgrim Church," 132–33.

134. Leo, *Great Encyclical Letters*, 371–72.

135. Ibid., 372–73.

136. Ibid., 378. As Meyendorff explains, the Council at Florence (1439) used all the "code words" justifying papal monarchy, namely the pope is "the successor of Peter," "the true vicar of Christ," "the head of the whole Church," and possesses full power in feeding and governing the universal Church, although a reference was made in the decree to the acts of the ecumenical councils and to holy canons as the framework in which the papal power should be exercised. Nevertheless, read by Westerners, this reference was quite innocuous, since all the papal terminology was integrated in the decree, *Rome, Constantinople, Moscow*, 97–98, 104.

137. Leo, *Great Encyclical Letters*, 357.

138. Ibid., 384–87.

139. Ibid., 373–74.

140. Ibid., 375–77.

141. Bermejo, *Toward Christian Reunion*, 117–20.

142. Terence Nichols, *That All May Be One*, 141; Demacopoulos, "Gregory the Great."

143. Leo, *Great Encyclical Letters*, 378–81.

144. Zizioulas's assessment, firmly anchored within eucharistic ecclesiology, is that, despite Cyprian's recognition of the primacy of Peter, "he does not recognise in any of the Bishops the right to express the unity of all the bishops. This is demonstrated, besides, by his constant struggle against Rome's view on baptism. . . . If the texts in his works which have provoked so much discussion had even the slightest sense of acknowledging in the Roman Church the property of expressing the unity of all the Churches throughout the world, these struggles of Cyprian's would be inexplicable," *Eucharist, Bishop, Church*, 154.

145. Schmemann, "Idea of Primacy," 163.

146. Terence Nichols, *That All May Be One*, 110. Nichols concludes that for Irenaeus the Roman Church "is not the source of orthodoxy—other churches also

NOTES TO PAGES 37-40   167

preserve the apostolic tradition—but it is the standard, the touchstone, of orthodoxy. Irenaeus mentions the Roman bishop (Eleutherius) later in this same passage, but he clearly does not see apostolic orthodoxy as vested only in the *bishop* of Rome; it is also vested in the *church* at Rome" (110).

147. Leo, *Great Encyclical Letters*, 379.

148. Ibid., 380–81.

149. Bermejo, *Toward Christian Reunion*, 114–16.

150. Ibid., 118–19.

151. Leo, *Great Encyclical Letters*, 382 (emphasis in original).

152. Ibid., 388.

153. Ibid., 386–87 (emphasis in original).

154. Ibid., 387.

155. Gelasius, in claiming that the Roman see was considered to be the supreme court of appeal, referred to several canons. These were Canons 3, 4, and 5 of the Council of Sardica (343), which granted to the bishop of Rome the right to judge whether or not there were grounds for revising the trial in the case of deposition of bishops and thus having a second hearing. The Pope did not judge in case of appeal. He could annul the rendered judgement and send his legates to this second hearing if he wished to do so. However, he could not annul the second judgement, which was to be enacted by a tribunal composed of neighboring bishops from the province where the conflict existed (see Meyendorff, *Orthodoxy and Catholicity*, 60).

156. See Dvornik, *Idea of Apostolicity*, 117–19.

157. Schatz, *Papal Primacy*, 73; Terence Nichols, *That All May Be One*, 116.

158. Terence Nichols, *That All May Be One*, 324.

159. Leo, *Great Encyclical Letters*, 387.

160. Terence Nichols, *That All May Be One*, 126.

161. The False Decretals advocated this idea (cf. Schatz, *Papal Primacy*, 70).

162. Terence Nichols, *That All May Be One*, 323; see also 125–26.

163. Ware, "Ecumenical Councils," 220.

164. Schatz, *Papal Primacy*, 51, 60–61.

165. Leo, *Great Encyclical Letters*, 387.

166. For the Seventh Ecumenical Council, see Papadopoulos, *Τὸ Πρωτεῖον τοῦ Ἐπισκόπου Ῥώμης*, 150–51.

167. Ibid., 150. The Robber's Synod of Ephesus was rejected not only by Rome, but also by the Patriarch of Constantinople, Flavian, and his synod (72), and finally by the whole Church.

168. Terence Nichols, *That All May Be One*, 119–20.

169. Ibid., 118.

170. Meyendorff, *Orthodoxy and Catholicity*, 73.

171. Schatz, *Papal Primacy*, 48.

172. Meyendorff, *Orthodoxy and Catholicity*, 73.

173. Leo, *Great Encyclical Letters*, 387.

174. Terence Nichols, *That All May Be One*, 118.

175. Malataki, Ἀπάντησις [*Answer*].

176. Baur, Διατριβαί [*Essays*].

177. Brandi, Ἀπάντησις [*Answer*]. This answer was published in Civiltà Cattolica (Nov. 26, 1895) and was translated into Romanian, French, Slavonic, and English.

178. Germain Trinadtzatsky considers *Satis Cognitum* itself as an attempt to answer the Orthodox position on the papal primacy found in the letter of the Patriarch of Constantinople issued in 1895 (*L'Eglise Russe*, 180).

179. Malataki, Ἀπάντησις, 78–151. Drawing upon the petrine texts, on some Fathers, and on some cases from Church history, Brandi claimed that Peter and his successors were the principle of unity and the foundation of the Church, and the infallible authority that determines the faith of all Christians; and that the Bishop of Rome, the church of Rome and the see of Rome exercised an authority over the whole Church (Ἀπάντησις, 55–78). Baur appealed likewise to the petrine texts and to the Fathers and to ancient councils to prove Peter's and papal primacy of jurisdiction over the whole Church (Διατριβαί, 95–124).

2—The Aftermath of Vatican I

1. Butler, *Vatican Council*, 74–75. For the reply of the Patriarch to the invitation, see Karmiris, Τά Δογματικά καί Συμβολικά Μνημεῖα [*The Dogmatic and Symbolic Documents*], 927–30.

2. Karmiris, Τά Δογματικά καί Συμβολικά Μνημεῖα, 928.

3. Ibid.

4. Ibid., 929.

5. See De Wyels, "Le Concile du Vatican," 492–508.

6. The encyclical says: "Since, however, from a certain period the Papal Church, having abandoned the method of persuasion and discussion, began, to our general astonishment and perplexity, to lay traps for the consciences of the more simple orthodox Christians by means of deceitful workers transformed into apostles of Christ, sending into the East clerics with the dress and head covering of orthodox priests, inventing also divers other artful means to obtain her proselytizing objects; *for this reason, as in sacred duty bound, we issue this patriarchal and synodical encyclical, for a safeguard of the orthodox faith and piety,* knowing 'that the observance of the true canons is a duty for every good man, and much more for those who have been thought worthy by Providence to direct the affairs of others'" (Mettallinos, *Answer of the Great Church*, 19, emphasis added). I refer to this English translation.

7. Ibid., 17, 19.

8. Ibid., 37.

9. Ibid., 45.

10. Ibid., 51.

11. Ibid., 53.

12. Ibid., 37, 39.

13. Zigavinos, Ἀπάντησις [Answer], 34; for St. Chrysostom, cf. his homily on the Gospel of Matthew 54:2 (PG 58, 534).

14. Malataki, Ἀπάντησις, 100.

15. See Meyendorff, "St. Peter in Byzantine Theology," 72.

16. See chapter 1.

17. Mettallinos, Answer of the Great Church, 39. Malataki agrees with the Patriarchal Letter in stating that Christ is the foundation of the Church. However, Malataki considers that the above statement of the Patriarchal Letter cannot be taken as contradicting the jurisdictional primacy of Peter. Thus, he states that Peter by the ordinance and by the grace and power of Christ is the second foundation of the Church in relation to Him, by Whom Peter became the foundation, namely the center and the principle of unity of the Church (Malataki, Ἀπάντησις, 86–87).

18. Ἀπάντησις, 58, 60, 62.

19. Ibid., 32.

20. Meyendorff, "St. Peter in Byzantine Theology," 75–79.

21. Ibid., 71–72.

22. Ἀπάντησις , 22–23.

23. Ibid., 46.

24. Ibid., 49.

25. Ibid., 71–72.

26. Ibid., 72.

27. Ibid., 80–81.

28. Ibid., 81.

29. Ibid., 82.

30. Ibid., 84.

31. See chapter 1.

32. Ἀπάντησις, 88–90. In order to refute the position expressed in the Patriarchal encyclical letter, namely that the Church of the first nine centuries did not recognize the jurisdictional primacy of the Roman bishop, Malataki contended that the above passage from St. Irenaeus proved that the ancient Church recognized the Roman bishop as a successor of Peter and visible head of the Church, and the Roman Church as a center and principle of unity (Malataki, Ἀπάντησις, 108–9, 159).

33. See chapter 1.

34. Ἀπάντησις, 105–9.

35. See chapter 1.

36. Ἀπάντησις, 116–17. On the other hand, we have seen that Meyendorff considers that, for patristic thought and for the Orthodox ecclesiastical writers after the schism, Peter had a distinct and particular function in the foundation of the Church and not just a primacy of honor.

37. Ibid., 115–16. With regard to these two instances, Ware notes that "according to Pope Julius, Athanasius 'did not come on his own initiative, but after being summoned and receiving letters from us'" (PG 25, 297A). It should be noted

that Chrysostom appealed not only to Pope Innocent I but also to bishop Venerius of Milan and Chromatius of Aquileia, so that this action need not necessarily involve any special recognition of unique papal prerogatives: he wrote to anyone in the West who he thought might be able to intervene effectively on his behalf" (Ware, "Primacy, Collegiality," 121n8). The Roman Catholic, Brandi, in his treatise against the Patriarchal Letter considers these cases as indication of the exercise of papal jurisdictional primacy (Ἀπάντησις, 76–77).

38. Ware, "Primacy, Collegiality," 121–22.

39. See chapter 1.

40. Mettallinos, *Answer of the Great Church*, 37.

41. See, for example, the Orthodox confession of Peter Mogila (1640), which stated that Christ is the head of the Church and that the bishops are called heads of their own churches, and heads and vicars of Christ in their own province (Karmiris, *Τὰ Δογματικὰ καὶ Συμβολικὰ Μνημεῖα*, 631). These confessions were reactions of the Orthodox Church to the Reformation (see Meyendorff, *Orthodox Church*, 84–87).

42. Jugie, *Theologia Dogmatica*, 416.

43. Afanassieff, "Church Which Presides," 99–100. We will see in chapter 4 that Afanassieff does not accept the idea of universal primacy in his eucharistic ecclesiology. For Afanassieff, acceptance of a universal primacy equates to acceptance of universalistic ecclesiology, which he did not accept.

44. Mesoloras, *Συμβολική* [*Symbolic*], 40.

45. *Συμβολική* , 41–43. Similarly, the Serbian canonist Nikodime Milash believes that the Church as spiritual kingdom cannot have an earthly head and as such has only a spiritual head, who has governmental power over the Church. Also, the Russian theologian Eugenius Akvilonov asserts that the Church has no use for a visible head because Christ is invisibly present, performs the sacraments, and governs the Church (quoted from Jugie, *Theologia Dogmatica*, 413). Schmemann criticizes the argument invoked by Mesoloras and other Greek Orthodox polemicists as follows: "The idea, popular in Orthodox apologetics, that the Church can have no visible head because Christ is her invisible head is theological nonsense. If applied consistently, it should also eliminate the necessity for the visible head of each local church, i.e., the bishop" ("Idea of Primacy," 151).

46.Ibid., 43.

47. Ibid., 46.

48. Ibid., 53–54.

49. Ibid., 53.

50. For certain Greek Orthodox of the nineteenth century, such as Metropolitan Nektarios Kefalas (1846–1920), the Roman Catholic theory that the pope is the center of the Church presupposes that Christ, who is in fact the center of unity of the Church, is absent from the Church and is replaced by the pope (Kefala, *Μελέτη Ἱστορικὴ περὶ τῶν αἰτίων τοῦ σχίσματος*, Τόμος 2 [*Historical Study on the Causes of the Schism*, vol. 2], 8. Although it was published in 1912, Metropolitan Nectarios first wrote this book in 1895, and it is considered to be an answer to *Praeclara Gratu-*

lationis; see Athanasius (Bishop Jevtic), *Бог Отаца Нашиx* [*God of Our Fathers*], 258n3, 260. Jevtic considers that this "theory" points out the deviation of the Latin Church from the christological mystery of the Church (ibid., 308); see also 311–12, where he refers to the similar opinions of the Orthodox theologians of the twentieth century, Georges Florovsky and Justin Popovic.

51. Schmemann, "Idea of Primacy," 163.

52. Ibid., 161–63.

53. Ibid., 164. Peter was also a primate and center of unity among the college of the apostles of the early Church. Terence Nichols says of Peter: "Thus, in Matthew, Luke, John and Acts, Peter is given a role of primacy among the apostles and disciples. . . . In Mark and in Matthew especially, Peter is the spokesman for the disciples, the one who proclaims the consensus. This role is continued in Acts. In Acts 1, 6 and 15, Peter serves as the facilitator of and the spokesman for the consensus of the Twelve, or the apostolic college. . . . It is not a primacy of individual, separate jurisdiction *over* the other apostles" (*That All May Be One*, 67–68). He then concludes that "the charism of the Bishop of Rome, I have argued, is to be a facilitator of consensus and a center of unity among the episcopal college, as Peter was among the apostles" (ibid., 325).

54. Tipaldos's treatise is found in Metallinos, Ἑλλαδικοῦ Αὐτοκεφάλου Παραλειπόμενα [*Missing Chronicles of the Greek Autocephaly*], 103–18.

55. Ibid., 102.

56. Ibid., 105.

57. Ibid., 107.

58. Ibid., 108.

59. Ibid., 108–9.

60. Ibid., 107.

61. Kiriakos, Ἀντιπαπικά [*Antipapal*, vol. 1], 26.

62. Ibid., 142.

63. Zizioulas, *Being as Communion*, 136.

64. Papageorgiou, Περί τῆς ἑνότητος τῆς Ἐκκλησίας [*On the Unity of the Church*].

65. Ἐκκλησιαστική Ἀλήθεια [*Ecclesiastical Truth*] (1896–1897), 327. *Ecclesiastical Truth* was the official periodical of the Ecumenical Patriarchate at that time. The Ecumenical Patriarchate did not respond to *Satis Cognitum*, because the Patriarchate claimed that in vain would it occupy itself with the rebuttal of the encyclical since the main issue in the encyclical was the primacy of the pope, which had been refuted many times with irrefutable arguments. The Patriarchate concluded that not the papal encyclical but simply the circumstances compelled the Patriarchate to respond, for the protection of its flock from error (ibid.).

66. Περί τῆς Ἑνότητος, 4–6.

67. Ibid., 7–17.

68. Ibid., 15.

69. Ibid., 16–17.

70. Ibid., 18.

71. Ibid., 18-26.

72. Ibid., 26.

73. Ibid., 27-37.

74. Ibid., 27.

75. Ibid., 43-44; cf. the papal encyclical, in Leo, *Great Encyclical Letters*, 308: "The true union between Christians is that which Jesus Christ, the author of the Church, instituted and desired and which consists in a unity of faith and a unity of government."

76. Schmemann says that this Roman Catholic teaching is an ecclesiological error and distortion ("Idea of Primacy," 163).

77. Mettallinos, *Answer of the Great Church*, 43.

78. Cf. Zizioulas, *Eucharist, Bishop, Church*, 33n32; 252. The patriarchal letter also, in arguing against the papal primacy of jurisdiction, states that the bishops were independent of each other, and each entirely free within his own bounds, obeying and being subject only to the synodical decrees (Mettallinos, *Answer of the Great Church*, 43, 45). This is an oversimplified picture. Though it is true that each bishop was free to conduct the affairs of his diocese, this independence was limited to the strictly local affairs of each diocese. Also, the authority of a council or synod was limited to affairs pertaining to communion between the local churches (Zizioulas, "Primacy in the Church," 120); see Zizioulas, Θέματα Ἐκκλησιολογίας [*Themes of Ecclesiology*], 70-71. Also, synods are not to be understood in juridical terms of obedience and subjection as the patriarchal letter implies. Zizioulas stresses that they are not a legalistic institution but rather an event of communion. See Zizioulas, "Ὁ Συνοδικός Θεσμός" ["The Synodical Institution"], 181.

79. Mettallinos, *Answer of the Great Church*, 63.

80. See Meyendorff, *Byzantine Legacy*, 226.

81. Ibid.

82. The Greek Church, which was declared autocephalous by the Ecumenical Patriarchate for political and nationalistic reasons, was an example of a state-controlled church. However, the Ecumenical Patriarchate, in the Great Local Synod held in Constantinople in 1872, condemned nationalism on the occasion of the so-called Bulgarian Schism; cf. Maximos, *Ecumenical Patriarchate*, 303-9. The Greek Orthodox theologian, Hamilkas Alivizatos, admits that nationalism, which caused the creation of the individual autocephalous churches, has deeply and seriously wounded the internal unity of Orthodoxy (ibid., 302n2).

83. Maximos, *Ecumenical Patriarchate*, 300-301 (emphasis in original).

84. See Erickson, "Local Churches and Catholicity," 491, 493.

85. Mettallinos, *Answer of the Great Church*, 49, 51.

86. Ibid., 41.

87. Leo, *Great Encyclical Letters*, 374.

88. Zizioulas, "Recent Discussions on Primacy," 234-35.

89. Ibid., 235.

90. For an ecclesiological analysis of the 34th apostolic canon, see Rodopoulos, *Μελέται Α' [Essays I]*, 155-75; also Daley, "Primacy and Collegiality," 5-21.

91. Zizioulas, "Recent Discussions on Primacy," 235; see also Daley, "Position and Patronage."

92. Maximos, *Ecumenical Patriarchate*, 115-16.

93. See Phidas, *Ὁ Θεσμός τῆς Πενταρχίας τῶν Πατριαρχῶν [The Institution of the Pentarchy]*, 307.

94. Zigavinos, *Ἀπάντησις*, 134-35.

95. Ibid., 143.

96. Ibid., 135.

97. Ibid., 135-38.

98. The canon says: "Therefore, if anyone says that blessed Peter the apostle was not appointed by Christ the lord as prince of all the apostles and visible head of the whole church militant; or that it was a primacy of honour only and not one of true and proper jurisdiction that he directly and immediately received from our lord Jesus Christ himself: let him be anathema" (Tanner, *Decrees*, 813: 21-24).

99. Karmiris, *Ὀρθόδοξος Ἐκκλησιολογία [Orthodox Ecclesiology]*, 552-89. In line with Karmiris, other Greek Orthodox theologians deny explicitly the support these scriptural passages give to Vatican I's doctrine of petrine primacy, e.g., Androutsos, *Συμβολική [Symbolic]*, 91-92. J. Michael Miller states that contemporary Roman Catholic theologians do not consider themselves bound by the interpretation and use of the petrine texts proposed by Vatican I (Miller, *Divine Right of the Papacy*, 189).

100. Karmiris, *Ὀρθόδοξος Ἐκκλησιολογία*, 552-53.

101. Ibid., 564, 576.

102. Ibid., 554.

103. Ibid., 564.

104. Karmiris refers to Meyendorff's article "St. Peter in Byzantine Theology" without taking into consideration Meyendorff's critical evaluation of those polemical arguments (Karmiris, *Ὀρθόδοξος Ἐκκλησιολογία*, 570).

105. See above.

106. Karmiris, *Ὀρθόδοξος Ἐκκλησιολογία*, 555-61.

107. Ibid., 557.

108. Ibid., 565, 579-81. Androutsos and Papadopoulos repeat these same polemical arguments (Androutsos, *Συμβολική*, 91; Papadopoulos, *Τό Πρωτεῖον τοῦ Ἐπισκόπου Ρώμης*, 4-10).

109. Karmiris, *Ὀρθόδοξος Ἐκκλησιολογία*, 582-88.

110. Ibid., 578-83. For instance, Karmiris refers to St. Chrysostom, who calls Peter the mouth of the disciples and *coryphaeus* in the choir of the apostles, while he mentions James as being appointed by Christ as a teacher of the whole universe (583n1).

111. Cf. Meyendorff, "St. Peter in Byzantine Theology," 72.

112. Karmiris, *Ὀρθόδοξος Ἐκκλησιολογία*, 567-68.

113. See above. St. Gregory Palamas, who lived after the schism, called Peter

"supreme pastor of the whole Church" and the "foundation of the church" (for quotations, see Meyendorff, "St. Peter in Byzantine Theology," 74). In sharp contrast, Vatican I uses the same terms exclusively to define papal primacy in juridical terms: "And it was to Peter alone that Jesus, after his resurrection, confined the jurisdiction of supreme pastor and ruler of his whole fold, saying: *Feed my lambs, feed my sheep*" (Tanner, *Decrees*, 812). Like Meyendorff, Karmiris considers that all bishops are successors to Peter. For Karmiris, all bishops, who with their ordination received the certain charisma of truth (i.e., *charisma veritatis*), of confession and of teaching the faith, are *ex officio* successors of the petrine ministry in their local churches (Karmiris, Ὀρθόδοξος Ἐκκλησιολογία, 593). Nevertheless, Karmiris differs from Meyendorff when he invokes the polemical arguments against the petrine primacy which, for Meyendorff, contradict the preeminent function of Peter recognized by the patristic tradition.

114. Karmiris, Ὀρθόδοξος Ἐκκλησιολογία, 564–65, 589.

115. Ibid., 607.

116. See chapter 1.

117. Karmiris, Ὀρθόδοξος Ἐκκλησιολογία, 608–9. Karmiris also quotes various Roman Catholic theologians, who agree with him that the Fathers were unaware of such a primacy.

118. Ibid., 593.

119. Ibid., 620–21.

120. Ibid., 619–20.

121. Karmiris, Θεολογικά Θέματα [*Theological issues*], 6.

122. Karmiris, Ὀρθόδοξος Ἐκκλησιολογία, 524.

123. Ibid., 524–25, 620n2.

124. See above.

125. Karmiris, Ὀρθόδοξος Ἐκκλησιολογία, 659–60. In fact, conciliarism is a diverse phenomenon with many authors taking many positions, as the work of Oakley has shown (*The Conciliarist Tradition*).

126. Ibid., 527.

127. Zizioulas, "Recent Discussions on Primacy," 238 (emphasis in original).

128. Zizioulas, "Conciliarity," 25, 30n13 (emphasis in original).

129. Ibid., 24. Thus, for Zizioulas, the fact that the Council of Ephesus held in 449 thought of itself as ecumenical but finally was not accepted by the Church as an ecumenical council shows that the ecumenical councils cannot be considered as an institution. Although Karmiris considers an ecumenical council as an institution, he also accepts the historical fact that the ecumenicity of a council depends on its recognition as such by the conscience of the Church (Karmiris, Ὀρθόδοξος Ἐκκλησιολογία, 676–77).

130. Tanner, *Decrees*, 816.

131. Karmiris, Ὀρθόδοξος Ἐκκλησιολογία, 631.

132. Ibid., 528. Among the main accusations that Karmiris directs against the dogmas of papal primacy and infallibility is that they overturned the apostolic and traditional episcopal-synodical constitution of the ancient Church and changed

this constitution from a democratic one into a monarchical, autocratic, centralized ecclesiastical *imperium*, that is, into a secular state with rigorous juridical organization and discipline (ibid., 631). Yet while he makes this criticism, he himself could also be criticized for adopting juridical views because he understands, as we have seen, the synodical institution in juridical terms as a highest authority. On the other hand, by accepting the fact that ecumenical councils have to be accepted by the conscience of the church, he implies that an ecumenical council is not a juridical thing, but a matter of recognition (ibid., 676–84). The internal contradiction in Karmiris's thought is therefore obvious.

133. Ibid., 526.

134. Ibid., 526n2.

135. Karmiris, Ὀρθόδοξος Ἐκκλησιολογία, 668. Karmiris refers to Androutsos's Συμβολική, 92.

136. Karmiris, Ὀρθόδοξος Ἐκκλησιολογία, 545–46. Karmiris agrees with Zizioulas's assessment that the unity of the Church in the ancient Church of the first three centuries was manifested in time through identity with what the Lord and the apostles taught (by the apostolic succession of bishops) and in space through identity with what the other churches around the world lived and taught (by the institution of councils). It was a unity of the faithful through the bishop and the church to which they belong. The living cell of Church unity was the one Eucharist under the leadership of the Bishop and the Catholic Church. Through this consciousness of unity, the Church of the first three centuries recognized the Lord Jesus Christ as the one center of the unity of the Catholic Church throughout the world (ibid., 252, 252n5); Karmiris quotes from Zizioulas's thesis, Ἡ ἑνότης τῆς Ἐκκλησίας ἐν τῇ θείᾳ Εὐχαριστίᾳ [*The Unity of the Church*], 147–48.

137. Karmiris, Ὀρθόδοξος Ἐκκλησιολογία, 602.

138. Ibid., 537.

139. Ibid., 590; see also Mettallinos, *Answer of the Great Church*, 41.

140. See above, chapter 2.

141. Karmiris, Ὀρθόδοξος Ἐκκλησιολογία, 535n1. Karmiris refers to Phidas's work Ἰστορικοκανονικὰ προβλήματα περὶ τὴν λειτουργίαν τοῦ θεσμοῦ τῆς Πενταρχίας τῶν Πατριαρχῶν [*Historical-Canonical Problems regarding the Function of the Institution of the Pentarchy of Patriarchs*], 69.

142. Karmiris, Ὀρθόδοξος Ἐκκλησιολογία, 591, 593.

143. In interpreting the meaning of the privileges in the Sixth Canon of Nicea, Meyendorff points out that these privileges rested not just on moral authority, but they could materialize in a legal power that consisted essentially in the right to ordain all the bishops within a group of secular provinces (*Orthodoxy and Catholicity*, 54–55).

144. Zizioulas, "Recent Discussions on Primacy," 233 (emphasis in original). Zizioulas quotes from Karmiris's Ὀρθόδοξος Ἐκκλησιολογία, 590.

145. Zizioulas, "Recent Discussions on Primacy," 234.

146. Ibid.

147. Ibid., 235 (emphasis in original).

148. Ibid.

149. Ibid.

150. Karmiris, Ὀρθόδοξος Ἐκκλησιολογία, 651.

151. Zizioulas, "Primacy in the Church," 123.

152. Ibid., 122.

153. Karmiris, Ὀρθόδοξος Ἐκκλησιολογία, 529.

154. Karmiris, Ὀρθόδοξος Ἐκκλησιολογία, 533—34.

155. Erickson, *Challenge of Our Past*, 82.

156. Ibid.

157. Karmiris, Ὀρθόδοξος Ἐκκλησιολογία, 527n1. Maximos of Sardes asserts that the Patriarch of Constantinople "holds not only privileges of honour, but also prerogatives of real ecclesiastical power. As a result he has been and is the supreme administrator and judge for the faithful of his own jurisdictional area. He also acts as such for the entire Orthodox East on general ecclesiastical matters, but always in cooperation with the other Patriarchs" (*Ecumenical Patriarchate*, 327); cf. also 115–21, where Metropolitan Maximos confirms from a canonical and historical point of view that the prerogatives of the metropolitans, including the prerogatives of the Patriarch of Constantinople, were not simply of honor, but involved a genuine power.

158. Karmiris, Ὀρθόδοξος Ἐκκλησιολογία, 527.

159. See above.

160. Zizioulas, "Recent Discussions on Primacy," 235–36.

161. Ibid., 236.

162. Ibid.

163. Ibid.

164. See above.

165. Karmiris, Ὀρθόδοξος Ἐκκλησιολογία, 602.

166. Zizioulas, "Recent Discussions on Primacy," 234.

167. With regard to Pentarchy, Meyendorff explains that "the shaping of the 'pentarchic' scheme took place already in the fourth century, with special privileges (πρεσβεῖα) being recognized as belonging to the primates of the most important cities of the empire: first to Rome, Alexandria, and Antioch (council of Nicea, 325); to Constantinople, as 'New Rome' (council of Constantinople I, 381); and finally, also to Jerusalem (Ephesus, 431)" (*Rome, Constantinople, Moscow*, 90).

168. Zizioulas, "Recent Discussions on Primacy," 234.

169. Ibid., 236–37. Thus Karmiris considers the synodical system as belonging to the essence of the Church and therefore existing *jure divino*, on the principle that the Church is a gathering—σύνοδος—of the People of God, called by God, its initial and simple form being the eucharistic gathering under the bishop (Ὀρθόδοξος Ἐκκλησιολογία, 521, 523, 653).

170. Zizioulas, "Recent Discussions on Primacy," 237.

171. Ibid.

172. Ibid.

173. Referring to the institution of the Patriarchates, originating with the

Pentarchy, he says: "The basis of this institution was political as well as historical and ecclesiastical—never theological in the strict sense. Certain local churches acquired pre-eminence, either because they were important in the political structure of the empire or because they had an historic significance in the establishment of the Christian faith and the emergence of new churches" (Zizioulas, "Primacy in the Church," 122).

174. Karmiris, Ὀρθόδοξος Ἐκκλησιολογία, 604. Karmiris refers to the first edition of Papadopoulos's book Τὸ Πρωτεῖον τοῦ Ἐπισκόπου Ῥώμης, 324.

3—Vatican II: Papal Primacy and Episcopal Collegiality

1. See McPartlan, "Eucharistic Ecclesiology," 316.

2. Himes, "Development of Ecclesiology," 63.

3. Gonzáles de Cardedal, "Development of a Theology," 12.

4. Ibid. For a brief account of Leo XIII's pneumatology, see O'Donnell, Ecclesia, 369.

5. O'Donnell notes that from St. Thomas until the nineteenth century, "though it was clear that the Eucharist as a sacrament and sacrifice was indeed a high point of the Church's life, there was little attempt to see it as encompassing the whole life of salvation, and hence of the Church" (Ecclesia, 160).

6. Quoted by Ratzinger in Church, Ecumenism, 3.

7. Ibid., 3–4.

8. Ibid.

9. McPartlan, "Eucharistic Ecclesiology," 316.

10. See McPartlan, Sacrament of Salvation, 41. Cf. also McPartlan, "Eucharistic Ecclesiology," 317–18. Thus de Lubac said that true eucharistic piety is not a "devout individualism." It cannot conceive of the breaking of bread "without fraternal communion" (Catholicism, 109–10). In that period de Lubac confronted the problem of individualism and self-centeredness in France of the 1930s. See McPartlan, "Liturgy, Church, and Society," 148.

11. De Lubac, Corpus Mysticum, 104. However, we must note at this point that de Lubac's principle is simultaneously conditioned by the other principle that "the Church makes the Eucharist." For a discussion on the problem from an Orthodox point of view, see Zizioulas, "Ecclesiological Presuppositions," 340–42.

12. Ratzinger, Church, Ecumenism, 7; see McPartlan, Sacrament of Salvation, 56–57: "he [i.e., de Lubac] spoke of the original perception of the relationship between the Church and the Eucharist according to which the Eucharist should properly be called Christ's 'mystical body', to encourage awareness that the Eucharist makes the Church."

13. Ratzinger, Church, Ecumenism, 7.

14. See LG 7, which speaks explicitly of the communal aspect of the Eucharist: "Really sharing in the body of the Lord in the breaking of the eucharistic bread, we

are taken up into communion with him and with one another." For a reflection on Vatican II's teaching on the Church as communion, see Walter Kasper, *Theology and the Church*, 148–65.

15. McPartlan, "Eucharistic Ecclesiology," 323.

16. McPartlan notes that "with these words the council returns to the early understanding that the Eucharist makes the Church" (*Sacrament of Salvation*, 42).

17. McPartlan says that de Lubac's eucharistic eccesiology comes first out of Augustine ("Eucharistic Ecclesiology," 319).

18. Ratzinger, *Church, Ecumenism*, 14.

19. McPartlan, *Sacrament of Salvation*, 37–38. In speaking of the significant contribution that de Lubac makes to Western ecclesiology, which is the recovery of the link between Eucharist and Church, McPartlan says: "By trying to re-open the ecclesial dimensions of the Eucharist, de Lubac was suspected by some of doubting transubstantiation, which was of course nonsense, but it was a damaging slur. What de Lubac had said, rather magnificently, regarding the real presence of Christ, was that eucharistic realism and ecclesial realism support one another, holy gifts for the holy people, as the Orthodox Liturgy proclaims. De Lubac wanted to restore this balance" ("Liturgy, Church, and Society," 156).

20. McPartlan, "Liturgy, Church, and Society," 156.

21. Kasper, "Church as Communio," 107.

22. Philip Sherrard notes that by the twelfth century the term *corpus mysticum*, instead of designating the Eucharist, designated the Church as a corporate, juristic, sociological entity in its own right that had to be governed along political lines in the same way as other corporate human societies. The term was assimilated to the visible structure of the Church as a supracollectivity with the pope at its head (*Church, Papacy and Schism*, 93–94).

23. McPartlan, *Sacrament of Salvation*, 38–39.

24. Duffy, *Saints and Sinners*, 100.

25. Gonzáles de Cardedal, "Development of a Theology," 20–21.

26. Ibid., 20–22.

27. McPartlan, "Eucharistic Ecclesiology," 326. Gonzáles de Cardedal notes that "the name of Afanassieff became a symbol which would appear in the very acts of the council" ("Development of a Theology," 22).

28. Gonzáles de Cardedal, "Development of a Theology," 38. Gonzáles de Cardedal refers to other figures from Protestant and Roman Catholic theology who contributed to the development of a theology of the local church within Roman Catholic ecclesiology (14–17).

29. See McPartlan, "Liturgy, Church, and Society," 157–58; for the famous article of Congar, "De la communion des églises à une ecclésiologie de l'Eglise universelle," see Congar & Dupuy, *L'Episcopat et l'Eglise universelle*, 227–60.

30. Gonzáles de Cardedal, "Development of a Theology," 32.

31. McPartlan, "Liturgy, Church, and Society," 149.

32. Ibid., 152.

33. Ibid.

34. Beauduin, *Liturgy*, 5; quoted by McPartlan, "Liturgy, Church, and Society," 155.

35. McPartlan, "Liturgy, Church and Society," 157.

36. Ibid., 152.

37. Ibid.

38. Ibid., 161–62.

39. Ibid., 150.

40. Ibid.

41. Quoted in ibid., 151. Avery Dulles also says that shortly before Vatican II, in 1950, neo-scholastic manuals of theology were juridical in tone, and the Church was seen as a "perfect society," in which the officeholders had jurisdiction over the members; the pope as vicar of Christ, was depicted as ruler of the entire society. The bishops were seen as deriving their jurisdiction from the pope. Many of these manuals were directed against the Protestants, who envisaged the Church as essentially invisible and charismatic (Dulles, "Half-Century of Ecclesiology," 419–20).

42. Dulles, "Half-Century of Ecclesiology," 421–23.

43. Ibid., 422.

44. McPartlan, "Liturgy, Church, and Society," 158.

45. Ibid.

46. McPartlan, *Sacrament of Salvation*, 38. The Scholastic theologians taught that the episcopate was not an order, nor was episcopal consecration a sacrament (cf. Terence Nichols, *That All May Be One*, 242). However, among the theologians of the High Middle Ages, there was a variety of views with regard to the episcopacy (Pottmeyer, "Episcopacy," 345). Pottmeyer says that among canonists of the Middle Ages the opinion still prevailed that the episcopacy constituted a rank of orders (ibid.).

47. McPartlan, *Sacrament of Salvation*, 38.

48. Terence Nichols, *That All May Be One*, 242.

49. Pottmeyer, "Episcopacy," 345.

50. Henn, *Honor of My Brothers*, 110.

51. Ibid., 110–13. This dependence of the bishops on the pope's authority cannot be merely understood as Rome's will to power. Rather, underlying this dependence was Rome's effort to free the bishops from their dependence on political powers (Pottmeyer, "Episcopacy," 345).

52. Henn, *Honor of My Brothers*, 113. Nevertheless, Henn notes that the theological and canonical opinion that all jurisdiction derived from the pope "was never finally adopted by the ecumenical councils held in the West during the second millennium" (ibid.).

53. Botte, "Collegial Character," 90; cf. McPartlan, "Eucharistic Ecclesiology," 321–22.

54. Botte, "Collegial Character," 89. However, as Pottmeyer notes, "Pope Pius XII was the first officially to determine, in his apostolic constitution *Sacramentum*

ordinis (1947), that the episcopate, the presbyterate, and the diaconate constitute each a proper rank of the sacraments of orders ("Episcopacy," 345).

55. McPartlan, "Eucharistic Ecclesiology," 322.

56. Botte, "Collegial Character," 89.

57. Ibid., 88.

58. McPartlan, *Sacrament of Salvation*, 58–59.

59. Ibid., 58.

60. Botte, "Collegial Character," 89.

61. Ibid., 88–89, here at 88.

62. McPartlan, "Eucharistic Ecclesiology," 323.

63. McPartlan, "Liturgy, Church, and Society," 160.

64. Botte, "Collegial Character," 88.

65. McPartlan, "Eucharistic Ecclesiology," 323.

66. McPartlan, "Liturgy, Church, Society," 21.

67. Botte, "Collegial Character," 89–90.

68. Ratzinger, *Church, Ecumenism*, 11.

69. Gérard Philips, "History of the Constitution on the Church," in H. Vorgrimler, ed., *Commentary on the Documents of Vatican II*, 1: 106; cf. Terence Nichols, *That All May Be One*, 239.

70. Philips, "History of the Constitution," 106.

71. Tourneux, "L'éveque," 111; cf. Terence Nichols, *That All May Be One*, 239.

72. Tourneux, "L'éveque," 111.

73. Ibid., 112–13.

74. Terence Nichols, *That All May Be One*, 240.

75. Ibid.

76. Philips, "History of the Constitution," 106.

77. O'Neil, "General Introduction," 10; cf. Terence Nichols, *That All May Be One*, 240.

78. Ibid.

79. Quoted in Philips, "History of the Constitution," 108.

80. Ibid.

81. O'Neil, "General Introduction," 11.

82. Williams, "Church Is Hierarchical," 85.

83. Philips, "History of the Constitution," 110.

84. O'Neil, "General Introduction," 12.

85. Ibid.

86. Philips, "History of the Constitution," 110–12.

87. O'Neil, "General Introduction," 13.

88. Philips notes that "this chapter was by far the most hotly debated" ("History of the Constitution," 112).

89. Ibid., 112–13.

90. Ibid., 112–15.

91. Henn, *Honor of My Brothers*, 148.

92. Williams, "Church Is Hierarchical," 86.

93. Philips, "History of the Constitution," 115–16.

94. Ibid., 116.

95. Philips, "History of the Constitution," 116–17.

96. O'Neil, "General Introduction," 15.

97. Terence Nichols, *That All May Be One*, 241–42.

98. O'Neil, "General Introduction," 15. During the period between the second and the third session, the task of the Theological Commission was to bring the text of the draft into line with the desires of the bishops (Philips, "History of the Constitution," 126).

99. See Joseph Ratzinger, "Announcements and Prefatory Notes of Explanation," in Vorgrimler, ed., *Commentary on the Documents of Vatican II*, 1: 298.

100. Philips, "History of the Constitution on the Church," 131, 137.

101. For the implications of such a linear conception of apostolic succession in ecclesiology, see Zizioulas, *Being as Communion*, 171–208, and "Apostolic Continuity," 153–68.

102. Pottmeyer, "Episcopacy," 349.

103. Ad Cor. 44,2 in Funk, *Patres Apostolici*, 1: 514f. Zizioulas notes that this text of St. Clement has been widely used to support the notion of apostolic succession in terms of linear history (*Being as Communion*, 154).

104. So Pottmeyer notes: "The council grounds the existence of the episcopal office in the sending and the empowerment of the apostles by Jesus and risen one" ("Episcopacy," 347).

105. Zizioulas, *Being as Communion*, 173.

106. Zizioulas, "Apostolic Continuity," 154.

107. Ibid., 153.

108. Ibid., 154–55.

109. Zizioulas, *Being as Communion*, 194.

110. "That divine mission, which was committed by Christ to the apostles, is destined to last until the end of the world (cf. Mt. 28:20), since the Gospel, which they were charged to hand on, is, for the Church, the principle of all its life for all time. For that very reason the apostles were careful to appoint successors in this hierarchically constituted society" (*LG* 20). As mentioned above, Congar admits that although Vatican II considers the Church predominantly as a mystery and as a communion, it contains a juridical notion of the Church, i.e., in terms of hierarchically structured society (Congar, "Pilgrim Church," 135–36).

111. We shall see in chapter 4 that Zizioulas considers that an approach to apostolic succession which moves along a merely linear historical line, as shown in the teaching of Vatican II, is the result of a priority of Christology over pneumatology and of a weak theology of the Holy Spirit.

112. See chapter 1.

113. Zizioulas, "Apostolic Continuity," 165, 168.

114. Ibid., 167.

115. Ibid., 158–59.

116. Ibid., 159.

117. Zizioulas evokes the letters of Ignatius as an example of the eschatological notion of apostolic succession, which he considers as stemming from the eschatological state of the Church's convocation in the same place, which is understood in connection with the eucharistic gathering (*Being as Communion*, 176–77). Here continuity is not expressed through individuals "but in and through the convocation of the Church in one place, through its Eucharistic structure" (177). Although this eschatological image of succession has been criticized, McPartlan thinks that Zizioulas "intends only to suggest that the standard missionary approach to apostolic succession needs a convocational corrective" (McPartlan, *Eucharist Makes the Church*, 201n89).

118. Hervé Legrand criticizes Vatican II for not containing a paragraph on placing the bishop within his Church. For Legrand this is a limitation on the ecclesiology of communion as a communion of local Churches ("Collégialite des évêques," 555–56).

119. Zizioulas, "Apostolic Continuity," 166.

120. McPartlan explains that the picture of the eucharistic assembly, which *SC* 41 paints with reference to Ignatius, is understood within an eschatological context, namely it is an image of the community that is gathered around Christ in heaven (McPartlan, *Sacrament of Salvation*, 64–65); cf. McPartlan, "Presbyteral Ministry," 13–14.

121. Buckley, *Papal Primacy*, 80.

122. Also, for Charles M. Murphy, even Vatican II's definition of collegiality is a limited one which "has meaning for the whole Church, as well, beyond the bishops, for the Church herself is a communion of persons united in a reciprocity of gifts in the same Spirit; the episcopal collegiality grows out of such a communion and is intended to serve and preserve it." He further comments that, to highlight the communal meaning of collegiality, the Dogmatic Constitution on the Church places chapter 3 on the hierarchical structure of the Church within the broader text of the Mystery of the Church (chap. 1) and the People of God (chap. 2) (Murphy, "Collegiality," 39).

123. Pottmeyer, "Episcopacy," 351; Pottmeyer, *Towards a Papacy*, 119: "Special attention is due to the texts that show the ecclesiological meaning of communion as communion of churches. In grounding the collegiality of the episcopate, reference is made directly to the practice of communion in the early Church (*LG* 22). The basis of that practice is the fact that the Catholic Church consists in, and of, the particular Churches."

124. *LG* 22–23; cf. Pottmeyer, *Towards a Papacy*, 120–21.

125. Thus for Legrand, the important passage from *LG* 23—"It is in these and formed out of them that the one and unique Catholic Church exists"—is undoubtedly an affirmation of the full catholicity of local churches (Legrand, "One Bishop per City," 370). Cf. Müller, "Local Church Lives," 344: "Since the Local Church is not only a part of the universal Church but rather in it 'the one, holy, catholic and

apostolic Church is truly operative and present' (*CD* 11, i.e., *Christus Dominus* the Decree of Vatican II on the Pastoral Office of Bishops in the Church), the universal Church is accordingly built from the local churches and is present in them."

126. Gonzáles de Cardedal, "Development of a Theology," 11. In commenting on the image of the "People of God," which signifies the notion of the Church as a communion, Aloys Grillmeier says: "One of the achievements of the Council was the re-discovery of the universal Church as the sum and communion of the local churches, understood as fully themselves, and the re-discovery of the universal Church in the local Church" (Grillmeier, "People of God," 1:167).

127. We will see in chapter 4 that Olivier Clement points implicitly to the tension between these two concepts that are present in *Lumen Gentium*.

128. Joseph A. Komonchak admits that "not only did the council begin its work within the perspective of the universalistic ecclesiology long dominant in the West, but its recovery of an ecclesiology of communion that underlies a theology of the local Church was hesitant and unsystematic" ("Local Church," 427).

129. Legrand, "Collégialité des évêques," 555. However, he notes that both *LG* 23 and the theological and canonical recognition of the regional churches as structures of communion by Vatican II (cf. *LG* 23) provide the doctrinal orientation and practical recommendations that make an ecclesiology of communion the necessary context within which episcopal collegiality is understood (ibid.).

130. McPartlan, "Local Church," 22–23.

131. Cf. ibid., 23. *LG* 2 uses the term "universal Church" in the eschatological sense, namely the heavenly eschatological Church of all ages: "At that moment as the Fathers put it, all the just from the time of Adam, 'from Abel, the just one, to the last of the elect' will be gathered together with the Father, in the universal Church" (cf. ibid., 22–23).

132. For de Lubac, it is in the context of the worldwide meaning of "universal Church," namely the Church led by the bishop of Rome, that we should understand the two important texts, namely *LG* 23 and 26 when they speak of the "universal Church," "the catholic Church," or the "Church of Christ" (McPartlan, *Eucharist Makes the Church*, 109). Each local Church in the Eucharist realizes therefore the "universal," i.e., worldwide Church, which is actually entrusted to the pastoral charge of the Roman bishop. For de Lubac, however, this does not make the pope a kind of superbishop with neither local nor temporal roots of his ministry. This means, as McPartlan points out, that "the pope has pastoral care for the worldwide Church because he has pastoral care for that portion of the worldwide Church which belongs to the local Church of Rome" (ibid., 116). Still, *LG* 26 is more open to the eschatological understanding of the local Church, since it paints the picture of the eucharistic assembly around the local bishop with reference to Ignatius, like *SC* 41, which sees the eucharistic assembly around the bishop as a manifestation of the heavenly gathering around Christ.

133. Also, Karl Rahner understands the term "universal Church" as the worldwide Church under the leadership of the Pope when he says that the bishop is subject-

ed to the pope "because the universal Church is manifested in his diocese. This makes him (i.e., the bishop) at once subordinate and independent. Therefore the bishop, too, has a responsibility for the whole Church. Not in the sense that he directly governs her, something which is reserved to the pope alone" (Rahner and Ratzinger, *Episcopate and Primacy*, 33).

134. I gratefully draw from personal communications with Professor Pott-meyer.

135. I draw here on personal communications with Pottmeyer. Further-more, Pottmeyer explains that the Explanatory Note, in clarifying that "the word college . . . does not imply equality between the head and the members, but only a proportion between the two relationships: Peter-apostles and pope-bishops," un-derscores the special place of the pope in the college (Pottmeyer, *Towards a Papacy*, 114). For Pottmeyer, the expression "hierarchical communion" in the Constitution on the Church (*LG* 22) was added to avoid any misunderstanding that the relation-ship inside the college between its head and the other members would be one of equality. (This point is taken from personal communications with Professor Pott-meyer.) However, Pottmeyer thinks that the word "hierarchical" was an unfortunate addition that weakens the idea of communion (ibid., 113).

136. I draw from personal communications with Pottmeyer.

137. Zizioulas, "Institution of Episcopal Conferences," 380.

138. Zizioulas, "Ὁ Συνοδικός Θεσμός," 177.

139. I draw on personal communications with Professor Pottmeyer.

140. Pottmeyer, *Towards a Papacy*, 114; Schatz, *Papal Primacy*, 169-70.

141. Philips, "History of the Constitution," 129.

142. Schatz says that both the Constitution and the Explanatory Note affirm the authority of the head of the college: "What was new in the version of 1964 was an additional description of a 'supra-collegial' position of the pope as vicar of Christ. While it appeared in the 1963 draft that the college of bishops, of course in union with the pope, was the proper agency of the highest authority in the Church, there now appears once more to be a twofold authority: on the one hand the college of the bishops in union with its head, but on the other hand the head by itself. This was certainly strengthened still further by the *nota explicativa praevia*, which repeatedly emphasizes that the pope can exercise his office alone 'and freely'" (*Papal Primacy*, 169-70).

143. Ratzinger, "Announcements," 304: "Finally, it is significant that the *Nota*, while stressing the Pope's independence of the college, nevertheless expressly in-cludes him in the college by its interpretation of the word *consentiente*. Article 22 of the text (i.e., *LG* 22) now has *consentiente* instead of the original *independenter*; and the word is interpreted to mean not that the Pope is independent of the col-lege as an authority wholly apart from it, but there must be a *communion* between them as between head and members." Also, Philips considers this fourth part of the Explanatory Note to be in accordance with the ecclesiology of communion: "The fourth point explains the 'assent' of the Pope, which is required for a collegiate act.

This use of this concept, which also occurs in the Constitution itself, is perfectly justified. One could not be accused of pressing matters on apologetical grounds if one even said that it is more in accordance with the ecclesiology of the *communio* than, for instance, the term 'in dependence on the Pope'" (Philips, "History of the Constitution," 136).

144. I am drawing this point from personal communications with Professor Pottmeyer.

145. Here I draw again on personal communications with Professor Pottmeyer.

146. Pottmeyer, *Towards a Papacy*, 115.

147. Ibid., 116.

148. Henn, *Honor of My Brothers*, 146.

149. Ibid.

150. Ratzinger comments on *LG* 21 as follows: "The sharp distinction between the power of order and power of jurisdiction, which had for centuries been introduced in the thought of the larger part of western theologians, now is made more fluid, and the intimate connection of the two realities which, in the ultimate analysis, constitute one sole thing, appears clear before the eyes" (quoted in Henn, *Honor of My Brothers*, 146n6).

151. Pottmeyer, *Towards a Papacy*, 117. Pottmeyer notes that the minority considered this doctrine as calling into question the maximalist conception of the papal primacy according to which all episcopal jurisdiction comes immediately from the pope.

152. Henn, "Historical-Theological Synthesis," 255.

153. Henn, *Honor of My Brothers*, 147.

154. Ibid., 147–48.

155. Ibid., 151.

156. Ibid., 151n10: "The *Nota explicativa praevia*, 2, is especially clear in indicating that the phrase 'hierarchical communion' intends to express the fact that 'a canonical or juridical determination through hierarchical authority' is required for such [ontological] power ordered to action."

157. In his commentary to Explanatory Note 2, Ratzinger calls this subject "one of the thorniest legal and constitutional problems in all the history of the Church" (Ratzinger, "Announcements," 300).

158. Henn, *Honor of My Brothers*, 151.

4—Orthodox Reactions to Vatican II

1. For the reactions to the invitation, see Karmiris, Ὀρθοδοξία καί Ρωμαιοκαθολικισμός 1 [*Orthodoxy and Roman Catholicism*, vol. 1], 31.

2. Ware, "Primacy, Collegiality," 122–23.

3. Karmiris, "Τὸ Δογματικόν Σύνταγμα περί «Ἐκκλησίας»" ["The Dogmatic Constitution on the Church"], 15.

4. Ibid., 16.

5. Ibid.

6. Ibid., 17.

7. Ibid., 18; see the similar comments of Russian theologian Nicholas Arseniev on this point: "'*Christ is the Light of nations*'—so begins this document. . . . The ecclesiology—for it is an ecclesiological document—is here from the beginning deeply *subordinated to Christology*. So it ought to be always, but we know how very often ecclesiology becomes practically independent" (Arseniev, "Constitution de Ecclesia," 17).

8. Cf. Karmiris, "Τὸ Δογματικόν Σύνταγμα," 18.

9. Meyendorff, in his review of Karmiris's ecclesiology, considers Karmiris's formulations on the "celestial" and the "earthly" Church as rather scholastic (Meyendorff, "Dogmatics, part 5: Orthodox Ecclesiology," 226).

10. Karmiris, "Τὸ Δογματικόν Σύνταγμα," 18–19.

11. Ibid., 19.

12. Ibid.

13. Cf. Karmiris, "Τὸ Δογματικόν Σύνταγμα," 19. Karmiris accepts the notion of the pre-existing Church (Ὀρθόδοξος Ἐκκλησιολογία, 25–44). It is relevant to note here that Zizioulas considers that the idea of the preexisting Church, found in Origen and in the second epistle of Clement of Rome, is markedly Platonic; it envisages the Church as the icon of the beginning [i.e., of the past], and of the original state of things. On the contrary, for Zizioulas, the Bible and Ignatius present the Church as an eschatological reality (Θέματα Ἐκκλησιολογίας, 19, 27–29). Meyendorff, in his review of Karmiris's ecclesiology, notes that, "the eternal, pre-existing and cosmic aspect of the Church's nature could rather be seen as revealed through the Incarnation of the Logos and, therefore, be mentioned in an 'incarnational' context, rather as a preamble, which, as such, sounds Platonic" (Meyendorff, "Dogmatics, part 5: Orthodox Ecclesiology," 226).

14. Harkianakis, "Ecclesiology of Vatican II," 238. Elsewhere, he considers the first chapter of the Constitution as the most important of all the chapters: "The most successful and important of all chapters of the Constitution seems to be the first where by considering the Church as the par excellence 'mysterion' the juridicism of the Roman Catholic Church is overcome and its theological horizons are so widened that they permit now the recognition of the secret dimension of the Church of Christ beyond its confessional boundaries" (Harkianakis, Τὸ Περί Ἐκκλησίας Σύνταγμα τῆς Β΄ Βατικανῆς Συνόδου [*The Constitution on the Church of the Second Vatican Council*], 273–74).

15. Karmiris, Ὀρθοδοξία καί Ρωμαιοκαθολικισμός II [*Orthodoxy and Roman Catholicism*, vol. 2], 184n1. Also, Athanasius Delikostopoulos considers that the ecclesiology of Vatican II, by stressing the *jure divino* nonexistent rights and attributes of the Roman bishop, does not show any respect for the nature of the Church as a mystery in Christ (Delikostopoulos, Αἱ Ἐκκλησιολογικαί Θέσεις τῆς Ρωμαιοκαθολικῆς Ἐκκλησίας [*The Ecclesiological Positions of the Roman Catholic Church*], 146).

16. Harkianakis, Τὸ Περὶ Ἐκκλησίας Σύνταγμα, 128–29.

17. Karmiris, "Τὸ Δογματικόν Σύνταγμα," 20.

18. Willebrands, "Vatican II's Ecclesiology," 189. Zizioulas has an opinion similar to that of Willebrands. Praising, as an Orthodox, the importance of Vatican II's Decree on Ecumenism, Unitatis Redintegratio, for Roman Catholic–Orthodox relations, Zizioulas emphasizes the point that in the Decree "there is no hesitation to call the Orthodox Churches by the name of Church in the full sense" ("Unitatis Redintegratio: An Orthodox Reflection," a paper read to the meeting for the fortieth anniversary of the promulgation of the conciliar Decree, Unitatis Redintegratio, November 2004, 6).

19. Karmiris, "Τὸ Δογματικόν Σύνταγμα," 20.

20. Ibid., 21.

21. Ibid., 21–22.

22. Ibid., 23.

23. Ibid.

24. Thus, the Constitution seems to suggest implicitly that the recognition of papal primacy of jurisdiction is a necessary condition for unity with other Christians, including the Orthodox. However, Zizioulas significantly asserts that the Decree on Ecumenism does not say explicitly that the petrine office as seen from a Roman Catholic view is a necessary condition for unity with the Orthodox Church. Moreover, Zizioulas comments that the decree leaves open the discussion on the petrine ministry, while at the same time it seems to suggest that the canonical structure of the Orthodox Churches does not have to change in order to be united with the Roman Catholic Church ("Unitatis Redintegratio," 7–8).

25. Karmiris, "Τὸ Δογματικόν Σύνταγμα," 24.

26. Ibid., 25. In so saying, he cites the similar opinion of the Russian Orthodox theologian Arseniev, who also claims the following: "So that a certain duality came to be stated in the structure of the Church—duality in unity!—the Pope and the Bishops, both as detainers of the supreme power in the Church, but the Bishops only as long as they are in union with the Pope. It is not stated, however, that the Pope retains the supreme power only in union with the body of the Bishops. So that the duality turns again to be rather a unity: a unity in the Pope" ("Constitutio de Ecclesia," 25n1).

27. Karmiris, "Τὸ Δογματικόν Σύνταγμα," 25. For Karmiris, the concept of collegiality is insufficiently expounded in the Constitution on the Church, and it is not grounded in the New Testament, for in the New Testament the "twelve" apostles did not form a college (37).

28. Likewise, the Greek Orthodox theologians Nikos Nissiotis and Panagiotis Nellas are opposed to the notion of collegiality. Pierre Duprey gives a number of Orthodox theologians who are opposed to the notion of collegiality (Duprey, "Synodical Structure," 171–72). Harkianakis, on the other hand, reacted to this criticism and considered that, even if the actual expression is lacking in the New Testament, the doctrine itself is radically present and expressed (ibid., 172n57).

It is not my intention here, however, to address the question of whether or not the twelve formed a college in the New Testament.

29. For this I draw on personal discussions with Professor McPartlan.

30. Karmiris, "Τὸ Δογματικόν Σύνταγμα," 30.

31. Ibid., 30; Karmiris, Ὀρθόδοξος Ἐκκλησιολογία, 661–63.

32. Karmiris, "Τὸ Δογματικόν Σύνταγμα περὶ Ἐκκλησίας," 30–31.

33. Karmiris quotes from Nicholas Afanassieff's article "Reflections d'un Orthodoxe," 11: "Entre les conciles, la collégialité des évêques se trouve dans un état d'anabiose et elle ne peut en sortir que sur le désir du Pape. En revanche, selon la même «Note explicative», «le Souverain Pontife, en tant que le pasteur suprême de l'Eglise, peut exercer son pouvoir en tout temps, à son gré, comme cela est requis par sa charge». S'il en est ainsi, je doute que l'on puisse parler du pouvoir suprême et souverain de l'épiscopat. Ce pouvoir appartient entièrement au Pape qui peut à son gré et dans les cas déterminés par lui, associer à se pouvoir le collège épiscopal qui doit toujours agir avec le consentement du Pape."

34. Karmiris, "Τὸ Δογματικόν Σύνταγμα," 32. Despite Karmiris's assertions, however, his quotation from the Explanatory Note, which states that "the college engages in strictly collegiate activity and that only with the consent of the head," cannot in itself be taken as an affirmation of the pope's right to act outside of and independently of the college. As was seen before, the Explanatory Note explains the meaning "with the consent of the head" within the context of communion ecclesiology and therefore includes the pope in the college when it says that, "the phrase *with the consent of the* head is used in order to exclude the impression of dependence on something *external*: but the word 'consent' entails *communion* between head and members"; see above, chapter 3.

35. See above, chapter 3.

36. Harkianakis, "Ecclesiology of Vatican II," 239–40.

37. Ibid., 240.

38. Ibid., 240–41.

39. Karmiris, "Τὸ Δογματικόν Σύνταγμα," 33.

40. See above, chapter 1. The Armenian Archbishop Mesrop K. Krikorian asserts in similar terms, "In the documents of Vatican II, the bishop of Rome as successor of Peter is vested with all powers and rights and consequently he possesses the highest authority and enjoys the greatest honor in the Church. Even in case of the ecumenical councils their confirmation or acceptance by the pope is regarded as a prerequisite, whereas for the Eastern and Oriental Churches the universal reception of a council by the Churches is the most important condition for its ecumenical character. In *Lumen Gentium* we read 'the supreme authority with which this college is empowered over the whole Church is exercised in a solemn way through an ecumenical council. A council is never ecumenical unless it is confirmed or at least accepted as such by the successor of Peter. It is the prerogative of the Roman pontiff to convoke these councils, to preside over them, and to confirm them.' It is quite clear that I am not delegated to speak in the name of other Churches, but I

think at least the Oriental Orthodox will not be able to accept the sole and highest authority of the Roman pontiff in respect to the ecumenical councils. I can imagine that most of these Churches will accept the *primacy of honor* of the Bishop of Rome and probably they also will agree that in consulting the heads of other Churches, he could convoke an ecumenical council and preside over it" (Krikorian, "Primacy of the Successor," 96).

41. Zizioulas asserts that the right of convocation of an ecumenical council and the presidency over it belong to the primate of the whole Church, who, according to the system that was valid in the ancient Church, was the bishop of Rome. He considers that any interference of the emperors in the convocation of the ancient councils and the presidency over them was of historical and not of canonical and ecclesiological importance (Zizioulas, "Ὁ Συνοδικός Θεσμός," 189n52).

42. Karmiris, Ὀρθοδοξία καί Ῥωμαιοκαθολικισμός, 208.

43. Karmiris, "Τὸ Δογματικόν Σύνταγμα," 35.

44. Harkianakis, "Ecclesiology of Vatican II," 243. Similarly, the Greek Orthodox theologian Panteleimon Rodopoulos asserts that, from an Orthodox point of view, episcopal collegiality is not of great importance since, according to the Constitution on the Church, the bishop of Rome has full power over the bishops even when they are gathered and make decisions in an ecumenical council. In referring to the above passage from *LG* 22, which states, "A council is never ecumenical unless it is confirmed or at least accepted as such by the successor of Peter. . . . It is the prerogative of the Roman Pontiff to convoke these councils, to preside over them, and to confirm them," Rodopoulos comments that the Orthodox cannot compromise on this point and cannot abandon the ancient tradition and practice of the Church according to which even the bishops of Rome and of Constantinople are bound to accept the decisions of the ecumenical councils provided that these councils are recognized as ecumenical by the conscience of the whole Church (Rodopoulos, "Μία ἀξιολόγησις τῶν ἀποφάσεων τῆς Β΄Συνόδου τοῦ Βατικανοῦ" ["An assessment of Vatican II's decisions"], 649.

45. Karmiris, Ὀρθόδοξος Ἐκκλησιολογία, 660n4. Karmiris quotes from A. Delikostopoulos's doctoral thesis, Αἱ Ἐκκλησιολογικαί Θέσεις τῆς Ῥωμαιοκαθολικῆς Ἐκκλησίας, 116–17.

46. See chapter 2. Karmiris quotes Nissiotis's position that the lack of a pneumatological basis in the Constitution on the Church causes its exaggerated preoccupation with the hierarchical structure of the Church, the successor of Peter, the collegiality of the bishops, and the episcopacy as a separate sacrament. He further argues, in line with Nissiotis, that there is not sufficient reference to the totality, the whole, the pleroma of the Church, and that without any pneumatological basis the Church loses its openness and flexibility, and its unity is seen only as a matter of discipline and obedience of the less important "categories of the People of God" to the superior ones. Karmiris agrees with Nissiotis that a lack of pneumatology results in a one-sided institutionalist and hierarchical view of the Church (Karmiris, "Τὸ Δογματικόν Σύνταγμα," 33n5). Yet, by siding with conciliarism, which, as we have

seen, implies for Zizioulas an institutionalist and juridical view of the synodical institution, Karmiris himself adopts such an institutionalist view.

47. Karmiris, "Τὸ Δογματικόν Σύνταγμα," 26–27.

48. See chapter 2.

49. Karmiris, "Τὸ Δογματικόν Σύνταγμα," 26.

50. See chapter 2.

51. See chapter 2.

52. Harkianakis, Περί τό Ἀλάθητον τῆς Ἐκκλησίας ἐν τῇ Ὀρθοδόξῳ Θεολογίᾳ [On the Infallibility of the Church in Orthodox Theology], 124.

53. Harkianakis, Τὸ περί Ἐκκλησίας Σύνταγμα, 183.

54. Ibid.

55. Ibid., 183–84.

56. See chapter 3.

57. Harkianakis, Τὸ περί Ἐκκλησίας Σύνταγμα, 184.

58. Rodopoulos, Ἡ Ἱεραρχική Ὀργάνωσις [The Hierarchical Structure], 32, 38.

59. Ibid., 32.

60. Ibid., 38.

61. Ibid., 31–32.

62. Harkianakis, Τὸ περί Ἐκκλησίας Σύνταγμα, 184–85.

63. Ibid., 184n2.

64. Duprey, "Synodical Structure," 176–77.

65. Zizioulas, Being as Communion, 141.

66. Zizioulas, "Unitatis Redintegratio," 2.

67. Zizioulas, "Institution of Episcopal Conferences," 379.

68. Ibid.

69. Ibid.

70. Zizioulas, Eucharist, Bishop, Church, 190–91n331, where Zizioulas refers to certain Roman Catholic theologians. References here are to the English translation of Zizioulas's dissertation.

71. Ibid., 262.

72. Ibid.

73. Ibid.

74. Ibid., 262–63.

75. Ibid., 263.

76. Ibid.

77. Zizioulas, "Apostolic Continuity," 156–57 (emphasis in original); cf. Zizioulas, Eucharist, Bishop, Church, 142; 186–87n281; 190–91n331. It is clear, therefore, that St. Cyprian excludes any universalistic ecclesiology that considers the Church as a worldwide unity headed by one man, the sole successor of Peter. As Clark Carlton puts it: "Cyprian was not talking about the unity of the universal Church, but the unity of the local Church. The reference to the chair of Peter is not a reference to Rome alone, but to the bishops in each local Church. . . . The local bishop, the successor of Peter in each Church, is the centre of unity in each local Church. . . . Cyprian

does not conceive of the Catholic Church as a worldwide unity headed by one man, the sole successor of Peter, but as the local Church, organised around the bishop, who, together with all of the other catholic bishops of the world, shares in the 'Chair of Peter'" (Carlton, *Truth*, 124–25). Also, Zizioulas asserts that Cyprian in his work *De Catholicae Ecclesiae Unitate* talks about the unity within each local Church and therefore "the ecclesial unity founded on the one throne of Peter is to be found in the episcopal Church which does not admit a second altar" (Zizioulas, *Eucharist, Bishop, Church*, 191n331).

78. Zizioulas, "Apostolic Continuity," 157; cf. Zizioulas, "Δύο Ἀρχαῖαι Παραδόσεις" ["Two Ancient Traditions"], 12–13n28. Thus, Zizioulas criticizes Afanassieff's view that in the ancient Church of the first centuries each bishop was understood as a successor of an individual apostle. For Zizioulas, "such a view is wrongly attributed to sources of the first centuries" (Zizioulas, "Apostolic Continuity," 157n11).

79. Zizioulas, *Being as Communion*, 200n106, 204n116.

80. Ibid., 200–201.

81. Meyendorff, *Orthodoxy and Catholicity*, 163.

82. Zizioulas, "Institution of Episcopal Conferences," 379; McPartlan, *Eucharist Makes the Church*, 209n128. Antonio Acerbi's book, *Due ecclesiologie*, is relevant in connection with Zizioulas's judgement about there being two ecclesiologies operative at Vatican II.

83. Zizioulas, "Institution of Episcopal Conferences," 379.

84. See chapter 3. However, we have seen that *LG* 23 does not fully guarantee the catholicity of the local Church, although *LG* 26 seems to provide stronger recognition for the same. For Meyendorff, *LG* 26 recognizes the catholicity of the local Church on the basis of eucharistic ecclesiology, while other passages reject such a catholicity by stating that the local churches "are constituted after the model of the universal Church" or that the local Churches are portions of the universal Church (cf. *LG* 23) (Meyendorff, *Orthodoxy and Catholicity*, 159). Meyendorff criticizes Vatican II's understanding of the universal Church as the current worldwide Church led by the Roman Bishop (McPartlan, *Eucharist Makes the Church*, 107–8).

85. See chapter 2.

86. Clement, "Quelques remarques d'un orthodoxe," 112: "Et certes; fondamentalement, la collégialité épiscopale est pensée dans le cadre d'une ecclésiologie universaliste comme un «pouvoir» analogue à celui du pape; et non comme l'expression universelle d'une ecclésiologie eucharistique. L'ordre des évêques constitue «le sujet d'un pouvoir suprême et plénier sur toute l'Eglise» (22). Pourtant, le sens de la diversité des églises se fait jour «par sa composition multiple, ce collège exprime la diversité et l'universalité du peuple de Dieu.»

87. See chapter 3.

88. Zizioulas, *Being as Communion*, 179.

89. Olivier Clement asserts that the ecclesiology of the above passage from *LG* 21 is clearly "filioquistic" (Clement, "Quelques remarques d'un orthodoxe," 109).

90. Zizioulas, *Being as Communion*, 179n29.

91. Ibid., 123.

92. *LG* 22: "The order of the bishops is the successor to the college of the apostles in their role as teachers and pastors, and in it the apostolic college is perpetuated. Together with their head, the Supreme Pontiff, and never apart from him, they have supreme and full authority over the universal Church."

93. Zizioulas, "Church as Communion," 11.

94. Zizioulas, "Primacy in the Church," 117.

95. Ibid.

96. Zizioulas, "Recent Discussions on Primacy," 244.

97. Ibid.

98. See chapter 2.

99. Zizioulas, "Primacy in the Church," 117.

100. Ibid.

101. Ibid.

102. Zizioulas, "Recent Discussions on Primacy," 245; quotation from Congar, *L'Eglise de Saint Augustin*, 78–79.

103. Zizioulas, "Recent Discussions on Primacy," 245.

104. Ibid.

105. Ibid., 244.

106. Ibid., 246, reference to Congar, *L'Eglise de Saint Augustin*, 78f.

107. Zizioulas, "Recent Discussions on Primacy," 246.

108. Zizioulas, "Primacy in the Church," 123.

109. Ibid., 118.

110. Zizioulas, "Orthodox Ecclesiology," 21.

111. He further indicates that, given that in the early Church the local eucharistic assembly was a revelation of the eschatological unity of all in Christ, "*no mutual exclusion* between the local and the universal was possible in a eucharistic context, but the one was automatically involved in the other" (Zizioulas, *Being as Communion*, 155, emphasis in original). In criticizing Afanassieff and Meyendorff for considering that the local church comes first, both historically and theologically, he expresses the view that the nature of the Eucharist points to the simultaneity of locality and universality. For Zizioulas, this prioritizing of the local church in eucharistic ecclesiology results from a lack of synthesis between Christology and pneumatology which leads to a kind of "congregationalism" in the Church. There is in fact no priority of the local over the universal nor of the universal over the local. The local/universal dilemma is transcended in the Eucharist, as is any dichotomy between Christology and pneumatology (Zizioulas, "Primacy in the Church," 119; Zizioulas, *Being as Communion*, 133).

112. Zizioulas, "Church as Communion," 10.

113. Ibid.

114. Ibid.

115. Zizioulas, Θέματα Ἐκκλησιολογίας, 86–87.

116. Ibid., 87–88.

117. Zizioulas, "Church as Communion," 10.

118. Ibid.

119. Ibid., 11–12.

120. Regarding the application of this principle in each local church, Zizioulas states that the person of the bishop in the local church represents the institution of unity—"the one"—*the primus*, while the many are represented through the other ministries and the laity. Both are understood as relational entities. In fact, it is in the Eucharist that "the one and the many" becomes a reality (Zizioulas, *Being as Communion*, 136; Zizioulas, "Primacy in the Church," 121).

121. Zizioulas, *Being as Communion*, 134–35 (emphasis in original).

122. Zizioulas, "Father as Cause," 118–19. In this important chapter of his book, Zizioulas responds critically to those theologians who object to his insistence on the teaching of the Cappadocians that the Father is the cause of the Son and the Holy Spirit (123–24). In particular, he is critical of certain theologians who identify the monarchy, the one *arche* in the Holy Trinity, not with the Father, but with the notion of the Triunity of God. Zizioulas considers that such a proposition cannot serve the purpose of indicating ontological derivation and puts at risk biblical monotheism because it implies that the relation between the ultimate giver (the Father) and recipient is a symmetrical one, allowing for the Father to be caused by the Son and the Spirit (134–36, 144n89, 149). While for Zizioulas, the Father as a person draws his identity from the relations to the other two persons and is conditioned by them (see below), the Father, as personal cause of the other two persons, freely and out of love constitutes this relation and communion with them (Zizioulas, *Being as Communion*, 44–46).

123. McPartlan, *Eucharist Makes the Church*, 179.

124. "But a relational being draws its identity, its personhood, from its relation with others. One person is no person. The spiritual character of God's own being lies in nothing else but in the relational nature of his existence: there is no Father unless there is a Son and the Spirit. And since the one God is the Father and not the one divine nature or *ousia*, the very identity of God depends on the Father's relationship with persons other than himself. There is no 'one' whose identity is not conditioned by the 'many,'" (Zizioulas, "Mystery of the Church," 299); see also Zizioulas, "Father as Cause," 13: "The Father as a relational entity is inconceivable without the Son and the Spirit."

125. Zizioulas, "Father as Cause," 140–49. In quoting St. Basil, Zizioulas asserts that there is an asymmetrical hierarchical ordering in the Holy Trinity, where the Father comes first and the Son is second in rank because he derives from the Father (140). Such a trinitarian ordering and causation does not threaten the equality of the other two persons, since this ordering and hierarchy implies that the causing one, the Father, who is higher, i.e., ontologically prior to the other two persons, brings forth the other two who are equal in nature and wholes of the whole (cf. 140, 143–44).

126. If there is not a hierarchical asymmetry and ordering but a polycentric symmetry in the structure of trinitarian relations, as Miroslav Volf, a theologian of the Free Church tradition, suggests, such a symmetry results in a structure of ecclesial unity, which cannot be conceived by way of the one, be it the pope, the patriarch, or the bishop. For Volf, at the trinitarian level, as well as at the ecclesiological level, unity does not presuppose the unifying one (Volf, *After Our Likeness*, 217, 219). Volf believes that the one cannot be part of the ecclesial community itself because this would contradict the analogy with the structure of trinitarian relations (see his paper, "Trinity, Unity, Primacy," 181). It seems then that from Volf's view of the Holy Trinity there is not an institution of unity, be it a bishop or a primate in the Church. We have already seen that for Zizioulas, if the relations between the persons were symmetrical, this would endanger monotheism. As we noted above, there is an order and a primate as an expression of unity (i.e., "the one") in the Church and in the apostolic college itself. As we shall see, Meyendorff asserts that the Church always recognized such an order.

127. I owe this important point to personal discussions with Zizioulas.

128. Zizioulas, "Father as Cause," 146–47.

129. Zizioulas, *Being as Communion*, 135. For the second principle, see below.

130. I draw on personal discussions with Zizioulas.

131. I owe this important point to personal discussions with Zizioulas.

132. Zizioulas, *Being as Communion*, 135–36.

133. Ibid., 136.

134. Zizioulas, "Nature of the Unity," 344–45.

135. Zizioulas, "Primacy in the Church," 124.

136. Zizioulas, "Recent Discussions on Primacy," 243.

137. Ibid.

138. Ibid. Nicholas Lossky notes that "some might say that canon 34 speaks of bishops and therefore concerns primacy and conciliarity among bishops only. Certainly in a limited sense this is true. However, as many of us say with insistence today, a bishop (theoretically at least) does not exist outside or above the Church" (Lossky, "Conciliarity," 131).

139. Zizioulas, "Recent Discussions on Primacy," 243.

140. Zizioulas, "Institution of Episcopal Conferences," 380–81.

141. Zizioulas, "Primacy in the Church," 125. If the universal primacy was exercised *over* the universal church this would imply a primacy of jurisdiction, which for Zizioulas would negate the catholicity of each local church (cf. 124).

142. Zizioulas, "Ὁ Συνοδικός Θεσμός," 188.

143. Ibid., 189.

144. Ibid., 189–90.

145. Ibid., 190.

146. Ibid.

147. Zizioulas, "Primacy in the Church," 120–21 (emphasis in original).

148. Zizioulas stresses the fact that a synod cannot impose any decision on a

local Church unless this Church participated through its bishop in taking the relevant decisions and agreed to their acceptance. He concludes that the synod derives its authority not as an institution in itself, but from the communion among the Churches, through their bishops, and that the Church is a body of communion and freedom and not of legal necessity (Zizioulas, "Ο Συνοδικός Θεσμός," 181).

149. Zizioulas, *Being as Communion*, 137.

150. Zizioulas, "Ecclesiology of Institutions," 7. Zizioulas here implies that this canonical structure of inter-Orthodox unity through a universal primate, i.e., the Patriarch of Constantinople, was not so visible in the past. It is for this reason that Zizioulas urges the Orthodox to accept the necessity of such a canonical unity within the Orthodox Church (I owe this clarification to personal discussions with Zizioulas). We have seen in chapter 2 that the creation of the nineteenth-century national autocephalous churches and the underlying ecclesiology did not provide effective structures for communion on the universal level, and this resulted in their division and fragmentation. On the other hand, in the twentieth century the convocation by the Ecumenical Patriarchate of Pan-Orthodox Councils contributed to the realization of the unity of all Orthodox churches on the universal level.

151. Zizioulas, *Being as Communion*, 133. McPartlan comments that this statement of Zizioulas "shows clearly that he does *not* think that Orthodoxy has replaced oneness in the Pope with oneness in conciliarity" (McPartlan, *Eucharist Makes the Church*, 205).

152. Zizioulas, "Orthodox Ecclesiology," 25–26.

153. McPartlan, *Eucharist Makes the Church*, 204.

154. Zizioulas, *Eucharist, Bishop, Church*, 161.

155. McPartlan, *Eucharist Makes the Church*, 204.

156. Ibid., 206–7.

157. See chapter 2.

158. Afanassieff, "Church Which Presides," 99.

159. Ibid., 115–16.

160. Ibid., 111–12.

161. Ibid., 112–13.

162. McPartlan, *Eucharist Makes the Church*, 233.

163. Ibid.

164. Ibid.

165. Zizioulas, *Eucharist, Bishop, Church*, 257–61; McPartlan, *Eucharist Makes the Church*, 227.

166. Afanassieff, "Church Which Presides," 111–12.

167. McPartlan, *Eucharist Makes the Church*, 233–34.

168. See above.

169. See above.

170. Zizioulas, *Being as Communion*, 133.

171. Zizioulas, "Orthodox Ecclesiology," 20–21; Zizioulas, *Being as Communion*, 24–25.

172. Zizioulas, "Orthodox Ecclesiology," 20.

173. Ibid., 20–21.

174. Afanassieff, "Church Which Presides," 102.

175. Zizioulas, "Ὁ Συνοδικός Θεσμός," 188n52.

176. See above.

177. Afanassieff, "Church Which Presides," 101.

178. Ibid., 102–3.

179. Ibid., 142.

180. Duprey, "Synodical Structure," 168–69.

181. Zizioulas, "Recent Discussions on Primacy," 233–35. It should be noted here that from a canonical point of view the term *"primus inter pares"* does not exist. The only term that the canons use is primate or the first one (πρῶτος); cf. for example, the Thirty-Fourth Apostolic Canon (I owe this point to personal discussions with Metropolitan Panteleimon of Tyroloe and Serention).

182. See chapter 2.

183. Zizioulas, "Institution of Episcopal Conferences," 380.

184. Afanassieff, "Church Which Presides," 113.

185. Ibid., 114.

186. See chapter 2.

187. Zizioulas, "Recent Discussions on Primacy," 240. Moreover, Zizioulas considers Afanassieff's principle, that the idea of primacy is a legalistic notion contradicting the idea of grace, to be influenced by Khomiakov and to some extent by liberal Protestant theology. For Afanassieff, priority is a concept founded on the idea of grace (Afanassieff, "Church Which Presides," 141).

188. Zizioulas, "Recent Discussions on Primacy," 244.

189. Ibid., 240. Zizioulas quotes from Schmemann's article, "Idea of Primacy," 163, 165. Though Zizioulas refers to the old edition of the book published in 1973, he in fact quotes from the new edition of 1992.

190. Zizioulas, "Recent Discussions on Primacy," 241. Zizioulas again quotes from the above-mentioned article by Schmemann at 166.

191. Schmemann, "Idea of Primacy," 165.

192. Zizioulas, "Primacy in the Church," 123.

193. Zizioulas, "Recent Discussions on Primacy," 259; Zizioulas quotes from Meyendorff, *Byzantine Legacy*, 243–45.

Bibliography

Acerbi, Antonio. *Due ecclesiologie. Ecclesiologia guiridica ed ecclesiologia di commu- nione nella "Lumen gentium."* Bologna: Edizioni Dehoniane, 1975.

Afanassieff, Nicholas. *The Church of the Holy Spirit.* Notre Dame, IN: University of Notre Dame Press, 2007.

——. "The Church Which Presides in Love." In *The Primacy of Peter*, edited by John Meyendorff, 91–143. Crestwood, NY: St. Vladimir's Seminary Press, 1992.

——. "Reflections d'un Orthodoxe sur la Collégialité des Évêques." *Le Messager Orthodoxe* 29–30, I–II (1965): 7–15.

Alberigo, Giuseppe, and Joseph A. Komonchak. *History of Vatican II: The Mature Council, Second Period and Intersession, September, 1963–September, 1964,* vol. 3. Maryknoll, NY: Orbis, 2000.

Amrich, M. Paracleta. *Catholicism and Orthodox: The "Struggle" for "Reunion" from the Second Vatican Council to the Holy Year 2000.* PhD diss., Duquesne University, 2006.

Androutsos, Christos. Συμβολική, Ἐκδόσεις Βασιλείου Ρηγοπούλου, Ἔκδοσις Τρίτη [*Symbolic*], 3rd ed. Thessaloniki: Vasilios Rigopoulos' Publishing, 1963.

Arseniev, Nicholas. "The Second Vatican Council's 'Constitutio de Ecclesia.'" *St. Vladimir's Seminary Quarterly* 9, no. 1 (1965): 16–25.

Athanasius, Bishop Jevtic. Бог Отаца Наших [*God of Our Fathers*]. Monastery Chilandar, 2000.

Aubert, Roger. *Le Saint Siège et l'Union des Eglises.* Brussells: Editions Universitaires, 1947.

Baur, John. Διατριβαί ἐπί τῆς ἐν ἔτει 1895 Ἐγκυκλίου Ἐπιστολῆς τοῦ Πατριάρχου Κωνσταντινουπόλεως καί περί τῆς ἐν γένει Ἀνατολικῆς Ἐκκλησίας καί ἰδίως κατά τούς συγγραφεῖς καί ὁμολογίας αὐτῆς, Τύποις ΡΕΝΙΕΡΗ ΠΡΙΝΤΕΖΗ [*Treatises about the encyclical letter of the patriarch of Constantinople and about the Eastern Church and in particular according to her authors and confessions*]. Siros: Renieri Printezi, 1898.

Beauduin, Dom Lambert. *Liturgy: The Life of the Church.* Collegeville, MN: Liturgical Press, 1926.

Berger, Calinic (Kevin M.). "Does the Eucharist Make the Church? An Ecclesiological Comparison of Stăniloae and Zizioulas." *St. Vladimir's Theological Quarterly* 51, no. 1 (2007): 23–70.

Bermejo, Luis. *Church, Conciliarity and Communion.* Anand, India: Gujarat Sahitya Prakash, 1984.

———. *Toward Christian Reunion, Vatican I: Obstacles and Opportunities.* Anand, India: Gujarat Sahitya Prakash, 1984.

Bordeianu, Radu. "Orthodox-Catholic Dialogue: Retrieving Eucharistic Ecclesiology." *Journal of Ecumenical Studies* 44, no. 2 (2009): 239–65.

Botte, Bernard, O.S.B. "The Collegial Character of the Priesthood and the Episcopate." *Concilium* 4 (Ecumenism), no. 1 (1965): 88–90.

Boutiras, Spiridon. Ἡ Παπικὴ Μοναρχία καὶ ἡ Ὀρθόδοξος Ἐκκλησία, Ἐκ τοῦ Τυπογραφείου Ἀποστολοπούλου [*The Papal Monarchy and the Orthodox Church*]. Athens: Apostolopoulou, 1902.

Brandi, Soterios. Ἀπάντησις τοῦ Αἰδ. πατρὸς Σωτῆρος Brandi πρὸς τὴν Ἐγκύκλιον Ἐπιστολὴν τῆς Α.Μ. τοῦ Πατριάρχου Κωνσταντινουπόλεως, Τύποις [*Answer of Reverend Father Soterios Brandi to the Encyclical Letter of his Beatitude the Patriarch of Constantinople*]. Siros: Renieri Printezi, 1896.

Buckley, Michael, S. J. *Papal Primacy and the Episcopate: Toward a Relational Understanding.* New York: Crossroad Publishing, 1998.

Bulgakov, Sergius. *The Vatican Dogma.* South Canaan, PA: St. Tikhon Press, 1959.

Butler, Dom Cuthbert. *The Vatican Council.* London: Collins and Harvill, 1962.

Cappellari, Mauro. *Il trionfo della Sancta Sede e della Chiese contro gli assalti de' novatori reprinti e commattuti colle stesse armi.* Rome: n.p., 1799.

Carlton, Clark. *The Truth: What Every Roman Catholic Should Know about the Orthodox Church.* Salisbury, MA: Regina Orthodox Press, 1998.

Chadwick, Owen. *A History of the Popes 1830–1914.* New York: Oxford University Press, 2003.

Clement, Olivier. "Orthodox Ecclesiology as an Ecclesiology of Communion." *One in Christ* 6 (1970): 101–22.

———. "Quelques remarques d'un orthodoxe sur la Constitution De Ecclesia." In *Oecumenica* (Annales de Recherche Oecuménique 1966), 97–116. Strasbourg: Centre d'Études Oecuménique de Strasbourg, 1966.

———. *You Are Peter: An Orthodox Theologian's Reflection on the Exercise of Papal Primacy.* New York: New City Press, 2003.

Congar, Yves. "De la communion des églises à une ecclésiologie de l'Eglise universelle." In *L'Episcopat et l'Eglise universelle,* edited by Y. Congar and B. D. Dupuy, 227–60. Paris: Editions du Cerf, 1964.

———, ed. *La collégialité épiscopale: Histoire et théologie.* Paris: Editions du Cerf, 1965.

———. *L'Eglise de Saint Augustin à l'époque moderne.* Paris: Editions du Cerf, 1970.

———. "Moving toward a Pilgrim Church." In *Vatican II by Those Who Were There,* edited by Alberic Stacpoole, 129–52. London: Geoffrey Chapman, 1986.

Cross, Lawrence B. J. *An Examination of the 'Dialogue of Love' between the Eastern Orthodox and Roman Catholic Churches.* PhD diss., Melbourne College of Divinity, 1999.

Cullmann, Oscar. *Peter: Disciple, Apostle, Martyr: A Historical and Theological Study*. London: SCM, 1953.

Daley, Brian E. "Position and Patronage in the Early Church: The Original Meaning of 'Primacy of Honour.'" *Theological Studies* 44 (1993): 529–53.

———. "Primacy and Collegiality in the Fourth Century: A Note on Apostolic Canon 34." *Jurist* 68 (2008): 5–21.

Dejaifve, George. *Pape et l'évêque au Premier Concile du Vatican*. Brussels: Desclée de Brouwer, 1961.

———. "Primauté et collegialité au premier concile du Vatican." In *L'Episcopat et l'Eglise Universelle*, 639–60.

Delikostopoulos, Athanasius. *Αἱ Ἐκκλησιολογικαί Θέσεις τῆς Ρωμαιοκαθολικῆς Ἐκκλησίας ὡς Δογματικόν Πρόβλημα τοῦ Θεολογικοῦ Διαλόγου [The Ecclesiological Positions of the Roman Catholic Church as the Dogmatic Problem in Theological Dialogue]*. Athens: n.p., 1969.

de Lubac, Henri. *Catholicism: Christ and the Common Destiny of Man*. San Francisco: Ignatius, 1988.

———. *Corpus Mysticum*. 2nd ed. Paris: Aubier, 1949.

Demacopoulos, George. "Gregory the Great and the Sixth-Century Dispute over the Ecumenical Title." *Theological Studies* 70 (2009): 600–21.

De Maistre, Joseph. *Du Pape*. Beaucé-Rusand: n.p., 1819.

De Ville, Adam A. J. *Orthodoxy and the Roman Papacy, Ut Unum Sint and the Prospects of East West Unity*. Notre Dame, IN: University of Notre Dame Press, 2011.

De Vries, Wilhelm. *Orthodoxie et Catholicisme: Unité et Vérité*. Paris: Desclee, 1967.

Dewan, F. Wilfrid. "Potestas vere episcopalis au Premier Concile du Vatican." In *L'Episcopat et l'Eglise Universelle*, 661–87.

———. "Preparation of the Vatican Council's Schema on the Power and Nature of the Primacy." *Ephemerides Theologicae Lovanienses* 36 (1960): 23–56.

De Wyels, Franco. "Le Concile du Vatican et l'Union." *Irénikon* 6 (1929): 366–96, 488–516, 655–65.

Documents of the Joint International Commission for the Theological Dialogue between the Roman Catholic Church and the Orthodox Church. Prepared by the Pontifical Council for Promoting Christian Unity 2007.

Duffy, Eamon. *Saints and Sinners: A History of the Popes*. New Haven, CT: Yale University Press, 1997.

Dulles, Avery. "A Half-Century of Ecclesiology." *Theological Studies* 50 (1989): 419–42.

Duprey, Pierre W. F. "The Synodical Structure of the Church in Eastern Theology." *One in Christ* 7 (1971): 152–79.

Dvornik, Francis. *The Idea of Apostolicity in Byzantium and the Legend of the Apostle Andrew*. Dumbarton Oaks Studies 4. Cambridge, MA: Harvard University Press, 1958.

Ἐκκλησιαστική Ἀλήθεια, τόμος 19 (1895–1896) [*Ecclesiastical Truth*] Ecclesiastical Truth, vol. 19 (1895–1896). The republished editions by Thessaloniki: Patriarchal Institute for Patristic Studies.

Erickson, H. John. *The Challenge of Our Past*. Crestwood, NY: St. Vladimir's Seminary Press, 1991.

———. "The Local Churches and Catholicity: An Orthodox Perspective." *Jurist* 52 (1992): 490–508.

Evdokimov, Paul. "Can a Petrine Office be Meaningful in the Church: A Russian Orthodox Reply." *Concilium* 4, no. 7 (1971): 122–26.

Eybel, J. V. *Was ist der Papst?* Vienna: n.p., 1782.

Farantos, Megas. "Τό Παπικόν Πρωτεῖον καί ἡ Ὀρθόδοξος Ἐκκλησία," Ἀνάτυπον ἐκ τοῦ Περιοδικοῦ Κοινωνία ["The Papal Primacy and the Orthodox Church"]. Athens, 1977. An offprint from the periodical *Koinonia*.

Fortino, Eleuterio. "The Theological Dialogue between the Catholic Church and the Orthodox Church." In *One in 2000? Toward Catholic-Orthodox Unity*, edited by Paul McPartlan, 15–36. St. Paul, MN: Slough, 1993.

Funk, F. X. *Patres Apostolici*, vol. 1. "Tubingae: H. Laupp, 1901.

Garuti, Adriano. *The Primacy of the Bishop of Rome and Ecumenical Dialogue*. San Francisco: Ignatius Press, 2004.

Gonzáles de Cardedal, Olegario. "Development of a Theology of the Local Church from the First to the Second Vatican Council." *Jurist* 52 (1992): 11–43.

Grillmeier, Aloys. "The People of God." In *Commentary on the Documents of Vatican II*, vol. 1, edited by H. Vorgrimler, 153–85. New York: Herder and Herder, 1967.

Hamer, Jerome. *The Church Is a Communion*. London: Geoffrey Chapman, 1964.

Harkianakis, Stylianos. "Can a Petrine Office be Meaningful in the Church: A Greek Orthodox Reply." *Concilium* 4, no. 7 (1971): 115–21.

———. "The Ecclesiology of Vatican II: An Orthodox summary." *Diaconia* 2, no. 3 (1967): 233–49.

———. Τό Περί Ἐκκλησίας Σύνταγμα τῆς Β΄ Βατικανῆς Συνόδου [*The Constitution on the Church of the Second Vatican Council*]. Thessaloniki: n.p., 1969.

———. Περί τό Ἀλάθητον τῆς Ἐκκλησίας ἐν τῇ Ὀρθοδόξῳ Θεολογίᾳ [*On the Infallibility of the Church in Orthodox Theology*]. Athens: n.p., 1965.

Henn, William. "Historical-Theological Synthesis of the Relation between Primacy and Episcopacy during the Second Millienium." In *Il primato del successore de Pietro: Atti del simposio teologico, Roma, dicembre 1996*. Vatican City: Libreria Editrice Vaticana, 1997.

———. *The Honor of My Brothers: A Short History of the Relationship between the Pope and the Bishops*. New York: Crossroad, 2000.

Himes, Michael. "The Development of Ecclesiology: Modernity to the Twentieth Century." In *The Gift of the Church: A Textbook on Ecclesiology in Honor of Patrick Granfield*, edited by Peter C. Phan. Collegeville, MN: Liturgical Press, 2000.

Jugie, Martin. *Theologia Dogmatica Christianorum Orientalium*, vol. 4. Paris: Sumptibus Letouzey et Ané, 1931.

Karavagelli, Germanos. *Πραγματεία Ἱστορική ἐπί τῆς κατά Ἰούνιον 1894, ἀπολυθείσης ἐγκυκλίου τοῦ Πάπα Λέοντος ΙΓ΄, Ἐκ τοῦ τυπογραφείου Ἀ. Καλαράκη* [*A historical treatise on the encyclical letter of Leo XIII issued in June 1894*]. Athens: A. Kalaraki, 1900.

Karmiris, John. *Τά Δογματικά καί Συμβολικά Μνημεῖα τῆς Ὀρθοδόξου Καθολικῆς Ἐκκλησίας* [*The Dogmatic and Symbolic Documents of the Orthodox Catholic Church*]. Gratz, Austria: Akademische Druck u. Verlagsanstalt, 1968.

——. "Τό Δογματικόν Σύνταγμα περί «Ἐκκλησίας» τῆς Β΄ Βατικανείου Συνόδου," Ἐπιστημονική Ἐπετηρίς τῆς Θεολογικῆς Σχολῆς["The Dogmatic Constitution on the Church of the Second Vatican Council"]. *Academic Review of the Theological School of Athens* 17. Athens: 1971, 15–58.

——. *Ὀρθόδοξος Ἐκκλησιολογία* [*Orthodox Ecclesiology*]. Athens: n.p., 1973.

——. *Ὀρθοδοξία καί Ῥωμαιοκαθολικισμός*, Ι [*Orthodoxy and Roman Catholicism, vol. 1*]. Athens: n.p., 1964.

——. *Ὀρθοδοξία καί Ῥωμαιοκαθολικισμός, ἡ Τρίτη Πανορθόδοξος Διάσκεψις τῆς Ῥόδου, καί ἡ Τρίτη φάσις τῆς Δευτέρας Βατικανῆς Συνόδου*, ΙΙ, Ἀνάτυπον ἐκ τοῦ Περιοδικοῦ Ἐκκλησία [*Orthodoxy and Roman Catholicism: The 3rd Pan-orthodox Conference of Rhodes, and the 3rd Session of the Second Vatican Council, vol. 2*]. Athens: n.p., 1965.

——. *Θεολογικά Θέματα, Ἀνάτυπον ἐκ τῆς ἐφημερίδος Ὀρθόδοξος Τύπος* [*Theological issues*]. An offprint from the newspaper *Orthodox Press*, Athens, 1979.

Kasper, Walter, ed. "Church as Communio." *Communio* 13 (1986): 100–117.

——. *The Petrine Ministry: Catholics and Orthodox in Dialogue*, edited by Walter Kasper. Academic symposium held at the Pontifical Council for Promoting Christian Unity. New York: Newman Press, 2006.

——. *Theology and the Church*. New York: Crossroad, 1989.

Kefalas, Nektarios. *Μελέτη Ἱστορική περί τῶν αἰτίων τοῦ σχίσματος*, Τόμος Β΄, Ἐκ τοῦ Τυπογραφείου Π. Λεώνη [*Historical Study on the Causes of the Schism, vol. 2*]. Athens: P. Leoni, 1912.

Kiriakos, D. Anastasios. *Ἀντιπαπικά*, Βιβλιοθήκη Συλλόγου Μικρασιατῶν, Τόμος Πρῶτος [*Antipapal*, Library of the Eastern Asia Minor Association, vol. 1]. Athens: n.p., 1893.

Komonchak, Joseph A. "The Local Church and the Church Catholic: The Contemporary Theological Problematic." *Jurist* 52 (1992): 416–47.

Krikorian, Mesrop K. "The Primacy of the Successor of the Apostle St. Peter from the Point of View of the Oriental Orthodox Churches." In *Petrine Ministry and the Unity of the Church*, 83–98.

Küng, Hans. *Structures of the Church*. London: Burns and Oats, 1965.

Lanne, Emmanuel. "To What Extent Is Roman Primacy Unacceptable to the Eastern Churches." *Concilium* 4, no. 7 (1971): 62–67.

Legrand, Hervé. "Collégialité des évêques et communion des églises dans la reception de Vatican II." *Revue des sciences philosophiques et théologiques* 75 (1991): 545–68.

———. "'One Bishop per City': Tensions around the Expression of the Catholicity of the Local Church since Vatican II." *Jurist* 52 (1992).

Leo. *The Great Encyclical Letters of Pope Leo XIII*. New York: Benzinger Brothers, 1903.

L'Huilier, Pierre. "A propos de la collégialité épiscopale." *Le Messager Orthodoxe* 4 (1963)–5(1965): 8–12.

Lossky, Nicolas. "Conciliarity: Primacy in a Russian Orthodox Perspective." In *Petrine Ministry and the Unity of the Church*, 127–35.

Malataki, M. Ἀπάντησις εἰς τήν περί τῶν χωριζουσῶν τάς δύο Ἐκκλησίας διαφορῶν Πατριαρχικήν καί Συνοδικήν Ἐγκύκλιον τῆς Ἐκκλησίας Κωνσταντινουπόλεως [*Answer to the patriarchal and Synodical letter of the Church of Constantinople about the differences which divide the two Churches*]. N.p., 1895. [Malataki seems to use an abbreviated form of his name, i.e., M.M.]

Mansi, G. D., et al., eds. *Sacrorum Conciliorum nova et amplissima Collectio*, ed. G.D. Mansi and others vols. 1–53. 1759–1798; 1901–1927.

Maret, Henri. *Du concile général et de la paix religieuse*. Paris: n.p., 1869.

Martin, C. *Omnium Concilii Vaticani Documentorum Collectio*. Paderborn: n.p., 1873.

Mavrichi, Ionut. "Rev. Dr. Dumitru Staniloae: Background, context and development of an Orthodox ecclesiological synthesis," http://works.bepress.com/cgi/viewcontent.cgi?article=1005&context=ionut_mavrichi

Maximos, Metropolitan of Sardes. *The Ecumenical Patriarchate in the Orthodox Church: A Study in the History and Canons of the Church*. Translated from the Greek by Gamon McLellan. Thessaloniki: Patriarchal Institute for Patristic Studies, 1976.

McPartlan, Paul. "Eucharistic Ecclesiology." *One in Christ* 22 (1986): 314–31.

———. *The Eucharist Makes the Church: Henri de Lubac and John Zizioulas in Dialogue*. Edinburgh: T&T Clark, 1993.

———. "Liturgy, Church, and Society." *Studia Liturgica* 34 (2004): 147–64.

———. "The Local Church and the Universal Church: Zizioulas and the Ratzinger-Kasper Debate." *International Journal for the Study of the Christian Church* 4, no.1 (March 2004): 21–33.

———. "Presbyteral Ministry in the Roman Catholic Church." *Ecclesiology* 1, no. 2 (2005): 11–24.

———. *Sacrament of Salvation: An Introduction to Eucharistic Ecclesiology*. Edinburgh: T&T Clark, 1995.

———. "Vatican I, Council of." In *The Oxford Companion to Christian Thought*, edited by Adrian Hastings, Alistair Mason, and Hugh Pyper, 737–38. New York: Oxford University Press, 2000.

Mesoloras, John. Συμβολική τῆς Ὀρθοδόξου Ἀνατολικῆς Ἐκκλησίας, Ἐκ τοῦ Τυπογραφείου Ἀθανασίου Γ. Δεληγιάννη [*Symbolic of the Eastern Orthodox Church*, vol. 2, part 2]. Athens: Athanasius G. Delligianis, 1904.

Metallinos, George. Ἑλλαδικοῦ Αὐτοκεφάλου Παραλειπόμενα, δεύτερη ἔκδοση,

Ἐκδόσεις Δόμος [*Missing Chronicles of the Greek Autocephaly*], 2nd ed. Athens: Domos, 1989].

Mettallinos, Eustathius, ed. (Very Reverend Archimandrite, Priest of the Greek Church). *Answer of the Great Church of Constantinople to the Papal Encyclical on Union in the Original Greek with an English translation*. Manchester, UK: Orthodox Greek Community, 1896.

Meyendorff, John. *The Byzantine Legacy in the Orthodox Church*. Crestwood, NY: St. Vladimir's Seminary Press, 1982.

———. "Dogmatics, part 5: Orthodox Ecclesiology, Athens, 1973." *St. Vladimir's Theological Quarterly* 18 (1974): 224–27.

———. *The Orthodox Church, Its Past and Its Role in the World Today*. Crestwood, NY: St. Vladimir's Seminary Press, 1996.

———. *Orthodoxy and Catholicity*. New York: Sheed and Ward, 1966.

———. *Rome, Constantinople, Moscow*. Crestwood, NY: St. Vladimir's Seminary Press, 1996.

———. "St. Peter in Byzantine Theology." In *The Primacy of Peter*, edited by John Meyendorff, 67–90. Crestwood, NY: St. Vladimir's Seminary Press, 1992.

———. "Vatican II: A Preliminary Reaction." *St. Vladimir's Theological Review* 9, no.1 (1965): 26–37.

———. "Vatican II: Definitions or search for unity?" *St. Vladimir's Theological Review* 7, no. 4 (1963): 164–68.

Miller, Michael J. *The Divine Right of the Papacy in Recent Ecumenical Theology*. Rome: Università Gregoriana Editrice, 1980.

Müller, Hubert. "How the Local Church Lives and Affirms Its Catholicity." *Jurist* 52 (1992): 340–64.

Murphy, Charles M. "Collegiality: An Essay toward Better Understanding." *Theological Studies* 46 (1985): 38–49.

Nellas, Panagiotis. "Collégialité épiscopale: Un problème nouveau?" *Le Messager Orthodoxe* 4 (1963)–5(1965): 12–21.

Nichols, Aidan. *Light from the East: Authors and Themes in Orthodox Theology*. London: Sheed and Ward, 1995.

———. *Theology in the Russian Diaspora: Church, Fathers, Eucharist in Nikolai Afanas'ev (1893–1966)*. New York: Cambridge University Press, 1990.

Nichols, Terence L. *That All May Be One: Hierarchy and Participation in the Church*. Collegeville, MN: Liturgical Press, 1997.

Nissiotis, Nikos. "Is the Vatican Council Really Ecumenical?" *Ecumenical Review* 16 (1964): 357–77.

———. "The Main Ecclesiological Problem of the Second Vatican Council and the Position of the Non-Roman Churches Facing It." *Journal of Ecumenical Studies* 2, no. 1 (Winter 1965): 31–62.

Oakley, Francis. *The Conciliarist Tradition: Constitutionalism in the Catholic Church 1300–1870*. New York: Oxford University Press, 2008.

O'Donnell, Christopher. *Ecclesia: A Theological Encyclopedia of the Church*. Collegeville, MN: Liturgical Press, 1996.

O'Neil, Colman. "General Introduction." In *Vatican II: The Church Constitution*, edited by A. Flannery. Dublin: Scepter Books, 1966.

———. "Ὀρθοδοξία καί ὁ Παπισμός." Ἐκκλησιαστική Ἀλήθεια τόμος 19 (1895–1896) (1896–1897) ["The Orthodoxy and the Papism"]. In *Ecclesiastical Truth*, vol. 19 (1895–1896): 356–58, 381–82, 387–89, 394–96; vol. 20 (1896–1897): 3–5, 12.

Papadopoulos, Chrysostom. Τὸ Πρωτεῖον τοῦ Ἐπισκόπου Ρώμης, Ἱστορική καί Κριτική Μελέτη, Δευτέρα Ἔκδοσις, Ἔκδοσις τοῦ Περιοδικοῦ Ἐκκλησία [The Primacy of the Bishop of Rome: A Historical and Critical Study]. Published by the periodical *Ecclesia*, 2nd ed. Athens: , 1964.

———. *The Third Ecumenical Council and the Primacy of the Bishop of Rome: A Reply to the Encyclical "Lux Veritatis" of Pius XI*. London: Faith Press, 1933.

Papageorgiou, Spiridon. Περί τῆς ἑνότητος τῆς Ἐκκλησίας, Ἐκ τοῦ Πατριαρχικοῦ Τυπογραφείου [On the Unity of the Church, Ecumenical Patriarchate's Press]. Constantinople: n.p., 1895.

Papanikolaou, Aristotle. "Integrating the Ascetical and the Eucharistic: Current Challenges in Orthodox Ecclesiology." *International Journal for the Study of the Christian Church* 11, nos. 2–3 (May–August 2011): 173–87.

Patelos, C. *Vatican I et les évêques Uniates*. Louvain: Bibliothèque de la Revue d'Histoire Ecclésiastique, 1981.

Phidas, Vlasios. Ἱστορικοκανονικά προβλήματα περί τήν λειτουργίαν τοῦ θεσμοῦ τῆς Πενταρχίας τῶν Πατριαρχῶν [Historical-Canonical Problems regarding the Function of the Institution of the Pentarchy of Patriarchs]. Athens: n.p., 1970.

———. Ὁ Θεσμός τῆς Πενταρχίας τῶν Πατριαρχῶν, I [The Institution of the Pentarchy, vol. 1]. Athens: n.p., 1977.

———. "Ὁ πρῶτος τῶν Ἐπισκόπων εἰς τήν κοινωνίαν τῶν τοπικῶν Ἐκκλησιῶν" ["The Place of the First of the Bishops within the Communion of the Local Churches"]. In *Eglise Locale et Eglise Universelle*, 151–75. Chambesy, Switzerland: Centre Orthodoxe, 1981.

———. "Ὁ Πρῶτος καί ἡ Συνοδικότης τῆς Ἐκκλησίας στήν Ὀρθόδοξη Παράδοση" ["The Primate and the Synodality of the Church in the Orthodox Tradition"]. *Episkepsis* 671 (2007): 40–46.

Philips, Gérard. "History of the Constitution on the Church." In *Commentary on the Documents of Vatican II*, vol. 1, edited by H. Vorgrimler, 105–37. New York: Herder and Herder, 1967.

Phougias Methodios. *Orthodoxy, Roman Catholicism and Anglicanism*. London: Oxford University Press, 1972.

Pietropaoli, David. *Visible Ecclesial Communion: Authority and Primacy in the Conciliar Church Roman Catholic and Orthodox Theologians in Dialogue*. Rome: Facultate Theologiae Pontificiae Universitatis Gregorianae, 1997.

Pottmeyer, Hermann. "The Episcopacy: The Conceptual, Structural, and Pastoral Renewal of the Church through Vatican II." In *The Gift of the Church: A Text-*

book on Ecclesiology in Honor of Patrick Granfield, OSB, edited by Peter C. Phan, 337–54. Collegeville, MN: Liturgical Press, 2000.

———. *Towards a Papacy in Communion: Perspectives from Vatican Councils I & II*. New York: Crossroad, 1998.

Puglisi, James, ed. *The Petrine Ministry and the Unity of the Church: "Toward a Patient and Fraternal Dialogue."* Collegeville, MN: Liturgical Press, 1999.

Rahner, Karl, and Joseph Ratzinger. *The Episcopate and the Primacy*. Edinburgh: Herder, Freiburg and Nelson, 1962.

Ratzinger, Joseph. "Announcements and Prefatory Notes of Explanation." In *Commentary on the Documents of Vatican II*, vol. 1, edited by H. Vorgrimler, 297–305. New York: Herder and Herder, 1967.

———. *Church, Ecumenism and Politics*. St. Paul, MN: Slough, 1988.

———. "Il Concetto della Chiesa nel Pensiero Patristico," in *I Grandi Temi del Concilio*. Rome: Paoline, 1965.

Rodopoulos, Panteleimon. *Μελέται, Α΄*, Πατριαρχικόν Ἵδρυμα Πατερικῶν Μελετῶν [*Essays* I]. Thessaloniki: Patriarchal Institute for Patristic Studies, 1993

———. "Μία ἀξιολόγησις τῶν ἀποφάσεων τῆς Β΄ Συνόδου τοῦ Βατικανοῦ", Μελέται, Α΄ ["An assessment of Vatican II's decisions," in *Essays I*], 643–53.

———. *Ἡ Ἱεραρχική Ὀργάνωσις τῆς Ἐκκλησίας κατά τό περί Ἐκκλησίας Σύνταγμα τῆς Β΄ ἐν Βατικανῷ Συνόδου* [*The Hierarchical Structure of the Church according to the Constitution on the Church of the Second Vatican Council*]. Thessaloniki: n.p., 1969.

Schatz, Klaus. *Papal Primacy from Its Origins to the Present*. Collegeville, MN: Liturgical Press, 1996.

Schmemann, Alexander. "The Idea of Primacy in Orthodox Ecclesiology." In *The Primacy of Peter*, edited by John Meyendorff, 145–71. Crestwood, NY: St. Vladimir's Seminary Press, 1992.

———. "O neo-papismie" ["On new-papism"]. *Tserkovnyi Vestnik* 5, no. 26 (1950): 11–18, in Russian.

———. "Vselensii Patriarkh i Pravoslavna Tserkov" ["The Ecumenical Patriarchate and the Orthodox Church"]. *Tserkovnyi Vestnik* 1, no. 28 (1951): 3–12, in Russian.

Sherrard, Philip. *Church, Papacy and Schism: A Theological Enquiry*. Limni, Evia, Greece: Denise Harvey, 1996.

———. *The Greek East and the Latin West: A Study in the Christian Tradition*. New York: Oxford University Press, 1959.

Spiropoulou, Mary, ed. *Ὀρθόδοξος Θεώρησις τῆς Β΄ Συνόδου τοῦ Βατικανοῦ* [*An Orthodox View of the Second Vatican Council*]. Athens: n.p., 1965.

Stilianopoulos, Theodore. "Concerning the Biblical Foundation of Primacy." In *The Petrine Ministry: Catholics and Orthodox in Dialogue*, edited by Walter Kasper, 37–64. *Academic symposium held at the Pontifical Council for Promoting Christian Unity*. New York: Newman Press, 2006.

Tamburini, Piero. *Vera idea de la Santa Sede*. Pavia: n.p., 1784.

Tanner, Norman P., ed. *Decrees of the Ecumenical Councils*, vol. 2. London: Sheed and Ward: Georgetown University Press, 1990.

Thils, Gustave. "Potestas Ordinaria." In *L'Episcopat et l'Eglise Universelle*, 690–707.

———. *La Primauté Pontificale: La doctrine de Vatican I, les voies d'une revision*. Gembloux, Belgium: Editions J. Duculot, 1972.

Tillard, J.M.R. *The Bishop of Rome*. London: SPCK, 1983.

———. *Church of Churches: The Ecclesiology of Communion*. Collegeville, MN: Liturgical Press, 1992.

Tourneux, André. "L'éveque, l'eucharistie et l'église locale dans *Lumen Gentium*." *Ephemerides Theologicae Lovanienses* 64 (1988): 106–41.

Trembelas, Panagiotis. *Αἱ μετά τό ἔργον τῆς Βατικανείας Συνόδου ὑποχρεώσεις μας, Ἀνάτυπον ἐκ τοῦ περιοδικοῦ Ἐκκλησία, [Our Obligations after the Work of Second Vatican Council]*. An offprint from periodical *Ecclesia*, Athens, 1967.

Trinadtzatsky, Germain. *L'Eglise Russe face a l'Occident*. Paris: OEIL, 1991.

Volf, Miroslav. *After Our Likeness: The Church as the Image of the Trinity*. Grand Rapids, MI: Wm. B. Eerdmans, 1998.

———. "Trinity, Unity, Primacy: On the Trinitarian Nature of Unity and Its Implications for the Question of Primacy." In *The Petrine Ministry and the Unity of the Church: "Toward a patient and fraternal dialogue,"* edited by James Puglisi, 171–84. Collegeville, MN: Liturgical Press, 1999.

Ware, Kallistos. "The Ecumenical Councils and the Conscience of the Church." In *Canon* II, 217–33. Freiburg, Germany: Verlag Herder, 1974.

———. "Primacy, Collegiality and the People of God." In *Orthodoxy: Life and Freedom, Essays in Honour of Archbishop Iakovos*, edited by A. J. Philippou, 116–29. Oxford: Studion Publications, 1973.

———. "*Sobornost* and Eucharistic Ecclesiology: Aleksei Khomiakov and His Successors." *International Journal for the Study of the Christian Church* 11, nos. 2–3 (May–August 2011): 216–35.

Wessel, Susan. *Leo the Great and the Spiritual Rebuilding of a Universal Rome*. Leiden, Netherlands: Brill, 2008.

Willebrands, Johannes. "Vatican II's Ecclesiology of Communion." *One in Christ* 3 (1987): 179–91.

Williams, Cornelius. "The Church Is Hierarchical." In *Vatican II: The Church Constitution*, edited by A. Flannery, 84–99. Dublin: Scepter Books, 1966.

Zigavinos, Gregory. *Ἀπάντησις εἰς τήν ἐγκύκλιον Ἐπιστολήν Λέοντος ΙΓ´ Πάπα Ῥώμης περί ἐνώσεως τῆς Ἀνατολικῆς Ἐκκλησίας μετά τῆς Δυτικῆς [Answer to the Papal Letter of the Roman Pope Leo XIII on the Unity of the Eastern Church with the Western]*. Marseille: n.p., 1894.

Zizioulas, John. "Apostolic Continuity of the Church and Apostolic Succession in the First Five Centuries of the Church." In *Louvain Studies* 21 (1996): 153–68.

———. *Being as Communion*. Crestwood, NY: St. Vladimir's Seminary Press, 1997.

———. "The Church as Communion." *St. Vladimir's Theological Review* 38 (1994): 3–16.

————. *Communion and Otherness: Further Studies in Personhood and the Church*, edited by Paul McPartlan. London: T&T Clark, 2006.

————. "Conciliarity and the Way to Unity: An Orthodox Point of View." In *Churches in Conciliar Fellowship*, 20–31. Geneva: Conference of European Churches, 1978.

————. "The Ecclesiological Presuppositions of the Holy Eucharist." *Nicolaus* 10 (1982): 333–49.

————. "The Ecclesiology of Institutions and the Unity of the Church." Unpublished paper read at an Orthodox conference on the topic of contemporary Orthodox ecclesiastical legislation, held in Belgrade, 2003.

————. "Eucharistic Ecclesiology in the Orthodox Tradition." In *L'ecclesiologie eucharistique*, ed. by Jean-Marie Van Cangh, 163–79. Brussels: Academie Internationale des Sciences Religieuses-Cerf, 2009. Translated into Greek as "Ἡ Εὐχαριστιακή Ἐκκλησιολογία στήν Ὀρθόδοξη Παράδοση," Θεολογία 4 (2009).

————. "The Father as Cause." In *Communion and Otherness: Further Studies in Personhood and the Church*, edited by Paul McPartlan. London: T&T Clark, 2006.

————. "The Institution of Episcopal Conferences: An Orthodox Reflection." *Jurist* 48 (1988): 376–83.

————. *Εὐχαριστίας Ἐξεμπλάριον, Ἱερά Ἀνδρῴα Κοινοβιακή Μονή Ἁγ. Παρασκευῆς Μαζίου, [Manifestation of Gratitude]*, edited by the Holy Monastery of St. Paraskevi Megara, 2006.

————. "The Mystery of the Church in Orthodox Tradition." *One in Christ* 24 (1988): 294–303.

————. "The Nature of the Unity We Seek." *One in Christ* 24 (1988): 342–48.

————. "Orthodox Ecclesiology and the Ecumenical Movement." *Sourozh* 21 (August 1985): 17–27.

————. "Ortodossia." In *Enciclopedia del Novecento* 5: 1–18. Rome: Instituto della Enciclopedia Italiana, 1980.

————. "Primacy in the Church: An Orthodox Approach." In *The Petrine Ministry and the Unity of the Church: "Toward a Patient and Fraternal Dialogue,"* edited by James Puglisi, 115–25. Collegeville, MN: Liturgical Press, 1999.

————. "Recent Discussions on Primacy in Orthodox Theology." In *The Petrine Ministry: Catholics and Orthodox in Dialogue*, edited by Walter Kasper, 231–46. Academic symposium held at the Pontifical Council for Promoting Christian Unity. New York: Newman Press, 2006.

————. "Ὁ Συνοδικός Θεσμός. Ἱστορικά, Ἐκκλησιολογικά καί Κανονικά Προβλήματα" *Τιμητικόν Ἀφιέρωμα εἰς τόν Μητροπολίτην Κίτρους Βαρνάβαν ἐπί τῇ 25ετηρίδι τῆς Ἀρχιερατείας αὐτοῦ* ["The Synodical Institution: Historical, Ecclesiastical and Canonical Problems"]. In *Honorary Dedication to The Most Rev. Barnabas Metropolitan of Kitros on his 25th Anniversary as Hierarch*], 163–90. Athens: n.p., 1980.

————. *Θέματα Ἐκκλησιολογίας [Themes of Ecclesiology]*. Thessaloniki: n.p., 1991. University lecture notes.

————. "Δύο Ἀρχαῖαι Παραδόσεις περί Ἀποστολικῆς Διαδοχῆς καί ἡ σημασία των", Ἀνάτυπον ἐκ τοῦ Τιμητικοῦ Τόμου εἰς τόν Καθηγητήν Γεράσιμον Κονιδάρην ["Two Ancient Traditions concerning Apostolic Succession and Their Theological Significance"]. Offprint from the *Studies in Honour of Professor G. Konidaris*. Athens: n.p., 1981.

————. "Unitatis Redintegratio: An Orthodox Reflection." Unpublished paper read to a conference for the 40th anniversary of the promulgation of the conciliar degree, Unitatis Redintegratio, Rome, November 2004.

————. Ἡ ἑνότης τῆς Ἐκκλησίας ἐν τῇ θείᾳ Εὐχαριστίᾳ καί τῷ ἐπισκόπῳ κατά τούς τρεῖς πρώτους αἰῶνας τῆς Ἐκκλησίας [*The Unity of the Church in the Divine Eucharist and the Bishop during the First Three Centuries*]. Athens: n.p., 1965.

————. *Eucharist, Bishop, Church: The Unity of the Church in the Divine Eucharist and the Bishop during the First Three Centuries*. Brookline, MA: Holy Cross Orthodox Press, 2001. This book is a translation of the second edition (1990) of the above-mentioned source.

Index

Uniatism, 3, 42–43

unity of Church, 3, 42, 44, 51, 53–55, 64, 103, 122, 129, 133, 154, 172n75, 175n136, 187n24, 193n126; communion of churches, 5; duality in unity, 187n26; ecumenical center of unity, 144; juridical, 148; monarchical, 103, 144, 148; mystical unity, 53; unity of communion, 51; visible *versus* invisible head, 53

Unity of the Orthodox Eastern Church (Tipaldos), 51–52

universal church, 5, 7–8, 75, 89, 90, 113, 121, 182n125, 183nn131–33, 191n84, 192n111; mutual interiority, 8

universal primacy, 9, 17–18, 49–50, 67–68, 107, 116, 118–19, 127, 130–31, 135–36, 138–40, 143, 152, 154–55, 170n43, 194n141

Vatican (city-state), 11

Vatican I, 19–40; aftermath, 41–71, 142–48; Dogmatic Commission, 25; dogmatic definition of primacy, 24–40; exegesis of the petrine texts, 30–34; historical context of, 16, 19–24; invitation to Orthodox bishops, 42; mutual interiority, 8; papal primacy, 16 (*see also* primacy of the bishop of Rome)

Vatican II, 72–95; aftermath, 4–11, 96–140; collegiality, 84–86, 86–90, 182n122, 183n129; commissions, 81, 83, 181n98; constitution, 81–83 (*see also* Constitution of the Church (*Lumen Gentium*)); sacred liturgy, 88; theological context of, 72–80, 148–51

Venerius (bishop of Milan), 169n37

vicarius Christi, 35, 85

Victor (bishop of Rome), 46

Volf, Miroslav, 193n126

Ware, Kallistos (metropolitan), 13, 15, 38–39, 47, 160n55, 169n37

Willebrands, Johannes, 100–101

Zigavinos, Archimandrite Grigorius, 41, 141, 175n136; views on primacy of canons, 58–59; views on primacy of Peter, 44–47

Zizioulas, John (metropolitan of Pergamon), 4–11 *passim*, 12, 16–18, 41, 141, 191n78; critique of Orthodox arguments, 110–41, 141–42, 144–48; doctoral thesis, 12, 112; eucharist ecclesiology, 12, 14–15, 110–11, 152–53, 166n144; historical *versus* eschatological method, 85–90; historical *versus* theological approach, 116–31 *passim*; theology of primacy, 116–31 *passim*, 131–40, 149, 152–56; views on collegiality, 86–90, 91, 111–16, 150–51; views on conciliarism, 62–64, 174n129; views on honor, 57, 66–69; views on independence of churches, 54; views on pope, 50–51; views on power, 57–58; views on primacy, 131–40; views on synodality, 56, 194n148

www.ingramcontent.com/pod-product-compliance
Lightning Source LLC
Chambersburg PA
CBHW030304100426
42812CB00002B/564